ENGLISH PLACE-NAME SOCIETY

VOLUME LXXIII FOR 1995-1996

GENERAL EDITOR

VICTOR WATTS

THE PLACE-NAMES OF LINCOLNSHIRE

PART V

THE SURVEY OF ENGLISH PLACE-NAMES
UNDERTAKEN WITH THE APPROVAL AND SUPPORT OF
THE BRITISH ACADEMY

THE PLACE-NAMES OF

LINCOLNSHIRE

BY

KENNETH CAMERON

in collaboration with

JOHN FIELD and JOHN INSLEY

PART FIVE

THE WAPENTAKE OF BRADLEY

NOTTINGHAM
ENGLISH PLACE-NAME SOCIETY
1997

Published by the English Place-Name Society

Registered Charity No. 257891

© English Place-Name Society 1997

ISBN 0 904889 53 X

Typeset by Paul Cavill & Printed in Great Britain
by Woolnough Bookbinding, Irthlingborough, Northants.

This volume is dedicated to the memory of

Sir Francis (Frank) Hill FBA

for all his encouragement and help

CONTENTS

PREFACE

The fifth part of *The Place-Names of Lincolnshire* covers the Wapentake of Bradley and completes the survey of the North Riding of Lindsey. Yet again I have to thank my friends in the Lincolnshire Record Office for their constant help during the many years in which I have been collecting material there; in particular my especial thanks go to Mr Nigel Colley. I have remarked before on the fact that the text itself indicates how many Collections have been searched and the time and energy spent by members of the staff to place it all at my disposal.

Over a long period regular visits were made to the North-East Lincolnshire Archives (formerly SHARO) in Great Grimsby which houses the Grimsby Borough Records and other local collections. The wealth of material there is evident from the section on the place- and field-names of the borough. The Archivist, Mr John Wilson, and his assistant Mrs Carole Moss, have earned my very grateful thanks for all their help in advising me on the various collections and in producing the documents themselves. The staff in the Reference Section of Grimsby Public Library were most helpful too in collecting material for Cleethorpes.

On all my visits to Grimsby I was accompanied by my friend Jean Russell-Gebbett. She collected all the 18th and 19th century material both for Grimsby and for Cleethorpes in Grimsby Archives and Public Library and led me on our many "practical place-name" trips around both towns. In addition she has checked the text of this volume at least twice and has also prepared the Index. My debt of gratitude to her is considerable not least for her constant support and encouragement whilst "living" with Lincolnshire place-names over the years.

Once again, my friends Mr John Field and Dr John Insley have helped greatly in the preparation of this volume that their names appear as collaborators on the title-page. Mr Field prepared the draft of the field-names of each parish and made many suggestions of etymology, most of which have been silently incorporated into the text. Only he will know his contributions to the volume. Dr Insley has read the whole of the text and with his expertise in the field of personal names and in philology generally he has made a considerable contribution which enhances the scholarship of the book.

My grateful thanks go to Mrs Anne Tarver who has drawn the detailed map of the parishes of the wapentake, a particularly difficult task because of the boundary changes around Grimsby. I owe a considerable debt of gratitude to two local people. Dr Rod Ambler provided me with his own collection of field–names, particularly for Cleethorpes, from documents in Sidney Sussex College and also made comments on names in Grimsby and Cleethorpes. Mrs Bettie Watkinson has checked the draft of Cleethorpes and, from her own researches in the area, has provided numerous comments on the names. These are attributed to her in the text and I offer her my grateful thanks.

Finally, it is my very great pleasure to thank Mrs Janet Rudkin for all her help, and my colleague, Dr Paul Cavill, who has guided the text of this volume through the press. His patience, skill and attention to detail are remarkable. Nothing is too much trouble for him and he has certainly earned my very special thanks. All errors are of course my own.

University of Nottingham   KENNETH CAMERON

ADDITIONS to the ABBREVIATIONS and BIBLIOGRAPHY printed in THE PLACE–NAMES OF LINCOLNSHIRE PARTS 1–4

AddReg	Additional Registers in LAO
Austin	F. Roth, *English Austin Friars*, 2 vols., 1961–66
Baker	Frank Baker, *The Story of Cleethorpes and the Contribution of Methodism*, 1953
Bdgs	Building(s)
BH	Documents in the Brown, Hudson and Hudson Collection in LAO
BReg	*Bishops Registers* in LAO
B.W.	Information provided by Mrs Bettie Watkinson
Dobson	*Dobson's Directory to the Lodging houses at Cleethorpes*, 1850
Falk	Documents in the Falkners of Louth Collection in LAO
Gait	A. Gait, *The Grimsby and Cleethorpes Directory*, 1871
GDC	The Gray, Dodsworth and Cobb of York Deposit in LAO
Gillett	Edward Gillett, *A History of Grimsby*, 1970
GrimsBCB	Grimsby Bailiffs' Court Books in NELA
GrimsCB	Grimsby Mayors' Court Books, i–xiv in NELA
GrimsChamb	Grimsby Chamberlains' Rolls in NELA
GrimsCLeet	Grimsby Court Leet Verdicts in NELA
GrimsCt	Grimsby Court Rolls in NELA
GrimsExtent	Grimsby Bailiffs' Extents in NELA
GrimsFC	Grimsby Final Concords in NELA
GrimsLeases	Grimsby Borough Leases in NELA
GrimsMap	Maps of Grimsby in NELA
GrimsMap (*PRO*)	Map of Grimsby, c.1600 (MP B/14) in PRO, copy in NELA
GrimsMiscD	Grimsby Miscellaneous Deeds in NELA
GrimParlExp	Grimsby Parliamentary Expenses in NELA
GrimsQR	Grimsby Quietus Rolls in NELA
GrimsSR	Grimsby Subsidy Roll, 1297, in NELA
Hagar	Hagar & Co, *Directory of . . . Lincolnshire*, 1849

Heneage	Documents in the Heneage Collection in LAO
Hig	Documents in the Higgins Collection in LAO
HumbD	Humberstone Deeds in NELA
Kirkby	A.E. Kirkby, *Humberstone. The Story of a Village*, 1953
Letch	Deeds in the Letch Collection in NELA
LincsD	Lincolnshire Deeds in NELA
MapGrims	Maps of Great Coates in NELA
Marshall	Marshall of Humberston Papers in NELA
Morris	*Morris & Co's Commercial Directory and Gazetteer of Lincolnshire*, 1813
NELA	North–East Lincolnshire Archives in Grimsby
Oliver	G. Oliver, *The Monumental Antiquities of Great Grimsby*, 1825
PRStJ	*The Register Book of the Parish Church of Saint James, Great Grimsby*, ed. G.S. Stephenson, 1889
Rigby	S.H. Rigby, *Medieval Grimsby: Growth and Decline*, 1993
SHARO	South Humberside Area Record Office, now North–East Lincolnshire Archives
Shaw	The Shaw Papers in NELA
Skelton	*The Skelton Index, 1847–49* in Great Grimsby Public Library
Sq	Square
SSC	Documents in Sidney Sussex College, Cambridge, Library; forms supplied by Dr R.E. Ambler
SSCTerrier	Terriers in Sidney Sussex College, Cambridge, Library; forms supplied by Dr R.E. Ambler
TCC	Documents in Trinity College, Cambridge, Library
Ter	Terrace
ThorGrims	Documents in the Thorold Collection in NELA
Watson	C.E. Watson, *A History of Clee and the Thorpes of Clee*, 1901
Wild	J. Wild, *Tetney, Lincolnshire. A History*, 1901

NOTES ON ARRANGEMENT

(1) Following the name Bradley Wapentake, the parishes in the Wapentake are set out in alphabetical order.

(2) Each of the parish names is printed in bold type as a heading. Within each parish the names are arranged as follows: (i) the parish name; (ii) other major names (i.e. names of sizeable settlements and names of primary historical or linguistic interest), each treated separately in alphabetical order; (iii) all minor names (i.e. the remaining names recorded on the 1906 edition of the O.S. 6" map, as well as some names that are "lost" or "local", *v. infra*), again treated in alphabetical order but in a single paragraph; (iv) field–names (which include other unidentified minor names) in small type, (a) modern field–names, normally those recorded after 1750, with any older spellings of these names in brackets and printed in italics, (b) medieval and early modern field–names, i.e. those recorded before about 1750, printed in italics, the names in each group being arranged alphabetically.

(3) Place–names no longer current, i.e. those not recorded on the editions of the 1" and 6" maps are marked "lost". This does not mean that the site to which the name refers is unknown. Such names are normally printed in italics when referred to elsewhere.

(4) Place–names marked "(local)" are those not recorded on the 1" and 6" O.S. maps but which are still current locally.

(5) The local and standard pronunciations of a name, when of interest and not readily suggested by the modern spelling, are given in phonetic symbols in square brackets after the name.

(6) The early spellings of each name are presented in the order "spelling, date, source". When, however, the head–form of a name is followed only by a "date and source", e.g. AYLESBY GRANGE, 1828 Bry, the spelling in 1828 Bry is the same as that of the head–form.

(7) In explaining the various place–names and field–names, summary reference is frequently made, by printing the elements in bold type, to the analysis of elements which will appear in the final

volume of the Lincolnshire County Survey, and more particularly to *English Place-Name Elements* (EPNS 25, 26) and to *Addenda and Corrigenda* to these volumes in *English Place-Name Society Journal* 1. In many of the minor names and field-names, the meaning is so obvious as to need no comment or so uncertain as not to warrant it. For personal names which are cited without authority, reference should be made for Old English names to Redin, Searle and Feilitzen, for Old (Continental) German to Förstemann PN and Forssner, and for English surnames to Bardsley and Reaney (for details of these sources, *v*. Abbreviations and Bibliography in *The Place-Names of Lincolnshire*, Part 1 (EPNS 58).

(8) Unprinted sources of the early spellings of place-names are indicated by printing the abbreviation for the source in italics. The abbreviation for a printed source is printed in roman type. The exact page, folio or membrane is only given where the precise identification of an entry is of special importance or value, e.g. *AddReg i*, f. 71.

(9) Where two dates are given for a spelling, e.g. Hy2 (e13), 1190 (m13), the first is the date at which the document purports to have been composed and the second the date of the copy that has come down to us (in many cases the latter is a Cartulary, ecclesiastic or lay). Sources whose dates cannot be fixed to a particular year are dated by century, e.g. 11, 12, 13, 14 etc. (often more specifically e13, m13, l13 etc., early, mid and late 13th century respectively), by regnal date, e.g. Ed1, Eliz, Jas1 etc., or by a range of years, e.g. 1150–60, 1401–2 etc., although this last form of date may alternatively mean that the spellings belong to a particular year within the limit indicated.

(10) The sign (p) after the source indicates that the particular spelling given appears in that source as a person's surname, not primarily as a reference to a place.

(11) When a letter or letters (sometimes words or phrases) in an early place-name form are enclosed in brackets, it means that spellings with and without the enclosed letter(s), words or phrases occur. When only one part of a place-name spelling is given as a variant, preceded or followed by a hyphen, it means that the

particular spelling only differs in respect of the cited part from the preceding or following spelling. Occasional spellings given in inverted commas are usually editorial translations or modernisations, and whilst they have no authority linguistically they have chronologically.

(12) Cross–references to other names are given with *supra* or *infra*, the former referring to a name already dealt with, the latter to a name dealt with later in the text.

(13) Putative forms of personal names and place–name elements which will appear asterisked in the concluding volume of this survey are not always asterisked in the text, although the discussion will often make it clear which are on independent record and which are inferred.

(14) In order to save space in presenting the early spellings of a name, *et passim* and *et freq* are sometimes used to indicate that the preceding form(s) occur repectively from time to time or frequently from the date of the last quoted source to that of the following one, or to the present day.

ADDENDA AND CORRIGENDA

Volume 64/65

15	line 8	793 (15) BCS 1297 (S 792) should read 973 (15) BCS 1297 (S 792).
98	s.n.	Croxton, line 1, 1098 DB should read 1086 DB.
194	line 1	1183 O should read 1183 P.

Volume 66

36   line 10   for *Vtrebi* 1106 ChancR read 1206 ChancR.

52   line 3   for 12254 ValNor read 1254 ValNor.

152ff   Thoresway f.ns. (a) add, all 1457 *TCC*: Acre Rood Hill 1781 (cf. *Acrewellhyll* 1457); Caister Gate 1781 (*Castergate* 1457); Gibdale Wong 1781 (*Gybdale, Gypdale* 1457); Waingate 1781 (*Waynegate* 1457); f.ns. (b) *the becke* 1579 (*Bekke* 1457); *croxbye gatt* 1579 (cf. *Croxbyway* 1457); *depedale* 1579 (*Depedalehyll* 1457); *farsdalle* 1579 (cf. *Farsdalebothem* 1457); *the gares* 1579 (*leȝ Gares* 1457); *middle -, upper greenedikes* 1625 (*Grene dykes* 1457); *lyttyl dalle* 1579 (*Lyttylldale* 1457); *makames* 1579 (*Mawkans* 1457); *the moore* 1597 (*le More* 1457); *nunngarthe syde* 1579 (cf. *Nonnhole* 1457, *v.* **hol**[1]); *nordale* 1625 (*Northdale, -gate, -hyll, -mowth* 1457); *pease landes* 1579 (*peeslandes* 1457); *the Prieste dale* 1652 (*Prestdale* 1457); *Rothwell meere* 1625 (*Rothewellmere* 1457); *strypes* 1579 (*leȝ Strypes, Eststrypes* 1457); Additional names in f.ns. (b): *Batryldale furlang* 1457; *Burgh, Burgslyht* (*v.* **burh** 'a fortification', with **slétta** 'a smooth, level field' but the sigificance of **burh** here is not obvious); *Dexdalehyll* 1457 (obscure); *est feld* 1457 (one of the open fields of the village, *v.* **ēast, feld**); *Grene furlange* 1457 (*v.* **grēne**[1], **furlang**); *Grenefyrthes* 1457 from **grēne**[1] 'green' and ME *frith* (from OE **fyhrðe**) here probably 'a

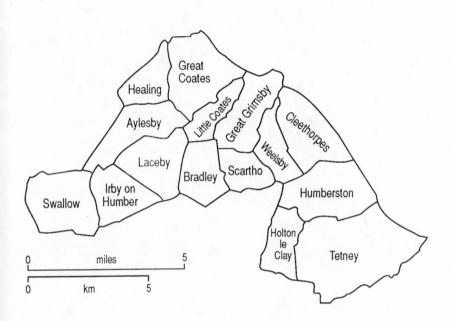

Great
Coates

Healing

Aylesby

Little Coates

Great Grimsby

Cleethorpes

Laceby

Weelsby

Bradley

Scartho

Swallow

Irby on
Humber

Humberston

Holton
le
Clay

Tetney

0 miles 5

0 km 5

THE WAPENTAKE OF BRADLEY

Based upon the 1963 Ordnance Survey four miles to one inch map,
with the permission of the controller of Her Majesty's Stationery Office.

© Crown Copyright

BRADLEY WAPENTAKE

Bradelai (2x) DB, 1177 P, *–lea* 1176 ChancR, *–lae* (sic) 1181
P, *–le* 1191 ib, 1196 ChancR, 1197, 1203 ib, 1242–43 Fees,
1265 Misc, 1298, 1305 Ass, 1338 Pat, *–lee* 1200 P, 1298
Ass, 1316 FA, 1332 *SR*
Bradel' 1198 P, 1237–38 RRG, 1275, 1276 RH
Bradle lHy3 *NCot*, 1296 *Ass*, 1373 Peace, 1409 Pat, 1431 FA
Bradeleye 1287, 1288 Ipm, 1327 *SR*
Bradley Haverstow 1653 *ParlSurv*
Bredelai c.1115 LS, 1166 P, *–la* 1182 ib

The forms are preceded or followed by Wapentake or Deanery,
usually in a Latin form, *v.* **vápnatak, wæpengetac.** The
Wapentake was named from Bradley, *infra*, where additional
forms of the name are given. Bradley was subsequently joined with
Haverstoe, PN L **4**, 47, to become known as Bradley Haverstoe
Wapentake.

Aylesby

AYLESBY

Alesbi (3x) 1086 DB, c.1115 LS, 1130 P (p), 1160–66 Dane,
1185 Templar, 1199, 1202 P (p), 1202 Ass, e13 *HarlCh*, *–
in Lindesia* 1212 FF, *–by* R1 (1318) Ch, 1221 Guis, 1221
Welles, 1225 Cur, 1226 FF, 1228 Cl (p), *– in Lindesya*
1229 Ch, 1232 Pat, 1240 FF, 1242–43 Fees, 1245 FF, 1254
ValNor, 1254, 1255 FF, 1276 RRGr, 1281 Ipm, 1281 QW,

1288 Ipm, 1291 Tax, 1293, 1294 RSu, 1295 Pat, c.1300
Guis, 1303, 1316 FA, 1318 Ipm, 1321 Cl, 1322 Pat, 1325
Cl *et freq* to 1634 *Terrier*, 1742 *Foster*, *-bye* 1536–37 Dugd
vi, 1563 *BT*, 1576 Saxton, 1563, 1589, 1595 *BT*, 1610
Speed, *-bie* 1592, 1598 *BT*, 1601 *DCLB*, 1604 *Foster*, 1616
BT, 1626 *Nelthorpe, Alysby* 1245 FF, 1278 RRGr, 1341
Extent, 1526 Sub, *-bye* 1551 Pat
Halesbi 115–60 Dane, 1218 Ass, *-by* 1210 RBE, *-bia* 1212
     Fees, *-b'* 1225 ClR
Alsebi c.1115 LS, 1736 *BT*
Aleby 1226 Cur, 1238–39, 1268 RRG, 1303 FA
Aylesby 1259 RRGr, 1331, 1414 Cl, 1461 Pat, 1598 *LCS*, 1620
     BT, 1634 *Foster*, 1678, 1686, 1701 *BT*, 1703 *Terrier et*
     passim, *-bie* 1566 LNQ xiv, 1586, 1622 *BT*, 1625 *Terrier*,
     1631 *BT*, *Aylsby* 1730 *ib*, *Ailesbie* 1627, 1631 *ib*, *-by* 1593,
     1595, 1609, 1612, 1810 *ib*, *Ailsbye* 1551 *Cragg*, *-bie* 1603,
     1623 *ib*, 1656 *Foster*, *-by* 1753 *BT*, 1767, 1770 *CCLeases*,
     1795, 1808 *BT*, 1826 *CCLeases*, 1840 *TA*

According to Ekwall, DEPN s.n., this is 'Áli's farmstead,
village', *v*. **bȳ**. The personal name would then be ON *Áli*, ON *Āli*,
discussed by Fellows–Jensen, SPNYL 9, and by Insley, SPNN 13.
It is the first el. also of Ailby LSR and Alby Nf, for which gen.sg.
spellings in *-es* are not found. In Aylesby itself *-es* presumably
represents a secondary ME gen.sg. form.

AYLESBY GRANGE, 1828 Bry, apparently an example of the later
dial. use of **grange** 'a homestead, small mansion or farmstead,
esp. one standing by itself remote from others', a sense quoted
from L, *v*. EDD s.v. 2. AYLESBY MILL HO, cf. *Aylesby Mill* 1824
O, 1831 *Monson*, 1838 *Brace*, *- Mills* 1828 Bry, cf. *Milne gate*,
- hill 1625 *Terrier*, *v*. **gata** 'a road, a way'. AYLESBY PARK, cf.
(*the*) *Park Green* 1766 *Tyr*, 1840 *TA*. BARTON STREET, *- strete*
1625 *Terrier*, *the street* 1634 *ib*; this is the name of a presumed
pre–Roman trackway along the eastern edge of the Wolds leading
to Barton upon Humber and found in other parishes in this
Wapentake. BEACH HOLT LANE. BRAMAHS HOLT (lost), 1818

Bry, cf. *Bramers* 1840 *TA*; it was just north of Pewet Fm. CARR
PLANTATION, cf. *The Carr* 1840 *TA*, *v*. **kjarr** 'brushwood', 'a
bog, a marsh, etc.'. CHURCH LANE cf. *Church Yard* 1840 *TA* and
Kirkemaire 1625 *Terrier*, *Kirkmares* 1840 *TA*; the latter may be
'the boundary, land on a boundary belonging to the church', *v*.
kirkja, **(ge)mǣre**. DRAKES GORSE is probably named from the
Rev. T.T. *Drake*, lord of the manor 1842 White. GRIMES HOLT
(lost), 1828 Bry, probably named from the family of Willam
Grime 1812 *BT*; it was south of Wybers Fm on the parish
boundary. MANOR HO is *Hall* 1828 Bry. MAUD HOLE COVERT,
– *Cover* 1824 O, cf. *maud hool* 1625 *Terrier*, *Maud Hole* 1828
Bry, – *hole* 1840 *TA*, presumably from the pers.n. *Maud* and **hol**
'a hole, a hollow'. NOOKING LANE, cf. *The nooking* 1840 *TA*,
from dial. *nooking* 'a nook', common in north L. NORTH FIELD
BARN (lost), 1824 O, cf. *North Feild* 1634 *Terrier*, – *feild* 1684
Tyr, named from one of the great fields of the village, *v*. **norð**,
feld, cf. *the West feild* in f.ns. (b) *infra*. PARSONAGE (lost), *the*
parsonage howse 1625 *Terrier*, *Parsonage House* 1656 *Foster*,
their parsonage of Ailsby 1767 *CCLeases, their parsonage* – 1801,
1826 *ib*. PEWET FM, *Pewet Hall* 1824 O, *Pyewipe Hall* 1828 Bry;
both *pewet* and *pyewipe* are common dial. names for the *lapwing*.
TEMPLE LANE, cf. *the temple sands* 1625, *Temple* – 1674, *ye*
Temple Sands 1686, *A close of pasture ground comonly called* ...
the Temples 1690, *the temples* 1698, *Temples* 1706, 1724 all
Terrier, 1840 *TA*, commemorating the holdings of the Knights
Templar, who held land here in 1185 Templar. WASHING DALES,
1840 *TA*, *Aylesby Washing Dales* 1824 O. WYBERS FM, *Wybers*
1824 O, *Wyburghs Fm* 1828 Bry, *Wyvers* 1841 *TA* (Great Coates),
cf. *wiberfurlong, –gate, –hedge* c.1590, *wyver hedge* (sic) 1634,
Wiber close, – Gate or Horse Way, – Hedge 1668, *Wyber Close,*
Wybur–gate 1686, *Weibur close, – gate, – hedge* 1706 all *Terrier*,
Wibers bottom, –close, Furzy Wibers, House Wibers 1840 *TA*;
Wybers, etc. is perhaps from the surn. *Wyber*, itself a derivative
of the OE fem. per.n. *Wīgburh*, *v*. Reaney s.n. *Wyber*. WYBERS
WOOD, *Wybers Covers* 1824 O, *Wyburghs Hole Pln* 1828 Bry.

FIELD-NAMES

Principal forms in (a) are 1840 *TA*. Forms dated 1212 are FF; c.1300 Guis; 1327, 1332 *SR*; 1586 *LincsD*; 1601, 1625, 1634, 1638, 1671, 1674, 1679, 1686, 1690, 1698, 1703, 1706, 1724, 1762 *Terrier*; 1656 *Foster*; 1684, 1685, 1757, 1766, 1771 *Tyr*.

(a) Bill Carr (*v.* **kjarr**); Blind hills (*blendhills* (sic) 1625, *blind hills* 1634, probably from ME **blind, blend** 'blind, hidden (by vegetation)' and **hyll**); Botom cl; Brick kiln & tup cl (*v.* **tup** 'a ram'); Brick kiln cl; Tom Brown fd; Channell plat (*v.* **plat**^{2} 'a small plot of ground', as elsewhere in the parish, the first el. being ME **chanel** 'a gutter, a drain, a ditch'); Chaulk pit cl; Clayton walks (named from the *Clayton* family, cf. David *Clayton* 1740 *BT*; with **walk** 'a stretch of grass used for pasturing sheep' in the pl., cf. **shepe-walk**); Close, Close heads (*Close heades* 1625, 1634, *v.* **clos(e)**, **hēafod**); Corn cl; Far –, Near corn cl; Cotcher platts (*cotcher plat* 1684, *Cotcher plats* 1685, 'the cottager's plot(s) of land', *cotcher* being frequently found for 'cottager' in north L); Gt – Lt doghams (*dogham heades* 1625, *v.* **dogga** 'dog', **holmr**; *ham* is a frequent modern form of **holmr** in north L); Dove Cote Yd (*v.* **douve–cote**); Far fd; Four cl; Garden & Garth, – & two Garth (sic); Garth, Garths (*v.* **garðr** 'an enclosure' as elsewhere in the parish); Great cl; Great fd; Great –, Little Garth (*v.* **garðr**); Hammer Leys (changes from *Hamner*) (*v.* **lea** (OE **lēah**) 'the meadow, pasture' in the pl.); Hassen Cl, – Garth; High cl; House & Garth, House cl; the Hundred Acres 1762, Part of hundred acres (2x) 1840; The inghams (*Ingham sid* (sic) 1625, *Ingham bancke* 1634, perhaps *v.* **innām** 'a piece of land taken in or enclosed'); King sleet (*v.* **slétta** 'a smooth, level field'); Kissing Carr (*v.* **kjarr**); Lane end cl; (Upr) Langmoor (*langmar Windinges*, *langmare hedge* 1625, 'the long boundary, land on a boundary' *v.* **(ge)mǣre**, changed to 'moor' in the modern form; for *Windinges*, *v.* *Wynedyngs* PN L **2**, 173); Little Garth (*v.* **garðr**); Far –, Near Lloyds walk (named from the *Lloyd* family, cf. John *Lloyd* 1763 *BT* and John *Lloyd* named in the document); Lords platt (*v.* **plat**^{2}); Low cl; Middle cl; Near fds; Old Garth (3x) (*v.* **garðr**); Orchard & plantn; Over lands (2x) (*Overlandes*, *litle Overlandes* 1625, 'the upper, higher selions', *v.* **uferra, land**); Ozier(s) holt (*v.* **holt**); Peter platt (from the pers.n. or surn. *Peter* with **plat**^{2}); Plantation; Rye cl; Scriveners Farm 1757 (named from the *Scrivener* family, cf. John *Scrivener* named in the document, George *Scrivener* 1723 *BT*); Slings Moor (*v.* **mōr**); Smith cl (named from the *Smyth* family, cf. John *Smyth* 1561 *BT*, Robert *Smyth* 1625); High –, Low –, Middle Snapp (*snape* 1625, *v.* **snæp** 'a boggy piece of land'); Stack cl; Gt –, Lt Swinesty (*swinsy nooke* 1671, *swinstie nooke* 1674, *Swinstye* – 1686, 1690, 1698, *Swinestienouke* 1703, *Swinesty Nooke* 1706, *Swinstye* – 1724 (*v.* **swīn, stigu** 'a sty, a pen', with **nōk**); Toft cl (*tofte* 1625, *v.* **toft** 'a messuage, a curtilage'); Toust cl (cf. *toust end* 1625, *the toustend* 1634); Tyggle Moor (*v.* **mōr**); Upper platt (*v.* **plat**[2] 'a small piece of land'); Well Bottom, – bottom (*well bottom* 1634, *v.* **wella, botm**); Winships cl (named from the *Winship* family, cf. *M*[r] *Winship* 1771); Gt –, Lt Wood cl.

(b) *campos de Aylesby* 1586, *Alsby feilde* 1601, *y*[e] *feild* 1679 (*v.* **feld**); *bagpip maire* 1625 (perhaps referring to a piece of land shaped like a bagpipe, with (**ge)mǣre** 'land on a boundary'; *blangsgare, blaunchger grene, blaunshger gate, blanshger* – 1625 (perhaps 'the white gore of land' *v.* **blanche, geiri,** with **grēne**[2] and **gata**); *blanshmarr* 1634 (*v.* (**ge)mǣre** and cf. prec.); *braken hill* 1625, *Braccon hill* (*v.* **brakni, hyll**); *Coats gate, coates leasses* 1625 (named from Great Coates, a neighbouring parish, with **gata** and **lǣs** in the pl.; *the comons* 1625; *Conygarthe* 1625 (*v.* **coni, garðr**); *Cowgarth hool* 1625 (*v.* **cū, garðr** with **hol**[l]); *Cristencare Windings* (sic) 1625, *Corsten Carr Winchinger* (sic) 1634 (obscure); *Curkle headland* 1625 (perhaps 'church hill', *v.* **kirkja, hyll** with **hēafod–land**); *The East Feild* 1634, *The East Feld* (sic) 1638, *y*[e] *East field* 1686 (*v.* **ēast, feld**, one of the great fields of the parish, cf. *the West feild infra*); *Estiby* 1327, *Estyby* 1332 both (p) ('east in the village', *v.* **ēast. í, bȳ**); *Foble mere sandes* 1625; *gare Wounge* 1625 (*v.* **geiri, vangr**); *Atte Grene* 1327, *atte* – 1332 both (p) (*v.* **grēne**[2]); *Grenedich* 1212 (*v.* **grēne**[1], **dīc**); *harpe* 1625 (alluding to the shape of the field); *Holmemares* 1634 (*v.* **holmr,** (**ge)mǣre**); *honey furlonge* 1634 (often a fanciful name for land with sticky soil); *lankinge pitts* (sic) 1625, *lampkyn pittes* 1634 (the first el. is probably the surn. *Lamnkin, v.* Reaney s.n.); *The Pasture ground* 1625; *Ribie close, – hedje* (sic) 1625 (on the boundary with Riby); *Roger Wheile maire* 1625 (*v.* (**ge)mǣre**); *rowsleits, the uper slates, the sleites* 1625 (*v.* **rūh** 'rough', **slétta** 'a level field' and cf. King sleet in f.ns. (a) *supra*); *sower hool* 1625 (*v.* **sūr, hol**[l]); *stond pits* (sic) 1625, *Stonepitt hill* 1634 (*v.* **stān, pytt**); *Suthcroft* c.1300 (*v.* **sūð, croft**); *tol mairre soule* (sic) 1625 (obscure); *Two leas* 1625 ('two allotments of grassland', *v.* **lea** (OE **lēah**) in the pl.); *Waterhouse farm* 1684, 1685 (named from the *Waterhouse* family, cf. *Widow Waterhouse* 1697 *BT*); *Watterfur* (sic) 1625 ('the water (i.e. wet) furrow', *v.* **wæter, furh**); *the west feild*

1625, – *Feild* 1634, – *Feld* (sic) 1638, *ye West field* 1686 (*v.* **west**, **feld**, one of the great fields of the parish, cf. *The East Feild supra*); *Wrengsleits* 1625 (Dr Insley suggests that this is 'the disputed level field', *v.* **slétta**, the first el. belonging to the ON verb (*v*)*rengja* in its legal sense 'to dispute, challenge'); *Wynd gripp* 1625 (perhaps 'the winding ditch', *v.* (**ge**)**wind**[2], **grype**).

Bradley

BRADLEY

> *Bredelou* 1086 DB
> *Bredelai* c.1115 LS, *–lay* 1177 P, *–la* lHy2 Dane, c.1189 LAAS v, *–l'* 1197 FF, 1254 ValNor
> *Bradela* 1163 P (p), *–lai* 1170 ib (p) *et freq* to 1210 all P (p), *–lay* 1179 ib (p), *–lea* 1177 ChancR (p), 1180, 1199 ib (p), *–le* 1176–86 YCh ii, a1183 Dane, 1199 Memo (p), 1212 Fees, 1232 Cl, 1234 Ch, 1242–43 Fees, 1259 Ipm, 1265 Pat, 1266 Misc, 1276 RH, 1282 QW, 1284 *HarlCh*, 1291 Tax, 1308 AD, 1311 Pat, 1311, 1314 Fine *et freq* to 1374 Pat, *–lee* 1308 AD, 1316 FA, 1332 *SR*, *–lay* 1179, 1180, 1181 P all (p) *et freq* to 1197 ib all (p), 1533 *Nelthorpe*, *–leia* 1196 ChancR, 1200, 1201, 1203 P, *–leg'* 1196 ChancR, 1197 FF (p), 1223 Cur, 1251 Ipm, *–l'* 1197, 1198 P, 1200 OblR, 1205, 1211, 1212, 1214, 1230 P, 1232, 1234 Cl, 1275 RH, *–leya* 1201 ChR, *–leye* 1268, 1270 Pat, 1292 Ipm, 1311 Orig, 1327 *SR*, 1336 Ch, 1349 Pat, 1351 Fine, *–legh'* 1261 Cl, 1291 Ipm, (– "by" *Grymesby*) 1297 Pat. *–ley* (– *juxta Grymesby*) 1274 Inqaqd, 1387 Pat, 1402, 1404 Cl, 1439 AD, (– *next Great Grymesbye*) 1558 *Nelthorpe*, 1679, 1694, 1698 *BT*, *–leigh* 1287 Ipm
> *Braidela* 1175–81 Dane, *–lai* 112 RA ix, *–le* 1232 Pat, *Braydeley* 1538 *Nelthorpe*
> *Braithela* a1180 (e13) *NCot*
> *Bradleie* 1196 Cur, *–le* 1361 Ipm, 1381 Peace, 1431 FA, *–lee* 1428 FA, *–ley* 1385 Misc, 1386 Fine, 1402 FA, 1419, 1421,

1450 *Nelthorpe*, 1475 Pat, 1506 Cl, 1526 Sub, 1535 VE iv,
1554 Pat *et freq*, *-lay* 1501 *Nelthorpe*, 1505 NCWills,
(*- juxta Grymesby*) 1519 *Nelthorpe*
Braddele ("by" *Grymmesby*) 1310, 1317 Pat, *-ley* 1396 ib
Braydlay 1543 *Nelthorpe*, *-ley* 1574 *ib*
Brodley 1610 Speed
Broadley 1662, 1663 *BT*, 1688 *Nelthorpe*

'The broad, wide wood or clearing', *v.* **brād, lēah**; it should be
noted that a fairly extensive wood still survives in the parish.
Forms in *Braide-*, *Brayd-* and *Braithe-* are due to Scand.
influence. Bradley is occasionally described as near Great Grimsby
and it gave its name to the wapentake in which it is situated, *v.*
Bradley Wapentake *supra*.

BRADLEY GAIRS, *the Gares* 1634, 1709 *Nelthorpe*, *Gairs* 1811,
1838 *ib*, 1839 *TA*, *Bradley Gears* 1828 Bry, cf. *Gaire Close* 1641
Nelthorpe, *Gare* - 1710 *ib*, 'the triangular plots of ground', *v.*
geiri. BRADLEY GROVE is *Kirks Farm* 1828 Bry, named from the
surn. *Kirk*, cf. Thomas *Kirk* 1846 White, where he is described as
a farmer. BRADLEY MANOR, *the nowe cheife manner howse in
Bradley*, *the Cheife Mansion house* 1638 *Nelthorpe*, cf. *the Lord
Wells mannor* 1583 *ib*, *Lordwells manner* 1611 *ib*. BRADLEY
WOOD, 1828 Bry, *- woode* 1535–46 *MinAcct*, 1537 *AOMB 209*,
Silvas de Bradley 1600 *Nelthorpe*, *Bradley wood* 1601 *LCS*, *Bosco
in Bradley* 1620 *ib*, *the great wood or Bradley Woods* 1688
Nelthorpe, cf. *Vnderwode* 1294 *Ass* (p), *Attewode* 1327 *SR* (p),
Atte Wode 1332 *ib* (p), and note *a wood called Bradeley Wood
which belonged to Wellowe* [i.e. Wellow Abbey] *lying in welloo,
Clee, Grymmesbye & Scarthowe* 1544 LP xix, cf. Bradley *supra*.
DASH WOOD, 1824 O, c.1835 *MiscDep 233A*, 1839 *TA*,
Dashwood Wood 1811 *Nelthorpe*. GREAT WOOD, 1811 *ib*, 1824
O, 1828 Bry, 1838 *Brace*; it is part of Bradley Wood *supra*. LOW
WOOD is *Farmstead* 1828 Bry. LOW WOOD (lost), 1811 *Nelthorpe*,
1824 O, 1831 *Monson*, *- Plantation* 1839 *TA*; it was part of
Bradley Gairs *supra*. NOTTY CAKE WOOD (lost), *- Wd* 1828 Bry;
Notty Cake is not recorded in dictionaries, but MED records *notti*

as 'nutlike in taste or colour, nutty', so perhaps a *notty cake* was 'a cake with a nutty taste'. Its significance in f.ns. is obscure. RECTORY, *y* *parsonage* 1577 *Terrier*, 1595 *Nelthorpe, the* – 1638, *parsonage hows* 1601, *the parsonage howse* 1612, *The Parsonage House* 1703 all *Terrier, Pars*. 1828 Bry, *the vicarage House* 1822 *Terrier, The old Mantion House . . . has been taken away, and in their place a new Rectory House was built in the year 1849 in the pingle lying north of the Lane which leadeth to Grimsby* 1864 *ib*. SCARTHO WOOD, 1824 O, 1831 *Monson*, 1838 *Brace*; it is part of Bradley Wood named from Scartho *infra*. SOURWELLS (lost), 1824 O, 1831 *Monson*, 1838 *Brace*, – *Wells* 1811, 1838 *Nelthorpe*, 1839 *TA*, cf. *Sowre lea furrelong* 1628, *Sower Le Well Close* 1634, *Sowrely well* 1654, *Sowereliwell chase* 1685, *Sower Lewell Close* 1709 all *Nelthorpe*; the earlier name is 'the sour meadow, pasture', *v*. **sūr, lea** (OE **lēah**), to which was added **wella** 'a well, a spring'. TEAM GATE DRAIN, 1828 O, 1831 *Monson*, 1838 *Brace*; it forms the boundary with Barnoldby le Beck, PN L **4**, 54.

FIELD–NAMES

Undated forms in (a) are 1839 *TA*; forms dated Hy3 are *HarlCh*; 1274 Inqaqd; 1292, 1293, 1311 Ipm; a1300, 1316, 1329, 1331, 1332, 1421, 1450, 1501, 1527, 1538, 1540, 1541, 1543, 1544, 1545, 1546, 1551, 1553, 1574, 1575, 1577[1], 1578, 1583, 1592, 1593, 1595, 1596, e17, 1600, 1628, 1633, 1634[1], 1638, 1641[1], 1654, 1673, 1685, 1686, 1709, 1710, 1776, 1777, 1811, 1838 *Nelthorpe*; 1309 AD; 1457 *TCC*; 1624 HMCRep; 1577[2], 1601, 1612, c.1625, 1634[2], 1638, 1662, 1664, 1671, 1674, 1679, 1686, 1690, 1692, 1703, 1718, 1724, 1781, 1822 *Terrier*; 1638 VisitN.

(a) Barn Cl 1811, 1838, 1839; Beechers Cl 1811, 1839 (probably from the surn. *Beecher*); Blue–caps 1811, Blue Cop 1838, – Caps 1839 (*blew cox hill* (sic) 1682, *Blew cop hill* 1634[1], *Blue copphill* 1654, *Blewcophill* 1709, *blue Copp hill* 1711, *v*. **copp** 'the top of a hill, a peak, a summit'; the first el. is obscure); Bottom Cl 1811, 1838, 1839; Church Holes 1838, 1839 (*a Plot of ground callled y* *church hole* 1664, *y* *Church* – 1674); Church Yard

Cl 1839; East –, West Clover fd 1811, 1838, – Fd 1838, 1839; Crow Fd; East Walk 1811, 1839 (*v.* **walk** 'a stretch of grass for pasturing sheep' cf. **shepe–walk** and West Walk *infra*); Forehouse Cl ('(the close) in front of the house', *v.* **fore, hūs**); Four Pound Cl 1838, – and Hills 1839 (*four pound Close* 1634[1], *foure pound close* 1709, doubtless alluding to a rent, cf. Seven Pound Cl *infra*); Fourteen Acres 1811, 1838, 1839; Glebe Cl 1838; Hall Cl 1838, 1839 (*the Old Hall garthes* 1634[1], – *garths* 1654, – *garth* 1673, 1685, *the old hall Garths* 1709, *the Hall Garth* 1668, *Hall Garths* 1710, *v.* **hall, garðr** 'an enclosure', as elsewhere in the parish); Hill Cl 1811, 1838, 1839, Hills 1811, 1838 (cf. *otthe Hill de Bradley* 1428 *GrimsCt* (p)); Home Cl 1838, 1839; Homestead 1839; Horse Cl 1811, 1838, 1839 (*the horse Closes* 1668, *ye Horse Close*, *ye north Horse close* 1674, *horse closes* 1710); Far House Cl 1811, 1839; Hundred Acres 1838, – Acres 1839 (an ironic name, well–evidenced elsewhere, for a small field; the area here is 2r. 11p.); Jack Daw Fd 1811, 1838, 1839 (referring to the bird, the jackdaw (*Corvus monedula*)); Jeykells 1811, (Great –, Little –) 1811, 1839 (*Jekells closes* 1654, *Jeck hills closes*, *Jeckills close* 1710, named from the *Jekell* family, cf. John *Jickell* 1634, John and William *Jeckhill* 1641); Kings Cl (cf. *Kings ground* e1700; probably from the surn. *King*, cf. Thomas *King* 1739 *BT*); Kitchen Fd 1811, 1838, 1839; (Furze) Knowles Cl 1811, 1838, 1839 (*v. the Innams* in (b) *infra*); Lessoe's Cl 1776, Lessoes – 1777; Little Fd 1811, 1838, 1839; Little Wd 1811, 1838; (Little) Mathew Cl 1811, Mathew Cl or Ascough Cl 1811, 1838, 1839 (probably from the surn. *Mathew*, the alternative name being no doubt from a surn. too); Meadow Fd; Moor dale 1781, Moordale 1822, 1839 (*More dayles* 1457, *the moore –*, *the more dales* e17, *moare dale* 1625, *Moore dales*, *Moredale* 1628, *–dales* 1634[1], *Moore dale*1634[2], *the more daile* 1662, *More dale* 1668, *the –* 1671, *y^e –* 1679, *the moredale* 1686, – *Moredales* 1709, *Moor Dale* 1718, 1724, *v.* **mōr, deill**, sometimes in the pl.); Moor Hill 1811, 1838, 1839; Narrow Lds 1811, 1838, 1839 (*v.* **land**); New Crofts 1811, 1838, 1839 (*newcroft* 1595, *newe Crofte* 1596, *Newcrof* (sic), *Newcroft* 1628, *the Newcroftes* 1634[1], *Newcrofts* 1638, *little –*, *North new Croft(e)s* 1654, *the New Crofts* 1709, *the little –*, *North New Crofts* 1710, *v.* **nīwe, croft**); Nine Acres, Nine Ac[r] Field 1811, 1838, Nine Acres (Fd) 1839; Pearson's Yd 1811, Pearsons – 1839 (from the surn. *Pearson*, cf. John *Pearson* 1755 *BT*); Pingle 1811, 1838, 1839 (*on* [i.e. one] *close called a pyngle* 1577[2], *vno clauso vocat' a Pingle* 1634[1], *a little piece of ground comonly called a Pingle* 1703, *the pingle* 1709, *v.* **pingel** 'a small enclosure', as described in 1701, cf. *pingle nooke* 1628); Rhodes Cl 1811, 1838, 1839 (from the surn. *Rhodes*); Ruckles 1811, 1839 (obscure); Rye

Grass 1811, 1838, 1839 (alluding to the pasture grass, *Lolium perenne*); Scartho Cl 1828, Scarthoe Cl, – Fd 1811, 1839 (cf. *Scarthow dikes* 1316, *Scartho Dikes* 1628 (*v*. **dík**), *le Scarthow meare* 1574 (*v*. **(ge)mǣre**, the boundary with Scartho, a neighbouring parish); Scrub Cl 1776, Scrub Dale 1811, 1838, Scrubdale 1839 (cf. *Scrubwood* 1634[1], *Scrub wood* 1709, *v*. **scrubb**); Seven Acres 1811, 1838, 1839 (*Seven Acres plott* 1654); Seven Pound Cl 1838, 1839 (presumably a reference to the rent, cf. Four Pound Cl *supra*); Sheffields 1811, 1838, 1839, High –, Low Sheffield 1811, 1838, – Sheffields 1839 (presumably from the surn. *Sheffield*); Shift Cl 1811, 1838, 1839 (probably referring to *shifts* in crop–rotation, discussed s.n. *a shift–acre* in the f.ns. (b) of South Ferriby, PN L **2**, 116); Spooner Cl 1811, 1838, 1839 (from the surn. *Spooner*); Standmoor 1811, Stanmoor 1838, 1839 (*the furlong called stanmaire, Stanmayre dyk* 1536 (*v*. **dík**), *Stangmare nooke, Stanmore* – 1628, *Stanmore* 1628, 1634[1], 1709 ('the stony boundary, land forming a boundary', *v*. **stān, (ge)mǣre**); Ten Pound Cl 1811, 1834, – pound Cl 1839 (probably referring to the rent of the land, cf. Four Pound Cl and Seven Pound Cl *supra*); Tofts 1811, Toft 1838, 1839 (*long tofte* 1577[2], *a furlong callede the tofte* 1601, *the Tofte–furlonge* 1612, *long* –, *short Toft, Toftgreene* 1628, *a furlonge called tofts* 1634[1], 1634[2], *toft–furlong* 1638, *A furlong called tofts*, *yᵉ Plot of Ground calld Tofts* 1664, *the Close called the Toffts* 1668, *yᵉ Toffts* 1674, *One other of them* [i.e. Closes] *called by the name of Toft's* 1710 (*v*. **toft** 'a curtilage, a messuage'; it was situated in the extreme north–west corner of the parish); Twenty Acres 1811, 1838, 1839 (*yᵉ Twentiacres* 1664, *the twenty Acres* 1668, 1674); Waltham Fd (*Waltham feilds meare* e17, cf. *Waltham Mere* 1457, *Wattham* (sic) *meare* 1628 (*v*. **(ge)mǣre**, 'a boundary, boundary land', alluding to the adjoining parish of Waltham); West Fd 1811, 1838, 1839 (*the west felld* 1546, *the West feild* 1628, *v*. **west, feld**, one of the great fields of Bradley, cf. *the north feelde, the south felld'* in (b) *infra*); West Walk 1811, 1839 (*v*. **west, walk**, cf. East Walk *supra*); Wood Cl 1811, 1838, 1839 (cf. *the wood end* e17, *Wood gate, the furlong under wood side* 1628, *le Wood lane end close* 1634[1], *the wood land close* 1709, named from Bradley Wood *supra*).

(b) *the abbey close* 1593, *the Abbey lane, the Abbey wood* 1628, *Abbey close* 1641, *Abbotts Close* 1575, *the Abbottes close, the abbottes close being parcell of the possessions of the late dissolued monasterie of Welhowe* 1577[1] (*v*. **abbbaye, abbat**; the reference is to Wellow Abbey in Great Grimsby); *bad acres furlong* e17, *bad Acres* 1628 (presumably self–explanatory); *barbowr greyn* 1546 (from the surn. *Barber* or *Barbour*, cf. William *Barber*

1620 *BT*, with **grēne**[2]; for the spelling *greyn*, cf. *the common greyn infra*);
barlyng mayre heylle 1546 (named from the *Barlynge(s)* family, cf. William
Barlynges 1501, with (**ge**)**mǣre, hyll**); *Bassingbornedale* 1274 (from the
surn. *Bassingbourn*, with **deill**); *Beardshaws close* 1654, *Beardshawes Close*
1673, 1685 (named from the *Beardshaw* family, cf. William *Beardshaw*
1669); *Bimangrene* Hy3, *Bymanlease* 1628 (named from the *Beaman* family,
though this has not been noted before Anthony *Beaman* 1673 *BT*, with
grēne[2], **lea** 'meadow, grassland' (OE **lēah**) in the pl.; the surn. possibly
developed from *Biman* Hy3); *Bradleys garth* 1634[1], *Bradleyes garth* 1709,
bradlay more 1544 (perhaps named from the *Bradley* family, cf. Robert
Bradley 1602 *BT*, with **garðr** and **mōr**); *bryans land* 1543 (named from the
Bryan family, cf. John *Bryan* 1421); *burell howys* 1543 (*v.* **hūs**), *Burwels
garth* 1634[1], *Burwell garth* 1709 (named from the *Burwell* family, cf. John
Burwell 1576 *Nelthorpe*, with **garðr**); *burnt garthe* 1578 (*v.* **garðr**); *a
common land called the butt land* 1634[1], *the butt lane* (sic) 1634[2], 1638, –
Lane 1664 (*v.* **butte**); *Butt Marr furre* 1628 (*v.* **butte, marfur** 'a boundary
furrow'); *Butterþorn* Hy3, *short butter thorne* 1628 (*v.* **þorn**; the
significance of *butter* here is obscure); *Capham furres* 1593 (presumably
from the surn. *Capham* with **fyrs** or **furh** 'a furrow' in the pl.); *Cawther
syke* 1593, *Cautersike* 1628 (probably from the surn. *Cauther* or *Cawther*,
with **sík**); *kyreklayn, kyrkplace* 1501, *the church way* 1601, *the church
wonge* 1601, *the Church-furlonge* 1612 (*v.* **cirice** (Scandinavianized in the
1501 names), with **lane, place, weg, vangr, furlang**); *Clarks garth* 1634[1],
Clarkes Garth 1709 (named from the *Clark* family, cf. John *Clarke* 1570 *BT*,
with **garðr**); *Cockthorne greene* 1628 (presumably self-explanatory, cf.
Cockthorne Fm PN L **3**, 116; *v.* also **grēne**[2] 'a grassy spot'); (*ultra*) *the
comond grene* 1538, *the Common Greene* 1541, *coem le greyn* 1543, *the
common greyn* 1543, *lee Coem grene* 1545, *the common greyn* 1546 (*v.*
grēne[2] 'a green, a grassy spot'); *the commown marfowre* 1546 (*v.* **marfur**
'a boundary furrow'); *the Comon peece* 1628 (*v.* **pece**); *coem' venellam ex
occidental'* 1540 ('the common street from the west'), *coem viam versus
occidentem* 1421, *coem –* 1450, *coem viam versus occidental' et boream'*
1551 ('the common way towards the west and north'), *the Comond Waye*
1538, *the comman waye* 1541, *the common waye agaynst the West* 1543, *the
commown way of the West* 1546; *the Comons* 1628; *the corne lands* e17, *the
Corne-field* 1612, *Corne Feild* 1654, *the Corne Plott* 1710 (*v.* **corn**[1] 'grain');
the Cotagers Plott 1634[1], *the Cottages* (sic) *Plot* 1709; *Covil leas* 1628 (*v.*
lea (OE **lēah**) in the pl.; *Covil* is perhaps the surn. *Covill(e)*); *Cow Pasture*

1628; *the furlong called crakwell'* 1546 (*v.* **kráka** 'a crow, a raven', **wella** and cf. Crow Fd in (a) *supra*); *Crosse greene* 1628; *Daltons close* 1654, – *Close* 1673, 1685 (named from the *Dalton* family, cf. John *Dalton* 1596, William *Dallton* 1614 *Inv*); *Danegate* Hy3 (probably 'the Danes' way, road', *v.* **Danir**, **gata**, cf. Deansgate in Great Grimsby); *John Drapers plott* 1633, 1638, *Drapers Plott* 1634¹ (named from the **Draper** family of frequent occurrence locally, cf. Robert *Draper* 1552, *Isabell draper* 1589 *BT*, with **plot**); *on* [i.e. one] *merfour called dypdalle* 1546 (*v.* **dēop, dalr**); *Drixdales* (sic) 1628 (obscure); *the East feild* 1593 (*v.* **ēast, feld**; in view of the lack of documentation, this appears to be a late addition to the open fields); *Eastlandes* 1628 (*v.* **ēast, land**, cf. *Westlandes infra*); *Elbow dales* (*v.* **deill** 'a share of land' in the pl.; an allusion to their angular shape); *Estbrathel* (sic) 1332 (*v.* **ēast**; the second el. is obscure); *Eykholm* 1292, 1293, *Aykeholme* 1311, *one close commonly called Akehams* 1654 ('the raised land in marsh, water–meadow where oaks grow', *v.* **eik, holmr**, a Scand. compound); *Eschete leys*, – *leis* 1577 ('escheated grassland', *v.* **eschete, lea** (OE **lēah**) 'grassland, pasture' in the pl.); (*super*) *Eskes* Hy3 (*v.* **eski** 'a place growing with ash–trees'); *Eyngesheueds* a1300 (perhaps from **eng** 'meadow, pasture', with **hēafod** in the pl., though Dr Insley suggests that the first el. may be the ContGerm pers.n. **Einger*, recorded in Feilitzen 246 from Bk); *in campis de Bradele* 1331, *in campis* 1501, – *de Bradeley* 1575, *Bradley feild* e17, *the Feildes of Bradley* 1638, *the feilds of Bradley* 1709 (*v.* **feld**); *the foure litle Closes* 1638; *the grass headings* e17; *Grimsby feild side* e17 (*v.* **feld, sīde**); *Grymesby gate* 1457, *Grimsby gate* 1628 ('the road to Great Grimsby', *v.* **gata**); *the highway from Grimsby to Caster* 1628; *Hallan grene* 1457; *Halley greene* e17 (*v.* **grēne²**), *between Halley & landgreene, a place called Halley* 1628, *Hally wood Close* 1710 (probably named from the *Hall(e)y* family, cf. William *Halley* 1663 *BT*); *the hardes* 1628 ('the hard places', *v.* **heard**, presumably places hard to till); *Hededayles* 1457 (*v.* **hēafod, deill**); *boscum Georgii Henney milit'* 1592 (i.e. 'Sir George Henney's wood'); *the High feild* 1674, (*v.* **hēah, feld**); *hornelane* 1501, ... *adjoins Horner or Pingould Lane* (sic) 1624; *Horsington headland* 1628 (presumably from the surn. *Horsington* and **hēafod–land**); *the hows Close* 1664; *Hyldaylehedes* 1457, *Hyldaylle furlong* 1546 (*v.* **hyll, deill** with **hēafod** in the pl.); *the Innams, short Innams* 1628, *the Inmun Close* (sic) 1638, *Inhams close or Knoles Close* 1654, *Inholmes Close or Knowles Close* 1685 (*v.* **innām** 'a piece of land taken in'; the alternative name perhaps alludes to the family of Richard *Knowles Clerici* 1634); *the Intack* 1668, 1703, *yᵉ* – 1664, 1674, 1690, 1692 (*v.* **inntak** 'a piece of land taken in or enclosed', cf. *the Innams supra*); *Kelby howys* 1543 (named from the *Kelby* family, cf. Richard *Kelby* 1527); *the Kilnehouse Close* 1628; *Laceby hedge* 1628, 1634[1], 1638, 1709 (referring to Laceby, a neighbouring parish); *lady bridge dale* 1628; *Lamcroft wong* 1628 (*v.* **lamb, croft, vangr**); *Longmaire hyll* 1546, *Langmare hill*, *langmare hole*, *a wong called long mare* 1628, *Lang more Close* 1634[1], *great & little Langmore* 1654, *Great* -, *little lang more* 1710, *Langmore Close* 1709 'the long boundary, land forming a boundary', *v.* **lang, (ge)mære**); *Layrebergh mare* a1300 (*v.* **leirr** 'clay', **beorg** 'a hill, a mound', with **(ge)mære**); *Lenecroft* 1293 [*n* = *u*], *Levecroftes* 1308 ('Leve's croft', *v.* **croft**; the first el. is the ME pers.n. *Lēue*, from OE *Lēofa*, *v.* Feilitzen 310); *Lyncolgate* 1457, *Lincolne gate* e17 ('the road to Lincoln', *v.* **gata**); *the high way goinge to Litle Cotes* 1601, *the gate called Coates gate* 1628, *heigh way y[t] Leedeth from Bradley to Littell Coats* 1664, *the foote-way that leades to little Coates* 1668, *ye high way y[t] leads to little Coates* 1674 (self-explanatory, *v.* **gata**); *Coates hedge* 1628, *litle Coates hedge* 1654, *little Coats hedge* 1673, *little coats hedge* 1685 ('the (boundary) hedge with Little Coates', *v.* **hecg**); *Little wood or Hog-wood* 1686; *lodge furlong* 1628; *long greene* 1628 (*v.* **grēne**[2] 'a grassy place'); *long heid laynd* 1546 (*v.* **hēafod-land**); *longmekyll holm' gatte* 1544, *longmekelle holme gotte* 1553 (*v.* **gotu**); *long mickleholmes* 1628, *Michel holmes bottom* e17 (*v.* **botm**) ('the big piece of raised land in marsh', *v.* **mikill, holmr**, a Scand. compound, with **lang** 'long, big' prefixed); *Lucroft* 1457 (obscure); *Mason's garth* 1634[1], *Masons Garth* 1709 (named from the *Mason* family, cf. Peter *Mason* 1592 *BT*, with **garðr**); *the mawne close* e17, *the Mowing Close* 1634[1], *the mowing wood close* 1654; *the moorewell furlong* e17, *Morewell*, *the more well* 1628, *Morewell Close* 1634[1], 1709, *The More Well* - (*v.* **mōr, wella**); *muswellegrene* 1329, *Muswell greene* 1628 (from **mūs** 'a mouse', **wella** with **grēne**[2]); *Mr Mussenden Wood* 1600 (*v.* **wudu**; Francis *Mussenden de healinge* is mentioned in the document); *Mylne mares* 1457 (*v.* **myln, (ge)mære** in the pl.); *neitgait gren'* 1546 (from **nēat** 'cattle', **gata**, with **grēne**[2]); *Mr Richard Nelthropp's dwelling-house* 1634[2], *Mr Edward Nelthorpe Hall* 1664; *new dyk* 1546, *le Newdike* 1574, *ye New dike* 1664, *newe dike hedge* e17, *Newdike* - 1628, *New dike* - 1634[1], *the New dike* - 1709 (*v.* **dík**); *the New Intake* 1638 (*v.* **inntak**, cf. *the Intack supra*); *in boriali campo de Bradele* 1316, *Camp' bor'* 1457, *the north feelde* 1601, *the North feild* c.1625, *the Northfeeld* 1634[1], *the north feild* 1634[2], 1638, 1664, *the Northfeild* 1668 (one of the great fields of Bradley, cf. West Fd in (a) *supra*, *the south felld' infra*); *Oastwell* 1628, *-close* 1634[1], *- Close* 1709; *Odlyns garth* 1634[1], *Odlings* - 1709 (named from the *Odling* family, cf. John *Odling* 1602 *BT*, with **garðr**); *the orchard* 1612; *out est furlong* 1544, *Out est furlonge* 1553 ('the outer east furlong', *v.* **ūt, ēast, furlang**); *the Oxganginges* 1628 (*v.* **oxgang, eng**); *Oxe pasture* 1628; *Pale Yard* 1710; *a close of Pasture called Paradise* 1638 (*v.* **paradis**); *Peselandgrene* a1300, *Peasland greene* e17, *peasland* –, *peaseland* – 1628 (*v.* **pīse** 'pease', **land**, with **grēne**[2]); *Prestegare* 1457 (*v.* **prēost, geiri** 'a triangular plot of ground'); *Ridinges* 1634[1], *Ridings close* 1654, *Ridings* 1709, *rideings* 1710 (perhaps 'the clearings', *v.* **ryding**, though this word is rare in north L p.ns.); *Roe garre* 1628, *Rowes garth* 1634[1], *Rowses Garth* 1709 (named from the *Rowse* family, cf. George *Rowse* 1604 *BT*, with **garðr**); *Roger greene* 1628, *Roger Old Acres plott* 1654 (probably from the surn. *Roger* with **grēne**[2]); *Saltergate* 1457 ('the road used by salt-merchants', *v.* **saltere, gata**); *sawlter gayres* 1546, *Sautergares*, *Saltergaies* (sic) e17, *Sautergarres*, *Sawtergares* 1628 (from the occupational or derived surn. *Salter* with **geiri**); *Scadacre headland* 1628 (*v.* **hēafod–land**); *Segg hole* 1628 (*v.* **secg** in a Scandinavianized form, and **hol**[1]); *the Sheepe walkes* 1634[1], *the North* –, *the South sheepe walk*(*e*) 1654, 1673, *the north* –, *the South Sheepe Walke* 1685, *the South sheep walk or great Sheep walk* 1710 (*v.* **shepe–walk**); *Sheriffes Close* 1628 (no doubt from the surn. *Sheriff*); *short dales* 1628 (*v.* **deill**); *in territoris australi de bradele* Hy3, *in austali campo* (sic) 1332, *in australi campo de Bradele* a1300, 1329, *Campus austr'* 1457, – *de Bradley* 1554, – *de Bradleye more* 1553, – *de Braydley* 1574, *the south felld'* 1546, *the southfeild* e17, *the south feild* 1628 (one of the great fields of Bradley, *v.* **sūð, feld**, cf. *the north feelde supra* and West Fd in (a) *supra*); *Sqwyre howys* 1543 (named from the *Squyre* Family, cf. William *Sqwyre* 1546, with **hūs**); *the steppinge stones at the woodside* e17; *Swallowe garth* 1634[1], *Swallow Garth* 1709 (named from the *Swallow* family, cf. John *Swallow* 1589 *BT*, Richard *Swallowe* 1592 *ib*, with **garðr**); *Swan greyn* 1546 (for *greyn* cf. *the common greyn supra*); *the swath* 1628 (*v.* **swæð**); *Swelacres* a1300 (Dr Insley suggests that this is 'the fields with raised plots of ground', *v.* **swelle, (ge)swell, æcer**); *a wong called swyne lawer* 1628; *Symson' garth* 1634[1], *Sympsons Garth* 1709 (named from the *Simpson* family, cf. William *Simpson* 1625 *BT*, with **garðr**); *Tadacres* 1457 (perhaps 'the plots of arable land infested by toads', *v.* **tadde, æcer**); *Tatam wife garth* 1634[1], 1709 (named from a member of the *Tatam* family, cf. John *Taytam* 1577 *Inv*, Thomas *Tatham* 1596 *BT*); *Thomson's garth* 1634, *Thompson Garth* 1707 (named from the *Thomson* family, cf. Edward *Thomson* 1592 *BT*, with **garðr**); *the greene where the thorne tree standes* 1628; *þreþornes* Hy3 ('the three thorn-trees', *v.* **þrēo, þorn**); *Townend*

Close, the Townend furlong, the Townes end 1628; *Traneholm* 1329, *tranrow* 1628 (*v.* **trani** 'a heron, a crane', **holmr**, a Scand. compound); *viam regiam ex oriental'* 1546 ('the royal way from the east'), *super viam versus occident'* 1545 ('the way towards the west'); *waterswalls* 1628 (*v.* **wæter** and perhaps **swælg** 'a pit, a pool' or the like); *ye Vicarage Garth* 1662 (*v.* **garðr** and The Rectory *supra*); *the well, the furrelong under the well side* 1628, *the well garth* 1638 (*v.* **wella, garðr**); *the west end* 1593; *Westlandes* 1628 (*v.* **west, land**, cf. *Eastlandes supra*); *Wolvernedale* 1274 (Dr Insley suggests that this is 'the valley infested by wolves', *v.* **wylfen, dalr**. He notes that OE **wylfen** 'wolfish' would normally have given spellings in *wilf-* here, but perhaps the first el. has been remodelled through analogy with the substantive **wulf**); *the Wong* 1628 (*v.* **vangr**); *boscum Jacobi Wright* 1592 (i.e. 'James Wright's wood'), *Mr Wrighes Wood* 1628 (probably named from an ancestor of *Hustwait Wright*, named in the 1628 document, *v.* **wudu**).

Cleethorpes

OLD CLEE

Cleia (4x) 1986 DB, *Cleiam* 1191, 1192, 1193, 1194 P, *Cleie*
1206 Ass, *Cleye* 1314 Inqaqd, *Cley* 1362 *CottCh*
Cle (3x) c.1115 LS, 1155–58 (1334) Ch, 1196 ChancR, 1197,
1198, 1202, 1204, 1205, 1206 P, 1212 Fees, p1220
WellesLA, 1242–43 Fees, 1275, 1276 RH, 1281 QW, 1292
RSu, 1300 Abbr, 1303 FA, 1304 Fine *et passim* to 1594 *Inv*
Clee 1232 Welles, 1254 ValNor, 1281 QW, 1291 Tax, 1298
Ass, 1304 Ipm, 1310 AD ii, 1314 Pat, 1316 AD iii, 1316
FA, 1327 *SR*, 1328 Banco, 1332 *SR*, 1335 Pat, 1341 *Extent*,
1343 *AddCh*, 1346 FA, 1351 *Cor et freq*, – als *Cley* 1316
to 1759 all *BT Clye* 1537 LP, 1551 Pat, 1576, 1597 *Inv*

From OE **clæg** 'clay, clayey soil', topographically appropriate for the site of Old Clee, now the name of the old village. Clee was originally the name of the parish.

CLEETHORPES

Thorpe 1406 Pat
Clethorpe 1552 *Inv*, 1652 *Rad*
Cleethorpp 1581 HMCRep, *–thorp* 1593 *Inv,* 1606 Admin,
  1723 *Td'E*, *–thorpe* 1582 Admin, 1593 *Inv*, 1598–99 Lanc,
  1622 Admin, *Clee Thorpe* 1694 *Haigh*, *– als Itterbie* 1593
  Inv, 1831 *Monson*, 1838 *Brace*, 1840 *EnclA*, *Cleethorp
  called Itterbie in the parishe of Clee* 1593 *Inv*
Clethorpes 1588 *Inv*, 1588 Admin, 1588–89 Lanc, 1695 *NW*,
  – thorpes 1606 *Inv*, *– thorps* 1609 *DuLaMB 119*, 1670 *Inv*,
  –thorps 1685 *NW*, *– Thorps* 1707 *BT*, 1736 *Inv*
Clee thorpes 1598, 1599 *Inv*, *–thorps* 1604, 1606, 1690 *Inv*,
  –thorps 1643, 1644 *ib*, *–thorpes* 1612 HMCRep, 1648
  Admin, 1671 *Inv*, 1749 *Field*, 1838 *Brace et passim*, *–
  Thorpes* 1723, 1742 *Inv*, 1755 *NW*
Cleythorpes 1597 *Inv*, *– Thorps* 1684 *Td'E*
Cleythorp 1697 Pryme

The 1406 reference occurs in a Confirmation of grants and
confirmations made to the prioress and convent of *Grymmesby*. It
refers to rents and possessions in *Grymmesby*, *Scarthowe*, *Clee
Thorpe*, *Welesby*, *Houton*, etc., the commas being purely editorial.
All the places mentioned here are in Bradley Wapentake. From the
order of the names it seems clear that the edited text should read
Grymmesby, *Scarthowe*, *Clee*, *Thorpe*, *Welesby*, *Houton*, etc. If
this is so this would be the earliest reference so far found for
Cleethorpes and it occurs in a simplex form. It will be noted that
the name subsequently appears as a compound in both singular *and*
plural forms; so, presumably the name means 'the outlying
settlement of Clee', *v.* þorp. The plural form is no doubt to be
explained because there were two very adjacent places, *Hole* and
Itterby, now part of Cleethorpes, with *Thrunscoe* a little to the
south.

HOLE (lost)

Hol c.1115 LS, 1210–12 RBE, 1212 Fees, c.1220 de l'Isle,
1242–43 Fees, 1259, 1273 Ipm, 1275 RH, 1298 Ass (p)
Hole 1275, 1276 RH, 1282 FF, 1292 RSu (p), 1300 FF, 1309
Pat, 1328 Banco, 1332 SR (p), 1346 de l'Isle, 1351 Cor,
1373 Cl et freq to 1649 Admin, Ole 1345 Abbr
Hule 1372 Misc, Hulle 1545 Inv
Hool 1386 Misc, 1784 Terrier, 1787 ThorGrims, Hoole 1443
AD vi, 1475 HMCRep, 1518 GrimsCB, 1530–31 Lanc,
1551, 1557, 1559 Inv, 1609 DuLaMB 119, 1613 Td'E et
passim to 1822 Terrier, the hoole 1664, 1747 ThorGrims, –
Hoole 1725 Td'E, 1756 ThorGrims, Hooll 1562 Inv
Hoyll 1531 Wills iii
Howle 1538–44 ECP, 1579 Inv, 1582 Admin, 1603 Inv, 1635
Terrier, 1853 MiscDon 328, How(i)ll a1567 LNQ v, Houle
1558, 1583, 1584, 1613 Inv, 1631 MiscDep 118, Whole
1587 Inv
Oole Road 1843 Hig, 1846 EnclA, Oole Drain 1846 ib

'The hollow', v. hol[1], topographically appropriate for the site of
the original settlement. For details v. Baker 10–11 and Watson
98–100. The name survives today in Oole Road in Cleethorpes and
was alternatively known as Fore Thorpe, Low Thorpe and Near
Cleethorpes.

HOLME HILL

Sotholm 1182, 1183 P, Sud– 1184, 1185 ib, Sutholm' 1212 FF
(p), 1282 FF, –holme c.1300 Guis
Saltholm 1191, 1192, 1193, 1194, 1195 P, 1196 ChancR, 1197,
1198, 1199 P
Holm 1275 RH, 1287 Ipm, 1313 Pat, 1332 SR (p), 1366
GrimsFC (p), 1372 Misc, Eliz ChancP, Holme 1276 RH,
1314 Inqaqd, 1314 Pat, 1327 SR (p), 1335 Fine (p), 1387 Cl
et passim to 1547 Pat

Hulm 1313 Inqaqd
Cleholme 1316 Pat
Holm' Hyll 1508 *GrimsCB ii*, *Holm hill* 1518 *GrimsCLeet*,
  holme - 1635 *Terrier*, 1720 *GrimsCLeet*, *Holme Hill* 1709
  LindDep 95, 1710, 1719 *Td'E*, 1828 Bry

The earliest forms indicate that this is 'the southern piece of higher ground amidst the marsh', *v.* **sūð**, **holmr**, presumably in relation to Grimsby. The late 12th century forms from P seem to belong here suggesting *Saltholm* was an alternative name 'the salty holme', *v.* **salt**, **holmr**. From 1275 onwards the name appears in a simplex form. The spelling *Cleholme* 1316 is unique and must mean 'the holme belonging to Clee' in which parish it was situated.

The site is described by Oliver 30 (1825), who states "Holm Hill is the most extraordinary monument which Grimsby can boast. It is more than 2000 feet long by 300 broad, —180 feet sloping height, from the most elevated point—and contains upwards of twelve acres of land". Today, there is only a slight rise and Foster, LRS 17, lii, 1920, comments "the site now forms part of the municipal borough of Grimsby and the name Holme Hill survives to specify the district immediately to the east of Hainton square, in Grimsby, where St. Luke's church, St. Andrew's vicarage, the Holme Hill Council Schools etc., are situated. No more than a mound, the site of St. Mary's Roman church, now remains to represent Holme Hill; but a hundred years ago the hill was one hundred and sixty feet high, and covered twelve acres. Fifty years ago to anyone facing eastwards from what is now Hainton square it appeared as a nearly perpendicular cliff from forty to fifty feet high, which in about ten years time was levelled, the materials being used by builders."

ITTERBY (lost)

Itrebi (4x) 1086 DB, *Ittreby* 1459 AD vi
Iterby 1210–12 RBE
Yterby 1210–12 RBE

Utterby 1242–43 Fees, 1303, 1346 FA, 1544, 1662 *Inv*, *-bye*
1545 *ib*, *Vtterby* 1543, 1616, 1627 *ib*, *-bie* 1546, 1591 *ib*,
a1567 LNQ v
Ytterby 1273 Ipm, 1467 WillsPCC, *-bi* 1275 RH
Itterby 1294 *Ass*, 1309 Pat, 1327 *SR* (p), 1328 Banco, 1351
Cor, 1364 AD iii, 1372 Misc, 1373, 1375, 1387, 1395
Peace *et freq*, *-bye* 1530–31 Lanc, 1594, 1602 *Inv*, *-bie*
1564, 1584 *ib*, 1635 *Terrier*
Itterbie thorp (sic) 1587 *Inv*, *Itterby thorpe* 1589 *ib*

'The outer secondary, farmstead, village (of Clee)', *v.* **ytri**, **bȳ**.
This appears to be a unique Scand. compound. The forms in the
1587 and 1589 *Inv* are noteworthy and are apparently simply
alternative forms for Itterby itself. Itterby was situated a quarter
of a mile south of Hole, and was later known as Middle Thorpe,
Far Cleethorpes and Upper Thorpe, *v.* Baker 10, 18 etc.

THRUNSCOE (lost)

Ternescou (2x) 1086 DB, *-sco* 1086 ib, *-scrou* (sic) 1086 ib
Tirnesco c.1115 LS, 1194 P (p), *-scog* 1212 Fees
Tiernesco 1195 P
Thirnescho 1212 Fees, *-sco* 1273 Ipm, 1364 AD iii, 1372 Misc,
-scogh' 1300 *FF*, *Thirnessco* 14 AD vi, *Thyrnescho* 1440
Visit, *-scough* 1502 Ipm, *Thyrnscho* 1327 *SR* (p), *Thirnsco*
1373, 1376 Peace both (p), 1384 ib, 1421 *AD*, 1446 AD
Thernesco 1309 Pat, *Thrinesco* 1332 *SR* (p), *Thrynsco* 1395
Peace, *-scowe* 1443 AD vi, *-scoo* 1536–37 Dugd vi,
Thrinsco 1503 Ipm
Thurnsco 1535 VE iv, *Thurnescoe* a1567 LNQ v
Throunschow 1572 *Inv*, *Thronskow* 1581 *ib*
Thrunskoe 1594 *Inv*, 1758 *BT*, *-scoe* Eliz ChancP, 1645
BRA1293, 1663, 1677 *Inv et passim*, *- Farm* 1871 *Census*,
-scowe 1609 LRMB 256, *-scoo* 1611, 1636 *Foster*, 1846
EnclA, *-sco* 1627, 1635, 1690 *Inv*, 1842 White

Thrumscoe als Thrumstow als Thrumstowe (sic) 1636 *LincsD*,
Thronschothorp 1588 *Inv, the Thorpe of Thrunscoe* 1761 *Td'E*

'The thorn–bush wood', *v.* **þyrnir** 'a thorn–bush', **skógr**, a
Scand. compound. The site is now built over and the name is
represented today by Thrunscoe Rd.

BEACON HILL (lost), 1734 *SSCTerrier*, 1842 White, cf. *Beacon
Meer fur* (sic) 1784 *Terrier, the Beacon Murfor* 1822 *Terrier* (*v.*
marfur), the site of a beacon and now represented by Beacon
Avenue. B.W. points out that Beacon Hill is marked on 1890 O,
and is situated in Cleethorpes Cemetery. BEACONTHORPE (lost),
1851, 1871 *Census, Cleethorpes Beacon* 1835 Baker; this was an
area around Clee Ness (B.W.). It was named from a white beacon
erected in 1834 by the Admiralty to cut down the large number of
wrecks in the Humber, opposite what is now Poplar Road. It was
demolished in 1864, *v.* Baker 61–62. This is a very late example
of **þorp** in north L, but common in Cleethorpes, *v.* Fore Thorpe,
etc., *infra*. BESCARS (lost), 1842 White, *besker* 1457 *TCC, beskar*
1528 *GrimsBCB, great bescar* 1601 *Terrier, bescar* 1674 *ib, Bes-*
1678 *ib, -care* 1686 *ib, Biscar* 1734 *SSCTerrier*, cf. *Bescar Closes*
1749 Baker, – *Close* 1846 *EnclA*, perhaps 'the marsh where coarse
grass grows', *v.* **bēos, kjarr**; according to Watson 58, "on Trinity
Sunday . . . the church floor was wont to be freshly strewn with
rushes for the coming winter. These were cut from the 'Bescars'".
It was on the extreme western boundary of the parish. BLOW
WELLS, 1831 *Monson*, 1838 *Brace, the blowe well* 1601 *Terrier*,
on the Weelsby boundary; for Blow Wells, *v.* the same name in
Great Coates *infra*. BLUE STONE (lost), *the Blue Stone* 1822
Baker, 1846 *EnclA*; this is the same as Blue Stone in Great
Grimsby *infra*. BLUNDELL PARK, commemorating the name of
Peter *Blundell*, the founder of Blundell's School in Tiverton. In
1616, Baker 10, the manor of Itterby was purchased by Sidney
Sussex College, Cambridge, from money left to the College by
him. CARR LANE, *Carrs Road* 1846 *EnclA*, cf. *Clee karr* 1457
TCC, – Carre 1503 Ipm, 1540 *AOMB 212*, 1609 *DuLaMB 119*, –
Carres 1625 *Terrier, – Carr* 1710 *Td'E*, 1788 *ThorGrims*, 1799

GrimsCB xiv, 1822 *Terrier*, *Carr of Clee* 1740 *ThorGrims*, *the Carrs* 1824 *Yarb*, 1843 *TA*, 1846 *EnclA*, *Clee Great Carr*, – *Little Carr* 1749 Baker, cf. *Carr's Drain* c.1843 *Hig*, *Carrs* – 1846 *EnclA*, *Carr Dyke* 1734 *SSCTerrier*, – *Gap* 1749 *SSC*, – *Meadow*, – *Pasture* 1788 *Heneage*, *v.* **kjarr** 'a marsh' and *Ox Pasture Lane infra*. CLEE COMMON (lost), 1710 *Td'E*, 1825 Baker, 1831 *Monson*, 1838 *Brace*. CLEE FIELD (lost), *campis de . . . Clee* 1421 *AD*, *Clee Feilde* 1687 *Td'E*, – *feild* 1690 *ib*, – *Field* 1734 *SSCTerrier*, 1828 Bry, 1871 *Census*, *v.* **feld**. CLEE HALL FM, 1828 Bry, *Hall Farm* 1723 *ThorGrims*, 1734 *SSCTerrier*, 1802, 1810 *ThorGrims*, *Clee Hall* (*now a farm house*) 1842 White. CLEE MARSH (lost), 1840 *EnclA* (*Grimsby*), 1843 *TA*, 1846 *EnclA*, *Clee Common Marsh* 1749 Baker, cf. *Marshdyke* 1734 *SSCTerrier*, *the Marsh Dike* 1822 *Terrier*, *Marsh Bottom* c.1843 *Hig* and *Cleethorp Marsh* 1828 Bry, self-explanatory, *v.* **mersc**. CLEE MILL (lost), 1831 *Monson*, 1838 *Brace*, *molend' de Clee* 1535 VE iv, cf. (*the*) *Mill Field* 1784 *Terrier*, 1788 *ThorGrims*, *Mill Gate* 1734 *SSCTerrier*, 1822 *Terrier*, – *gate* 1784 *ib* (*v.* **gata**), *milne greene* 1601 *Terrier* (*v.* **grēne** 'a grassy place'), *Mill Hill* 1734 *SSCTerrier*, 1850 Dobson, *Windmill Buildings* 1843 *TA*, *v.* **myln**; the name is represented today by Mill Hill Crescent and stood "at the crest of Crow Hill in Mill Road", Baker 106. CLEE NESS (lost), 1773 *Map*, 1809 *GrimsCB xiv*, 1820 *ib xv*, 1828 Bry, 1831 *Monson*, 1838 *Brace*, *v.* **nes** 'a headland'. COLLEGE FM (lost), 1828 Bry, presumably referring to Sidney Sussex College which held land here. CROWHILL, 1851 *Census*, – *Hill* 1861, 1871 *ib*, 1872 White, cf. *Crowhill Terrace* 1861 *Census*; it is now represented by Crowhill Avenue; *v.* also *Clee Mill supra*. FAR CLEETHORPES (lost), 1842 White, – *Cleethorp* 1846 *ib*, an alternative name for Itterby. FORE THORPE (lost), 1861 *Census*, apparently an alternative name for Hole. HIGH THORPE (lost), 1749 Baker, 1866 Kelly, 1871 *Census*, – *Thorp* 1851 *ib*, an alternative name for Itterby. LOWS FM (lost), – *farm* 1625 *Heneage*, named from the family of Oliver *Low* 1565 *BT*. LOW THORPE (lost), 1871 *Census*, – *Thorp* 1851 *ib*, an alternative name for Hole. MARKET PLACE, *the* – 1846 *EnclA*, 1861, 1871 *Census*. MIDDLE THORPE (lost), – *Thorpe* 1749 Baker, – *Thorps* 1751 *BT*,

Mid–Thorp 1755 *ib*, *Mid–Thorps* 1757 *ib*, *Mid Thorps* 1766 *ib*, an alternative name for Itterby. NEAR CLEETHORPES (lost), 1842 White, – *Cleethorp* 1826 ib, an alternative name for Hole. NEEVES FM, 1822 *Terrier*, named from the family of Gabriel *Neve* 1780 *BT*. NEW BRIGHTON (lost), 1856 Baker, 1861, 1871 *Census*, 1872 White, now Brighton St. *infra*, presumably named from New Brighton (Ch). NEW CLEE, 1871 *Census*; a branch railway line from Grimsby was constructed in 1863 and the district around the station became known as New Clee. RACE GROUND (lost), 1831 *Monson*, 1838 *Brace*, *the race course* 1811 *GrimsCB xiv*, *Race Course* 1812 *ib*, *the –* 1816 *ib xv*, *Racing Ground* c.1820 *GrimsMap*, cf. *The Horse Course* 1749 Baker; races were already taking place here as early as c.1618, Gillett 124. On later maps it is shown as being in Great Grimsby. RAGGS FM (lost), 1749 *SSC*, named from the family of Richard *Ragge* 1605 *BT*. RECREATION GROUND (lost), c.1843 *Hig*, 1846 *EnclA*, cf. *Pleasure Ground* 1850 Dobson, *Clee Pleasure Gardens* 1871 *Census*; according to Watson 119, it was merged in the Cliff Gardens and its old name was Sea Field (1843 *Hig*, 1846 *EnclA*). SIMPSON HALL FM (lost), 1734 *SSCTerrier*, named from the *Simpson* family well-represented in Clee, cf. Katherine *Simpson* 1734 *BT*. SMALLFLEETS COMMON (lost), 1846 *EnclA*, *Smale flittes* 1601, *Smalflits* 1671, 1674, 1678, 1697, *the Small fleets* 1686, *Small flits* 1715 all *Terrier*, – *Fleets* 1749 Baker, 'the narrow streams, water-channels', *v*. **smæl**, **flēot** in the pl. On the plan, 1749 Baker, it lies immediately to the east of Clee village. VICARAGE, *one vickaridge house* 1601, *The vicaridge –* 1613, *ye vicarige –* 1635, *The vicarage howse* 1664 all *Terrier*, *Parsonage* 1734 *SSCTerrier*, *Vicarage* 1861, 1871 *Census*, 1872 White. WHITE HOUSE FM (lost), 1734 *SSCTerrier*, cf. *White House* 1749 *SSC*. WILTON FM (lost), 1734 *SSCTerrier*, *Nook Wilton Farm* 1734 *ib*, cf. *Wilton Headland* 1734 *ib* (*v*. **hēafod–land**), presumably from the surn. *Wilton*.

PUBLIC HOUSES and HOTELS

Names in this and the following sections for the most part include only those found up to and including 1872 White.

CLIFF HOTEL, 1866 Kelly, 1871 *Census*, – *Hotell* 1861 *ib*. It is *Cliff House* 1850 Dobson (B.W.). CROSS KEYS, 1826, 1842 White, 1850 Dobson, 1861 *Census*, 1866 Kelly, – *Inn* 1837 Baker, 1843 *TA*, 1846 *EnclA*. CROWN & ANCHOR (lost), 1826 White and was *the Crown Inn* 1829 Baker; it became the Leeds Arms in 1836, ib 57. DOLPHIN HOTEL, 1843 *TA*, 1846 *EnclA*, 1850 Dobson, 1851 *Census*; for details of its early history *v*. Baker 57–58. FISHERMAN'S ARMS, 1871 *Census*. LEEDS ARMS, 1842 White, 1851, 1861, 1871 *Census*, – *Inn* 1843 *TA*, 1849 Skelton, 1850 Dobson, and cf. *Crown & Anchor supra*. LIFE BOAT HOTEL, – *Inn* 1871 *Census*; Cleethorpes became a Life Boat station in 1868, Baker 108. MANCHESTER & SHEFFIELD HOTEL (lost), 1861 *Census*. QUEEN'S HEAD (lost), 1871 *ib*. TEMPERANCE HOTEL (lost), 1850 Dobson. VICTORIA HOTEL, 1871 *Census*.

STREETS, ROADS and WAYS

ALBERT RD, – *street* 1872 White, cf. – *Terrace* 1871 *Census*, – *House* 1871 *ib*, – *Parade* 1872 White. ALEXANDRA RD is *Itterby Road* c.1843 *Hig*, 1846 *EnclA*, 1871 *Census*, – *Lane* 1822 *Terrier*, cf. *Alexandra Terrace* 1871 *Census*, 1872 White. AMOS ST. (lost), 1871 *Census*, cf. – *Square* 1850 Dobson, 1871 *Census*, named from *Amos*, a member of the *Appleyard* family, prominent in Cleethorpes, *v*. Baker Index and cf. *Appleyards Buildings infra*. BEACONTHORPE RD (lost), 1871 *Census*, cf. *Beacon Terrace* 1861 ib, 1866 Kelly, cf. *Beaconthorpe supra*. BRIGHTON ST., – *Terrace* 1871 *Census*, *New Brighton terrace* 1862 White, cf. *New Brighton supra*. CHAPEL LANE (lost), 1850 Dobson, 1861 *Census*, cf. – *Yard* 1850 Dobson, 1861, 1871 *Census*, the site of the first Primitive Methodist Chapel in Cleethorpes. Chapel Yard, however, refers to the first Wesleyan Chapel, built in 1802 (B.W.). CHAPMAN RD, cf. *Chapman Row* 1850 Dobson, *Chapman's* – 1861 *Census*, *Chapman Square* 1871 *ib*, *Chapman's Buildings* 1861 *ib*, – *buildings* 1872 White; named from an old established Cleethorpes family, cf. Samuel *Chapman* 1704 *BT* and *v*. Baker, Index. CHARLES ST., cf. *Charles Square* 1850 Dobson. B.W. points out that *Charles Square* has nothing to do with Charles St., which survives today. *Charles Square* formed part of a complex of squares between Wardle St., North St. and Humber St. CHURCH ROAD (lost), 1871 *Census*, – *road* 1872 White. CLEETHORPES RD (lost), 1861, 1871 *Census*, – *road* White, apparently now Grimsby Rd. CROSS ST., 1845 Baker, 1850 Dobson. CUTTLEBY, *Cattleby Lane* (sic) 1784 *Terrier*, *Cuttleby* – 1861, 1871 *Census*, cf. – *Dale* 1734 *SSCTerrier*, obscure. ELM RD, cf. *Elm Terrace* 1871 *Census*, 1872 White. FISHERMENS RD (lost), 1846 *EnclA*, the name of a footpath along the cliffs. FRONT ST. (lost), 1861 *Census*. GRANT ST., 1871 *Census*, 1872 White, cf. *Grants Buildings* 1861, 1871 *Census*, named from the family of John *Grant* 1796 *BT*. GRIMSBY RD, 1871 *Census*, *Grimsby New Road* c.1843 *Hig*. HIGH CLIFF RD, 1850 Dobson, 1871 *Census*, *High Cliffe Terrace* 1849 Skelton. HIGHGATE, *Hygate* 1734 *SSCTerrier*, *the Highgate* 1784 *Terrier*, *High gate* 1822 *ib*, – *Gate* 1871 *Census*, *Highgate* 1872 White, cf. *highgate furlong* 1822 *Terrier*, *High Gate House*, – *Terrace* 1871 *Census*. HIGH ST., 1872 White. HUMBERSTON RD (lost), *Humberstone* – c.1843 *Hig*, 1871 *Census*, apparently an alternative name for Highgate, cf. also *Humberston waye* 1601 *Terrier*, *Humberstone Gate* 1734 *SSCTerrier* (*v*. **gata**). HUMBER ST., 1861, 1871 *Census*, 1862 White, cf. – *Terrace* 1871 *Census*. KIRK GATE (lost), 1850 Dobson and said to run from the "chapel" at Thrunscoe to Clee. KNOLL ST., *Knoll Road* 1871 *Census*, cf. – *Crescent* 1871 *ib*, – *crescent house* 1872 White, – *House* 1871 *Census*, *v*. **cnoll** 'a knoll, a hillock'. LONG LANE (lost), cf. – *End* 1734 *SSCTerrier*. MANGLE ST. (lost), 1871 *Census*, *Mangall St.* 1872 White. MARKET ST., 1850 Dobson, 1871 *Census*. MIDDLE ST. (lost), 1861 *ib*, 1871 Gait. MILLERS RD (lost), c.1843 *Hig*; it was off Weelsby Rd. MILL LANE (lost), 1871 *Census*, led to the

five-sailed mill in Mill Place, Baker 106, and cf. Mill House 1861
Census. MILL RD, 1846 *EnclA*, named from *Clee Mill supra*.
NEPTUNE ST., 1871 *Census*, cf. – *Terrace*. B.W. informs me that
this was the name of a Russian ship bought by Robert Keetley
p1852. NORFOLK LANE, cf. *Norfolk Cottages* 1871 *Census*, –
cottages 1872 White. NORTH ST., 1845 Baker, 1850 Dobson,
1861, 1871 *Census*, and perhaps cf. *the North Lane* 1784, 1822
Terrier. OSBORN ST., *Osbourne Terrace* 1861 *Census*, *Osborne* –
1871 *ib*, – *Square* 1871 *ib*, cf. *Mr Osborne's Barn* 1847 Skelton,
Osbourne Buildings 1850 Dobson, – *House* 1871 Gait, from an old
established family here, cf. John *Osborne* 1743 *BT* and *v*. Baker,
Index. OX PASTURE LANE (lost), 1846 *EnclA*, cf. *the oxe pasture*
1671, *ye* – 1674, – *Oxe Pasture* 1678, *the Oxepasture* 1686,
Oxpasture 1697 all *Terrier*, 1734 *SSCTerrier*, *ox paster* 1715
Terrier, *Ox Pasture* 1788 *Heneage et passim* to 1843 *TA*,
self-explanatory; it was an extension of Carr Rd, Watson 95.
PEAK'S LANE, 1846 *EnclA*, cf. *Peek lane End* 1749 Baker, leading
to Peaks (Fm) in Weelsby *infra*. PEARS LANE ROAD (lost), c.1843
Hig. PELHAM RD, – *Street* 1871 *Census*, – *St*. 1872 White, cf.
Pelham Villa 1872 ib, no doubt named from the *Pelhams*, Earls of
Yarborough, who held land here. QUEENS PARADE, *Queen's* –
1872 White. SCARBOROUGH RD, 1871 *Census*, – *Street* 1871 Gait,
– *St*. 1872 White, cf. *Scarborough House* 1871 *Census*, – *ho*. 1872
White. SEA RD, c.1843 *Hig*, 1846 *EnclA*; according to Watson
118, this was earlier Folly Hole. SEA VIEW ST., 1871 Gait, 1872
White, – *Lane*, – *Rd*. 1871 *Census*; "Sea View Street replaces the
quaint *Town Street*", Watson 119. SEGMERE ST., cf. *Segmare*
1687, 1690, 1725 *Td'E*, *Sege Mere* 1734 *SSCTerrier*, *Segmere
Drain* 1846 *EnclA*, and *Sigg Mare Dale* 1749 *SCC* (*v*. **deill** 'a
share, a portion of land'), perhaps 'the pool where sedge grows',
v. **secg, mere**, in a Scandinavianized form. This is in the position
of *Segmere Drain* which separated *Itterby* and *Thrunscoe* (B.W.).
SMITH ST. (lost), 1871 *Census*, presumably from a local family,
cf. Abraham *Smith* 1705 *BT*. SOUTH ST., 1861 *Census*, cf. *South
Parade* 1861 *ib*, 1871 Gait. STATION RD is probably *Railway
Street* 1871 *Census*. STIRLING ST., 1871 *Census*, 1872 White.
SUGGITTS LANE, – *Road* 1871 *Census*, named from the *Suggitt*

family, cf. Robert and William *Suggitt* 1861 *Census*. THOROLD ST., *Thorald* – 1871 *ib*; named from the *Thorold* family, who held land here. THRUNSCOE RD, 1846 *EnclA*. TOWN ST. (lost), 1846 *ib*, now Sea View Street. TRINITY RD, – *Street* 1871 *Census*, 1872 White, cf. – *Terrace* 1872 ib; this probably commemorates the holdings of Trinity College, Cambridge. WARDALL ST., *Wardle Street* 1871 *Census*, named from the family of John *Wardall* 1761 *BT*. WEELSBY RD, c.1843 *Hig*, cf. *Weelesbye lane ende* 1601 *Terrier, Wilsby Gate* 1734 *SSCTerrier* (*v.* **gata**). WEST PARADE (lost), 1861 *Census*. WEST ST., 1861 *ib*. YARRA RD, named from Yarra Ho "originally called Yarra Yarra House after a river in Australia", Baker 91.

BUILDINGS, COTTAGES, HOUSES and TERRACES

The names in this group are no longer in use, except where stated.

ALLISON COTTAGES, 1861 *Census*, for the *Allison* family, *v.* Baker 17–18. ALBION COTTAGE, 1871 ib, – *Cottages* 1871 Gait, 1872 White. ALCOCK'S HOUSES, 1871 *Census*, from the family of Charles *Alcock* 1868 Kelly. ALMA VILLA, – *villa* 1872 White, presumably named from the battle of Alma in the Crimean War, 1854; it was in Church St. APPLEYARDS BDGS, 1861 *Census*, – SQ., *Appleyard's* – 1861 ib, 1871 Gait; named from an old established Cleethorpes family, cf. James *Appleyard* 1704 *BT* and *v.* Baker, Index. BANCROFT BDG, 1861, 1871 *Census*, BANCROFT'S TER., 1871 Gait, cf. George and John *Bancroft* 1861 *Census*; Joseph *Bancroft* was a resident in the Terrace in 1871 *ib*. BATH HOUSES, 1850 Dobson. BELLE VUE TER., 1871 Gait. BELL'S BDGS, 1871 *Census*, – SQ., 1861 *ib*; for the *Bell* family, *v.* Baker, Index. BRICKYARD HO, 1861, 1871 *Census* and cf. Good's Houses *infra*. BROCKLESBY'S BDGS, 1871 *ib*, from the family of Mr David *Brocklesby* 1872 White. BROUGHTON'S BDGS, 1871 Gait, – SQ., 1850 Dobson, 1861 *Census*; Elizabeth *Broughton* was in residence in 1861 and for the family, *v.* Baker, Index. BROWN'S BDGS, 1850 Dobson, 1871 *Census*, – *Houses*

1871 *ib*. BROWN TER., 1871 *Census*, cf. Benjamin *Brown* 1850
Dobson and for the family, *v.* Baker, Index. BRUCES COTTAGES,
1871 *Census*, *Bruce* – 1871 Gait. CLEE TER., 1872 White. CLIFF
TER., 1861, 1871 *Census*, 1871 Gait, *Cliff Cottage* 1850 Dobson.
CLIFTON HO, 1871 *Census*, named from the family of Alfred
Clifton 1872 White. COAST GUARD TER., 1861 *Census*, cf.
Coastguard Station 1871 *ib*. COULBECK'S BDGS, 1871 *ib*, named
from an old established Cleethorpes family, cf. Thomas *Colbeck*
1725 *BT*. DEANSGATE HO, 1664 *Foster*; it was in Itterby.
DRIFFIELD YARD, 1850 Dobson, named from the family of
William *Driffield, v.* Baker 80–81. EMERSON'S BDGS, 1871
Census, 1872 White, named from the family of Thomas *Emmerson*
1868 Kelly. FRAGMENT COTTAGE, 1850 Dobson, 1871 *Census*,
later called Grafton Ho (B.W.). FRANCES BDGS, 1861 *ib*; for the
surn. *France*, cf. William *France* 1799 *BT*. GOOD'S HOUSES, 1871
Census; *Good* is a well–attested surn. in the area, cf. Thomas
Good 1748 *BT*; cf. also *Good's Corner* and *Good's Brick Yard*
1871 *Census* and note *Isaiah Good* is described as a *master
brickmaker* 1871 *ib*. GRANTHAM COTTAGE, 1871 *ib*. GUNNERS
HO, 1871 *ib*. HAINTON TER., 1871 *ib*. HEMBOROUGH BDGS, 1871
ib, named from the family of William *Hemborough* 1826 White.
HIGH FIELD HO, 1871 ib, *Highfield* 1872 White. HUGH COTTAGE,
1871 *Census*. ITTERBY TER., *Itterby Terrace 1875* is inscribed on
the wall of the house. IVY COTTAGE, 1871 *Census*. IVYMONT
COTTAGE, 1861 *ib*. JACKSON'S SQ., 1861 *ib*; John *Jackson* was in
residence here. JAMES BDGS, 1850 Dobson, – SQ., 1850 ib, 1861
Census, 1871 Gait; apparently named from *James* Appleyard, who
lived here. This appears to be the same as *St. James Square* 1871
Census. KEETLEY'S BDGS, 1871 Gait, 1872 White, named from
the *Keetley* family, cf. Thomas *Keetley* 1871 Gait. KINGSTON
TER., 1871 *Census*. LAVENDAR HO, 1843 *Hig*, cf. – *Cottage* 1850
Dobson, 1871 *Census*. LEAMINGTON VILLA, 1871 *ib*.
LUDBOROUGH TER., 1871 Gait. MACAULAY TER., 1872 White.
MANTELLS BDGS, 1850 Dobson; apparently named from the Rev.
E.R. *Mantell*, who became Vicar of Tetney in 1836 (B.W.).
MARINE COTTAGES, 1871 Gait. MARION COTTAGE, 1861 *Census*.
MARY'S TER., 1861 *ib*, *St*. – 1871 *ib*; there is no church dedicated

to St Mary in Cleethorpes, cf. James Bdgs *supra*. MUMBY TER., 1871 *Census*, named from the *Mumby* family, cf. Robert *Mumby* 1767 *BT*. NATIONAL SCHOOL HO, 1861 *Census*, *National School* 1826 White; the school was opened in 1815, *v*. Baker 70. NEWTON BDGS, 1871 *Census*, named from the *Newton* family, cf. James *Newton* 1861 *ib*. NORWICH VILLA, 1872 White. NOTTINGHAM TER., 1871 *Census*, 1872 White. ODD FELLOWS HALL, 1871 Gait; the local branch of "the Manchester Unity of Odd Fellows" was inaugurated in 1839 and the Hall was opened in 1854, Baker 109. Its outline can still be seen in part on the pavement at the junction of Yarra Rd and Cuttleby, beside dilapidated garages (B.W.). OYSTER HO, 1850 Dobson, 1851 *Census*; for the oyster fishing industry here, *v*. Baker 98–99. OYSTERSHELL COTTAGE, 1871 Gait. PAILTHORPS BDGS, 1871 *Census*, named from the family of George *Pailthorp* 1861 *ib*. PEAK'S TER., 1861, 1871 *ib*, – *terrace* 1872 White. POWERS SQ., 1861 *Census*, cf. *Powers Terrace* 1861 *ib*, no doubt named from the family of Mr Thomas *Power* 1863 Morris. PRIMITIVE ROW, 1871 *ib*. PROVIDENCE TER., *Providence Terrace 1871* is inscribed on the wall of the house. RANTER ROW, 1850 Dobson; apparently an alternative name for Chapel Lane *supra*, the site of the first Primitive Methodist Church in Cleethorpes (B.W.). RICHARD BDGS, 1850 ib, named from *Richard* Appleyard 1850 ib, cf. *Amos St*. and *James Bdgs supra*. ROBINSON ROW, 1861 *Census*, cf. *Robinson Square* 1861 *ib*; for the *Robinson* family, *v*. Baker, Index. ROWSON'S HO, 1851 *Census*. ROWSTON'S SQ., 1871 Gait, *Rowson* and *Rowston* are variants of the same surn. cf. John *Rowson* and John *Rowston*, the same man, 1705 *BT*. ST PETER'S TER., 1871 *Census*, – *terrace* 1872 White, from the church dedication; the name survives in St. Peter's Avenue. SANDFIELD HO, – *house* 1872 White. SAND HALL, 1861, 1871 *Census*. SAUNBY'S BDGS, *Saunby's Buildings 1864* is inscribed on the wall of the house, cf. *Saunby Villa* 1871 *Census*, where Thomas *Saunby* lived. SEMINARY, 1850 Dobson. SLIGHTS BDGS, 1861 *Census*, where William *Slight* lived. SPRING TER., 1861 *ib*, cf. *Spring Houses*, – *Villa* 1871 *ib*, – *row* 1872 White, from the *Spring* family, cf. Joseph *Spring* 1871 *Census*. SUNDERLAND TER., 1871 *ib*, – *terrace* 1872 White. SUNNYSIDE,

1871 *Census*. SWABY'S BDGS, 1871 Gait, – *Villas* 1871 ib, where
Robert *Swaby* lived. SYDNEY TER., 1861, 1871 *Census*, *Sidney* –
1872 White, cf. *Sidney Cottage* 1861 *Census*; presumably named
from Sidney Sussex College, Cambridge. TEA TREES COTTAGE,
1843 *Hig*. THATCH COTTAGE, 1850 Dobson. THOMAS BDGS, 1850
Dobson. THORPS VILLA, 1871 *Census*, *Thorpe* – 1872 White.
THRUNSCOE VILLAS, 1871 Gait. TUPLING'S BDG, 1871 Gait,
where William *Tupling* lived. VICTORIA TER., 1861, 1871 *Census*,
– *terrace* 1872 White; it was on the site of Stocks Hill in f.ns. (a)
infra (B.W.). WEBSTER'S TER., – *terrace* 1872 White, named
from the family of Michael *Webster* 1871 Gait. WHITES SQ., 1861
Census, cf. *White's Buildings* 1861 *ib* and *Mr White's Houses*
1871 *ib*, cf. Henry *White* 1872 White. WORSLEY HO, 1861
Census, – *hs* 1872 White; according to B.W., from the name of a
ship owned by Capt. Thomas Keetley, who lived here.

FIELD-NAMES

Forms dated 13, 1310, 1316, 1358, 1388, 14, 1443, 1459 are AD;
c.1300 are Guis; 1327, 1332 are *SR*; 1396, 1484 are *GrimsCt*;
1457, c.1600, 1787 *TCC*; 1457–59, 1535–46, 1574–75, 1594–96,
1609, 1632–33 are *MinAcct*; 1508, 1533 are *GrimsCB ii*; 1601,
1613, 1625, 1635, 1662, 1664, 1671, 1674, 1678, 1686, 1697,
1715, 1784, 1822 are *Terrier*; 1609 are *DuLaMB*; 1625 are
Heneage; 1652 are *Rad*; 1664 *Foster*; 1687, 1690, 1710, 1725,
1761, 1800 are *Td'E*; 1723, 1740, 1741, 1759, 1765, 1788, 1789,
1802, 1805, 1808, 1812, 1826 are *ThorGrims*; 1734 are
SSCTerrier; 1749[1] are *SSC*; 1749[2] are Baker; 1788 are *Heneage*;
1798, 1824 are *Yarb*; 1843, c.1843 are *Hig*; 1846 are *EnclA*; and
1873 are *Daubney*. B.W. indicates information provided by Mrs
Bettie Watkinson.

(a) Abby Pann 1787 (*y[e] abbey panne* c.1600, *Abba Pann* 1734, named
from Humberston Abbey and **panne** 'a pan' denoting some feature
resembling a pan; it was close to the Humberston boundary (B.W.)); Alfor
Meer 1784, Aufier Mier 1822 (*Aufrey mare* 1687, *–mare* 1690, *Aufry mare*

1725, *Aufraymare* 1734, *Aufere Mare* 1749, probably named from the surn. *Alfrey*, *v.* Reaney s.n., and (**ge**)**mǣre** 'a boundary, land on a boundary', as elsewhere in the parish); Anderson's Garth 1846 (named from the family of Robert *Anderson* 1590 *BT* and **garðr** 'an enclosure', as elsewhere in the parish); Bagbeaters 1784; Bagwater Grass 1784; the Bank Fd 1788, Clethorps East Field or . . . Bank Field 1822 (*Thorps Bank Field* 1749²); Beck Fd 1788, 1846 (*v.* **bekkr** 'a stream'); Brant Fm 1784; Braywater 1787 (*brawaters* 1601, 1687, *Bray-* 1652, *Braughters* 1690, probably 'the broad water(s)', *v.* **breiðr, wæter**); the Brick Bridge 1801, 1803 (it was built over *the Clee fresh Water drain infra*); Bridgate 1822 (*v.* **brycg, gata** 'a way, a road'); Brigholme 1787 (*v.* **brycg**, in a Scandinavianized form, **holmr**); Brown bank 1784 (probably named from the family of William *Brown* 1785 *BT*); Buntin Swaiths 1787 (*v.* **swæð** 'a strip of grassland', the first el. being obscure); Burnt Cl 1788 (cf. *Bornt Hill* 1734, *- Hole* 1734; Burnt Fm 1822; Cabbage Garth 1843 (*v.* **garðr**); Cadger's Cl; Chapel Nooken 1850 (*Chapill Nooking* 1734, *v.* **noking** 'a nook'); Church Well 1850 Dobson (it was in Thrunscoe and according to Dobson was stagnant water; it is described by Watson 61–62; today it is the site of a football field, adjacent to Buck Beck (B.W.)); Clee Fd 1787; Clee fresh Water Drain 1801; Clee Hedge Field 1846 (cf. Clee West Field *infra*); Cleethorpes Middle Fd 1784, 1822 (*Thorps Middle Field or Thorps Great Field* 1749, cf. *Middle Field Marfur* 1734, *v.* **marfur** 'a boundary furrow, etc.', as elsewhere in the parish); Cleethorpes Marsh 1843, 1846 (*Thorps Marsh* 1749); Cobblers Farm 1761 (*Cobler -* 1734, 1749); Cock Meer 1784, *- Mier* 1822 (*Cokmaar* 1459, *Cockmare* 1734, *- Mare* 1749¹, probably from **cocc** 'a cock' and (**ge**)**mǣre** 'a boundary, land on a boundary' or **marr**¹ 'a marsh'); the common Murfor 1822 (*v.* **marfur**); Conger Cl 1843, 1843 *TA* (*Cuninger Close* 1687, *Cungarr - 1690, 1725, *Conger Close* 1734 (from **coninger** 'a rabbit–warren' and **clos**(e)); Cow Cl 1759, 1808; Croft 1784, 1822, the *- 1788 (*loco voc' Croft* 1609, *Croft* 1652, *v.* **croft**); Croftgate 1784, *- Gate* 1822 (*croft gate* c.1600 *v.* **gata**); Croft Leys 1787 (*v.* **croft, lea** (OE **lēah**) 'meadow, pasture' in the pl.); Cruels Cl 1812, Cruels' *- 1826, Cruel *- 1831 Monson, 1838 *Brace*, 1843 *TA*, 1846 (*Cruels Close, Cruell Close* 1749²; this must have been an important piece of land for it appears on 19th century plans; perhaps it is a nickname of the uncomplimentary type denoting land difficult to work; B.W. comments that this is now allotments and is solid clay); the Dale Ground 1784, 1822 (*Dale Ground* 1734, 1749¹, *v.* **deill** 'a share of land, as elsewhere in the parish); Dod Mere 1787 (*v.* (**ge**)**mǣre**); Dog Mar, *- Meer* 1784, 1822 (*dogmare* c.1600, cf. Cock Meer *supra*); Dun Farm 1784,

Dunns Cl 1788 (*Field Leas Dun Farm* 1734, probably named from the family of Thomas *Dune* 1562 *BT*); the Easter Bank Field 1784 (cf. *Easter Gate, Ester Gate* 1734; probably from **eowestre** 'a sheep–fold', *v.* also **gata**); East Fd 1765, 1788, – field 1810, Clee East Field 1784, 1822 (*Eastfield* 1723, *Clee East Field* 1749², *v.* **ēast, feld**, one of the open fields of Clee); East Field Pingle 1759, Pasture formerly called East Field Pingle but now Sea Pingle 1808 (*v.* **pingel** 'a small enclosure', as elsewhere in the parish); East Sleight 1822 (*the East Slights* 1671, *yᵉ East sleights* 1674, – *Sleights* 1678, 1715, *East Slights* 1686, *east slights* 1697, *East Sleights* 1749¹, cf. *Sleytes* 1457, *the sleights* 1601, *Fare Slights, West* – 1734, *v.* **ēast, slétta** 'a smooth, level field'); Fallow Fd 1788, the – 1822; Farr Carr 1765, 1802, the – 1810 (*the far Carr* 1601, *the Farr Carr* 1723, *v.* **kjarr** and cf. Carr Lane *supra*); First–Sixth Field Cl 1843; Field Mdw 1788; Fresh Dales 1822 (1749¹, *fresdailes* 1457, *the fresh Dales* 1601, *Freshdales* 1734, *v.* **fersc** 'fresh (i.e. without salt)', **deill**); Frog Hall Garden 1843 *TA*, – Green 1846 (Frog Hall means literally 'land where frogs are found', but is also used ironically to denote poor land); the Garden 1788; Garth 1843, 1843 *TA*, 1846 (*le Garthes* 1535–46, *v.* **garðr**); piece or parcel of Land or Oyster Ground heretofore called Garthstead lying in the water of the River Humber in Cleethorpes 1798 (*v.* **garthstede (garðr, stede)**, a compound not found in Sandred; cf. *Oyster Ho supra*); the Gated Pasture of Clee 1808; Glebe Garth 1843 *TA* (*v.* **garðr**); Glentworth head dale 1822 (probably from the surn. *Glentworth* with **hēafod, deill**); Goose Paddle Drain 1843, 1846 (from *paddle* 'a wading place', in this case for *geese*, cf. Cow Paddle, PN L 1, 22; B.W. notes that this is now culverted under Taylor's Avenue, but joins Buck Beck as an open sewer); Great Carr 1788, 1822, Clee – 1824 (*the Greate Car* 1671, *yᵉ Great Carr* 1674, *the great Care* 1686, – *Carr* 1797, *v.* **kjarr** and cf. Carr Lane *supra*); Great Randall 1800 (probably identical with *Rundales* 1734, *v.* **rynel** 'a runnel, a small stream' in the pl.); Anthony Green Headland 1784, – Green's headland 1822 (*v.* **hēafod–land**); North –, South Holm Meer 1784, – Mier 1822 (*Northolmare* 1457, *North Holme Mare* 1734, 1749¹, *v.* **norð, holmr, (ge)mǣre**); Home Cl 1846 (in Thrunscoe; a building is marked here on the Plan); the Homestead 1788; a Headland called Hounton 1784; the Ings 1788 (1652, 1749, *thrunsco Ingges* c.1600, *v.* **eng** 'meadow, pasture'; it was on the southern boundary in Thrunscoe); the Kirkgate 1784, –gates 1822 (*v.* **kirkja, geat** 'a gate'); the Lea Bank 1784 (*v.* **lēah**) 'meadow', as elsewhere in the parish); Little Carr 1765, 1788, 1802, 1810, Clee Little Carr 1824 (*the little Car* 1671, *yᵉ little Carr* 1674, *the* – 1678, – *Little Care* 1686, – *Carr* 1697, 1723, cf. *Little Carr Dyke* 1734, *v.* **kjarr** and cf. Carr Lane *supra*); Little Cl 1824; Little Cow Pasture 1843; the Long Leas 1784, - long leys 1822 (*Long Leas* 1734, *v.* **lang, lea** (OE lēah)); Longmoor 1822; the Fields called Marfrays 1787 (*Marfray* is a variant form of *Marfer*, *v.* **marfur** 'a boundary furrow' and cf. *Marfor* in f.ns. (b) *infra*); Meadow 1843; the Middle Carr Dike 1822 (*the middle Carr* 1601, *Middle Carr Dicke* 1734, *v.* **middel, kjarr** and cf. Carr Lane *supra*); Middle Fd 1765, 1788, 1802, - fd 1810, Clee Middle Fd 1784, Middle Field Drain c.1843, 1846 (*the Middle feild* 1686, *Middlefield* 1723, *Midel Field* 1734, *Clee Middle Field* 1749, *v.* **middel, feld**; one of the great fields of the parish); Little Mouse Meer 1784, - Mier 1822 (*Little mouse mare* 1687, 1690, *Great Mouse Mare* 1734, the sense of *meer, mare* is uncertain); New Cl 1843 *TA* (1734); East -, West North Cl 1846; Nuns Furze 1824 (*v.* **fyrs**, and cf. *Nunns heade Dale* 1601, *Nuns Dale* 1749[1] (*v.* **deill**); no doubt named from the nuns of Grimsby who held land in Clee); Orley Hill 1822, - Meer 1784 (*Orley Mare* 1734); Peake Cl 1759, 1805, the Peak Cl 1788, Peakes Closes 1789, Pasture formerly called the Peaks Close but now the East Plough Close 1808 (presumably named from Peaks Fm in Weelsby *infra*); Pindar Piece 1822 (cf. *the pinder dale ende*, *the pinder heade dale* 1601, named from the village *pinder* with **hēafod** and **deill**); the Pinfold 1822 (*v.* **pynd–fald**); (the) Pingle 1784, 1788 (*v.* **pingel**); the Pit (*Pit, The Pitts* 1749[1], *v.* **pytt**); the Pontoon 1873; the Quarter Green 1784, - quarter green 1822 (*Quarter Green* 1734, *v.* **grēne**[2] 'a green, a grassy place' and for *quarter v.* Chapel Field Rd, PN L **2**, 121–22); Raven Leys 1846 (*v.* **hræfen, hrafn, lea** (OE lēah) in the pl.); Robert Leas (gate) 1784, Robert Leys (Gate) 1822 (*v.* **gata**) (from the forename or surn. *Robert* and **lea** (OE lēah) in the pl.); long -, short Rushams 1822 (*Rusholm* 1457, *russoms* 1601, *Long -, Short Rushams* 1734, *v.* **risc** 'a rush' and **holmr** 'raised land in marsh' in the pl.; *ham* and *om* are frequently found as reflexes of **holmr** in north L); Scalper Gate 1784, Scabor gate, Scauber Gate 1822 (*Scawbēgate* (sic) 1457, *Scawbor gate* 1601, *Scauber gate* 1671, *Scawber Gate* 1678, *Scabor gate* 1697, *Scar bor gate* 1715, earlier forms are needed to suggest an etymology); Scartho Gate 1822 (*Scarthoe gate* 1671, 1674, 1686, –*gate* 1678, *Scartho gate* 1697, - *Gate* 1734, *Scar–tho gate* 1715, 'the road to Scartho', *v.* **gata**); School Allotment 1843 *TA*, the School Green 1846; Scramlands (Headland) 1784, Scramblings (Headland) (sic) 1822; the Sea Bank 1784, 1822; Sea Fd, - Flg 1787 (cf. *Sedyke* (*hyrne*) 1457, *v.* **sǣ, dík**); the short Ings 1788 (*v.* **eng** and cf. the Ings *supra*); Short Lands 1784, short lands 1822 (*v.* **land** 'a selion, a strip of arable land'); the short wrongdales 1822 (*Short Wrongdale* 1734, - *Wrong Dales* 1749[1], *Wrongdales* 1734, 'the crooked shares of land' *v.* **vrangr, deill** in the pl., with the prefix *short*); Skin Garth 1843 *TA* (cf. *Skin Green* 1734, on the site of 63 Highgate and presumably where animals were killed and skinned (B.W.)); Spring Well Paddock 1843 *TA*; the Stock(s) Hill 1784, Stocks – 1822 (perhaps cf. *Stock Mare* 1734 and *v.* Victoria Ter. *supra*); the Stone Meer 1784, – Mier 1822 (*Staynmare*, *Stone Meare*, – *Mare* 1734, *Stone Mare Pit* 1734, 'the stony boundary, land on a boundary', *v.* **steinn**, **stān**, **(ge)mǣre**); Swift Headland 1784; the Syddike 1822 (*Sidike*, *Syddyke* 1734, cf. *the Siddick Ditch* 1601, *Sydick Bank*, *Siddick Dales* 1734, 'the spacious, long ditch', *v.* **sīd**, **dík**); the Syke 1784, 1822 (*le Sykes* 1358, *v.* **sík** 'a ditch'); Thorps Mill Field 1822 (*Thorpe Mill Field* 1734); the Three Carrs 1765, 1802, 1810 (*the Three carrs* 1723, *v.* **kjarr** and cf. Carr Lane *supra*); Three Stongs 1784 (*v.* **stong** 'a pole', a measure of land); Thrunscoe Beck Field 1822 (*le Bek* 1457, *yᵉ beck* c.1600, *v.* **bekkr**); Thrunscoe Drain c.1843, 1846; Thrunscoe Field 1843 (1734, *v.* **feld**); Thrunscoe Knowells, – Knowles 1784 (*v.* **cnoll**; B.W. states that this is topographically appropriate for a part of Bradford Avenue and Oxford St.); Thrunscoe Marsh 1784; Thrunscoe Middle Field 1784, 1822, East Middle and West Fields of Thrunscoe 1826 (referring to the three open fields of the township); Thrunscoe Occupation Rd 1843; Tithe Barn and Yard 1843 *TA*; a Green called Houl Totterel, West Totterel 1784, – Tot(t)erhill 1822, Totterhill 1822 (*Totternil hill* 1671, 1674, 1678, *Totternill hill* 1671, – *Hill* 1686, *totternill hill* 1697, *yᵉ west Totternill* 1671, *West* – 1686, *West totterill* 1697, *yᵉ west Totternil* 1674, 1678, *totterill hill* 1715, *West toterill* 1715, – *Tottrill* 1734, *Houl Tottrill*, 'the look–out house hill' from OE *tōt–ærn, **hyll**; OE **tōt–ærn** is not on record, but would be a perfectly regular formation and occurs in Totternhoe, PN Bd 139–40; for *Houl*, *v. Hole supra*); the Town spring well 1846; Trunscoe Town Side (sic) 1784; Two Foot Hole, – Meer 1784, two foot Mier 1822 (*Two Foot Mares* 1734); Vicarage Cl 1843 (*The vickaridge close* 1601, *the vicaridge lande and meadowe* 1635, *the vickaridge heade Dale* 1601, *Parsonage Head Dale* 1734, *v.* **hēafod**, **deill**); The Vicar's Croft 1846; Villa Drain 1843, 1846; a place called Wallboar, Wallboar Shift Headland 1784, Wallboar (Shift) 1822 (obscure); Washley Mier 1822 (*Washley*, – *Hedge* 1734); a place called Wat England 1784 (presumably *Wat England* is a person's name); Weelsby Drain c.1843 (cf. *Weelsby Hedge* 1734, both on the boundary with Weelsby *infra*); West Cl 1846; West Fd 1765, 1822, *yᵉ* – 1788, West field 1810, Clee West Field 1784, 1822 ("the west field" 14, *the west feelde* 1601, – *westfeilds* 1613, *yᵉ westfielde* 1635, *the west feild* 1662, 1671, *Westfield* 1723, – *Field* 1734, – *or Cow Pasture*, *Clee West Field or Clee Hedge Field* 1749², *West Field Dike* 1734 (*v.* **west**,

feld, one of the open fields of Clee); West Garth 1843 (*Westgayrthes* 1508, *v*. **west, garðr**); West head dale 1822 (*v*. **hēafod, deill**); West Middle and Beck Fields 1759; West Well Gate or Way 1784, West Well 1850 Dobson (*west well* c.1600; the well is said in Dobson to be stagnant); Wifie Mier (sic) 1822; Wild Goose Hill 1784, 1822 (self–explanatory); Wipe Meer 1784 (*Wypemere* 1457, – *Mare* 1784, obscure); Witch Lane Pingle 1759 (*Pasture formerly called Witch Lane Pingle but now Foal Pingle* 1608, *v*. **pingel**; the meaning of *witch* is uncertain); The Yard 1788.

(b) *Abbey Fees* 1749[1] (presumably this refers to Wellow Abbey in Great Grimsby); *Acre Piece* 1734; *Ambler Dale* 1749[1] (from the surn. *Ambler* and **deill** 'a portion, a share of land', as elsewhere in the parish); *Balls Land* 1734 (from the surn. *Ball* and **land** 'a selion'); *Barnet Dale* 1734 (*v*. **deill**); *Barron Hill Furlong* 1734 (Dr Insley points out that the first el. is probably ME *barain(e)* 'unproductive, bare, infertile' with **hyll** and **furlang**); *Bateland* 1388 from the ME surn. *Bate* and **land**); *Beggar Busk* 1734 (probably denoting worthless land); *Billiard Well* 1734, *Billerd –* 1749[1]; *Black Hat Marfur* 1734 (*v*. **marfur** 'a boundary furrow', as elsewhere in the parish); *Botham* 1734 (*v*. **botm** 'a bottom, a valley bottom'); *Boymare* c.1600 (*v*. **boia** 'a boy, a servant', **(ge)mære**); *brigdikes, bridgdike* 1601, *Brigdikes* 1674, 1678, *Briggdikes* 1686, *bridg. dikes* 1697, *Brigdike* 1715 (*v*. **brycg** (mostly in a Scandinavianized form), **dík**, cf. *Brigdikes furlong* 1671, *Bridgedicke Furlong* 1734); *Brit(t) Green* 1734; *Bundings* 1749[1]; *Burghill* 1358 (*v*. **burh, hyll**; the significance of **burh** here is not clear); *Butcher Green* 1734 (*v*. **grēne**[2] 'a grassy place', as elsewhere in the parish); *But Gate, – Green, Butt Bank* 1734 (the first el. is probably **butt** 'an archery butt', the *Green* being where the butts were situated); *Byegate* 1734 (Dr Insley suggests that this is possibly a variant of dial. *by(e)way* 'a back entrance'); *Cardyke* 1457 (*v*. **kjarr, dík**); *Castell Crofte* 1443 (perhaps cf. *Castelle* 1327, *Castell* 1332 both (p); the significance of **castel** here is unknown); *Chappill Farm* 1734; *Checker* 1734, 1749[1], *Chequer* 1749[1] (*v*. **cheker**, here no doubt denoting land with variegated soil, *v*. Field s.n.); *Clee Cow Marsh* 1749[2]; *Cleeholes* 1457 (from the village name and **hol**[1] 'a hollow' in the pl.); *Cliff Hill* 1734; *Corne feild* 1625; *Corneholmeshill'* 1475–77 (probably 'the raised land in marsh where herons are found', *v*. **cran, holmr**; names derived from **cran** frequently have forms in *corn*); *the Cowgates* 1686 ('the right of pasturage for cows', *v*. **cū, gata**); *ye Cow Pasture* 1671, 1697, 1734, *ye Cow pastur* 1674, – *Pasture* 1678, – *pester* 1768; *Cromwell cross* 1457 (from the surn. *Cromwell* and **cros**); *Danegat'* 1457 (from **Danir** 'Danes' and **gata** 'a road, a way' and cf. Deansgate in

Great Grimsby *infra*); *Dunmare* 1457 (*v.* (**ge**)**mǣre**); *the East Feild of Itterby* 1609; *Estgate* 1457 (*v.* **ēast**, **gata**); *the Field or South Carr of Clee* 1690, *the field* – 1687, *The Fields* – 1725 (cf. Carr Lane *supra*); *Four Acre Piece* 1734; *Furland* 1734 (a variant form of **furlang**); *ye garres* c.1600 (*v.* **geiri**); *golding hill* 1601, 1697, 1715, *Golding hill* 1671, 1674, 1678, *–hill* 1686; *Goose Pudding* 1734, *– Puddings* 1749[1] (no doubt a name for a sticky place); *gracian garth* c.1600 (*v.* **garðr**; the first el. in obscure); *Great Green* 1734 (*v.* **grēne**[2] 'a green, a grassy place'); *Edward Grymoldbys headland* 1687 (*v.* **hēafod–land** 'the head of a strip left for turning the plough'); *Le grypes* 1533 (*v.* **grype** 'a ditch, a drain', cf. *le grippe* PN L **4**, 91); *gunnel dyke* 1484, *Gunwelldyk* 1508, *Gunwells Dike*, *– Nook*, *– Nooking* 1734 (perhaps from the ON fem. pers.n. *Gunna* or masc. *Gunni* with **wella** 'a spring'; the 1484 form represents an early shortening of *Gunwell* to *Gunnel*; B.W. notes that this is probably an artesian spring; this is probably the same as Gunwells Cl in Weelsby *infra*); *Half Acre* 1734; *Hall Firze*, *– Headland*, *– Mare* 1734 (*v.* **fyrs** 'furze', **hēafod–land** and (**ge**)**mǣre**); *Hanggerholme* 1457 (*v.* **holmr**); *hawley medew* 1457 (probably from the surn. *Hawley* and **mǣdwe**); *Haycroft* 13, *–crofte* 1535–46, 1601, *Haycroftes dyke* 1457 (self–explanatory); *Head Dale* 1749[1] (the meaning of *head* is uncertain, but may well have the same sense as **hēafod–land** 'a headland in the common field'); *Henghou* 14 (the first el. is uncertain; the second is **haugr** 'a hill, a mound'; it was in Thrunscoe); *Hyll* 1327, *of the hill'* 1332 both (p) (*v.* **hyll**); *the hither Carr* 1601 (cf. Carr Lane *supra*); *Hoggescrofte* 1535–46 (the first el. is the ME surn. *Hogg* with **croft**); *Horley Hill'*, *– Mare* 1714 (presumably the first el. is a surn. *Horley*); *Hourmarhyll* 1310; *How Hill Gate* 1714 (cf. *Howmare* 1457, *How Mare 1714*; the first el. is **haugr**); *Hountaine Close* 1690 (it was in Hole); *in campis de . . . Itterby* 1421 *AD* (*v.* **feld**); *Kyrk dyke* 1457 (*v.* **kirkja**, **dík**); *the Leas* 1687, 1690, *– Leaz* 1725 (*v.* **lea** (OE **lēah**) 'meadow, pasture' in the pl.); *leecoynes* (sic) c.1600 (obscure); *le Lyttill Filde* 1535–46, *little feelde commonli called the west feelde* 1601 (self–explanatory); *Longemaers* 1686, *long maires* 1697, *Longmares* 1671, 1674, 1678, *– mairs* 1715 (*v.* **lang**, (**ge**)**mǣre** 'a boundary, land on a boundary', as elsewhere in the parish); *Long Slater* (sic) (obscure); *Long Stears* 1734 (Dr Insley wonders whether we are concerned with dial. *steer* (Cu, Y) 'a landing place, a wharf'); *a certain place called Lowsey* 1687, 1690, 1725 (a derogatory nickname for a piece of land); *Lytelmare* 1457 (*v.* **lȳtel**, (**ge**)**mǣre**); *Lythe Acre* 1734 (the first el. is derived from OE **hlið** or ON **hlíð** 'a slope, a hillside'); *in Camp' Margaretæ* c.1300 ('Margaret's field', *v.* **feld**); *Marfor* 1734 (*v.* **marfur**); *The Matcheses* 1749[1] (obscure);

Middle Dyke 1734 (self-explanatory); *Middle House mare* 1734; *Mratheth Swath* (sic) 1734; *Munckcroft* 1326 (1457) *TCC, Muncroft* 1388 (*v.* **munuc, croft**); *le Newdyke* 1457 (*v.* **nīwe, dík**); *(the) ninedáles* 1687, 1690, *Ninedales* 1725 ('nine shares of land', *v.* **deill**); *ye north–carre* 1635 (*v.* Carr Lane *supra*); *the northe feelde* 1601, *ye north–fielde* 1635, – *North feild* 1662, *the* – 1671, *North Field* 1749[2] (one of the great fields of Clee, *v.* **norð. feld**); *North Green* 1734 (*v.* **grēne**[2] 'a green, a grassy place'); *Ormelethe* 1316 (probably 'Orm's slope, hillside', from the ON pers.n. *Ormr* and **hlíð**); *Oxkardyke* 1457, *Oxcar hill* 1601, *Oxgarrhill* 1687, 1690, – *Hill* 1725 (*v.* **oxa** 'an ox', **kjarr** with **dík** and **hyll**); *pardyke* 1457 (*v.* **dík**); *Pigglane End* 1734; *Pipe Mare* 1749[1]; *Pitkerine Close* 1734, *Pitkin* – 1734 (obscure); *ad Portam* 1327, *ad portam* 1332 both (p) (*v.* **geat** 'a gate'); *pottmare Iggs* (sic) 1687, – *Ings* 1690, *Potmare Ings* 1725 (perhaps 'the boundary (land) at a pit or hole' *v.* **potte**, **(ge)mære**, with the pl. of **eng** 'meadow, pasture'); *Prestemare* 1457, *Preest Mare* 1734 (*v.* **prēost**, **(ge)mære**); *Pridgeon* (sic) 1734; *St. John's Land* 1734; *Saltmare* 1547 (*v.* **salt**, **(ge)mære** or **márr**); *Sandehouse* 1535–46 (no doubt a house on or near the sands); *Scatthowe gate* 1601, *Scattergate furlong* 1652 (*Scatthowe* and *Scatter* are no doubt forms of Scartho and so belong to Scartho Gate in f.ns. (a) *supra*); *The Shift* 1749[1] (cf. Shift cl North in Utterby, PN L **4**, 4); *Short Dales* 1749[1] *v.* **sc(e)ort, deill**); *Southiby* 1327 *SR*, *Sotheby* 1396 both (p) (literally 'south in the village' *v.* **sūð, í, bȳ**, a common formation in L, cf. *Estiby* PN L **3**, 76, *Northyby* ib, 92); *Stanber* 1734 (*v.* **stān, berg** 'a hill'); *Stephenson's Hedge* 1734 (named from the family of John Stephenson 1718 *BT*; *the stintinges* 1601 (*v.* **stinting** 'a portion of common land set apart for one man's use' and *v.* further *ye stintings* PN L **2**, 14); *The Stolne* (sic) *Pit* 1749[1]; *ye stone hill* c.1600; *Stounelees* 1457 (*v.* **stān, lea** (OE **lēah**) 'meadow, pasture' in the pl.); *Suthowemare* 1316 (*v.* **sūð, haugr, (ge)mære**); *Swath Lea* 1734 (*v.* **swæð** 'a strip of grassland', **lea** (OE **lēah**) 'meadow, pasture'); *Swin Moor* 1734; *Swynemaregate* 1457 (*v.* **swīn, (ge)mære** with **gata**); *Syth Acre* 1734; *Thornedyke* c.1300 (*v.* **þorn, dík**); *Thorpe Bank Field* 1734, *Thorpe Field, Thorpe Great Field* 1734, *thorps Marsh* 1662, *Thorp* – 1734 (the reference is to Cleethorpes); *Three Acre Piece*, – *Whong* 1734 (*v.* **vangr** 'a garden, an in–field'); *Thrunscoe Bank Field* 1749[2]; "the east field of" *Thirnessco* 14; *campis . . . de Thirnsco* 1421, *Thirnsco Feld* 1457 (*v.* **feld**); *Threstangge mare* 1457 ('the three poles (of land)', *v.* **þrēo, stong** with **(ge)mære**); *Thrunscoe Marsh*, – *Middle Field*, – *West Field* all 1749[2]; *Waddome* c.1600; *Walker Hill* 1734 (named from the family of Robert Walker 1676 *BT*); *Wardyke* 1749[1] (probably denoting a protection dyke, *v.* **weard, dík**); *Wash Carr Hill* 1749; *Waswelmore* 1457; *Watry Farm* 1734; *atte* *well'* 1332 (p) (*v.* **wella**); *Well Arme* 1749[1]; *West Arme* 1734 (the meaning of *Arme* is obscure); *West Closes* 1734; *West Willow feild* 1652; *Wilsby Ground*, – *Hedge* 1734 (the reference is to Weelsby *infra*); *Whatber* c.1600 (perhaps 'the hill, mound where wheat is grown', *v.* **hwǣte, beorg**); *Windings* 1734 (cf. *wynedyngs* in Immingham f.ns. (b), PN L **2**, 73); *le Wra* 13, *le Wraa* (*dyke*) (*v.* **vrá** 'a corner of land, etc.' with **dík**); *Yeldall* 1457 (perhaps from **helde** 'a slope' with prosthetic [j] and **deill** 'a share of land').

Great Coates

GREAT COATES

> *Cotes* (5x) 1086 DB, 1175 ChancR (p), 1176, 1191 P *et freq* to 1200 ib all (p), 1201 Ass (p), 1202 P (p), 1204 FF, 1204, 1205, 1206 P, 1209 FF, 1212 Fees, 1212, 1214 P, 1220 Cur, 1223, 1227 FF, 1230 P, 1249, 1262 FF, 1265 Misc *et passim* to (– "by" *Grymesby*) 1426 Cl, *Cotis* c.1115 LS
> *Cotun* c.1115 LS, 1183, 1184, 1185 P, *Kotun* 1182 ib, *Cothum* 1196 ChancR, *Cotom* 1374, 1375 Peace (p)
> *Magna Cotes* 1272 *Ass*, 1281, 1297 *FF*, 1242–43 Fees, 1254 ValNor, 1274 Abbr, 1275 RH, 1284, 1294 RSut, 1303, 1316 FA, 1318 *AD*, 1327, 1332 *SR et freq* to (– *juxta Grimesby*) 1584 *MiscDon 238*, – *Cotis* 1503 Ipm, *Cotes Magna* 1526 Sub, 1554 InstBen, – *magna* 1569 ib, 1590, 1594 *BT*, – *M:* 1576 Saxton, *Cotts Magna* 1535 VE iv, *Cots Mag* a1567 LNQ v, *Cootes magna* 1570 *BT*, *Coates magna* 1602, 1614, 1622, 1675 *ib*, 1686 *Terrier*, *Coats Magna* 1689, 1723 *BT*, 1697, 1709, 1724 *Terrier*
> "Great" *Cotes* 1282 Ipm, 1307 Pat, 1313 Ch, 1314 Ipm, 1319, 1329 Pat, 1347 Fine *et freq* to 1509 Ipm, – *Cothes* 1303 Pap, – *Cottes* 1561 Pat
> *Mikelcotes* 1329 *Ass* (p), *Mykel-* 1374 Peace, – *kotes* 1369 Misc, *Mekelcotes* 1413–26 ECP, *Mikyll Cotes* 1493–1500 *MinAcct*, *Mikkyl –* 1503 Brasses, *Mikell –* 1518 *GrimsCB*

Great Cootes 1562 *BT*, – *Cottes* 1576 LER, *greate Cotes*
c.1590 *Terrier*, 1596 *Foster*, *Great* – 1610 Speed, 1629 *Inv*,
1634 *Terrier*, 1639, 1645 *BT*, – *Coats* 1702 *ib*, 1706
Terrier, – *Coates* 1741 *PT*, 1756 *BT*, 1781 *Terrier*

'The cottages, the sheds or shelters', *v*. **cot**; forms in *Cotun* etc.
are from the dat.pl. **cotum** and for this variation, *v*. Ekwall,
Studies 31–32. Great Coates is distinguished as such from the
adjacent Little Coates *infra*. Spellings in *Mikel-*, *Mykel-* etc. are
from ON **mikill** 'big, great'. Forms in *Grawencotes*, *Grauncotes*
Hy3 (e14) Selby probably belong here, and contain ME *graunt*,
gra(u)nd, *gra(u)n* (in compounds) 'large, big; great' as first el., as
suggested by Dr Insley.

ATKIN'S FM is no doubt from the family name *Atkin*. BECK LANE,
cf. *the beck* 1686, *y*ᵉ – 1697, 1709, 1724, – *Beck* 1706 all *Terrier*,
Great Coates Beck 1703 *GrimsCB x*, *v*. **bekkr**. BLOW WELLS, cf.
Blow-well Plot 1841 *TA*; *v*. NED s.v. *blow* sb. 2. under *blow-well*
where the following quotation is given: "On the warp-lands of ...
the Humber estuary there bubble up with great vigour a series of
springs known as 'blow-wells' . . . A 'blow-well' is a natural
artesian discharge". BROWN'S FM, no doubt named from the
family of John *Browen* (sic) 1618 *BT*, Jane *Brown widdow* 1632
ib. BUTTS. CONK LANE. COOKS LANE (lost), 1828 Bry; named
from the local *Cook* family, cf. William *Cooke* 1775 *BT*; it is now
Town's Croft Drain. THE DECOY. FIELD HO, cf. *campum de
Cotes* Hy3 (14) Selby, *v*. **feld**. GREAT COATES BRIDGE, cf. *Bridge
Carr* 1841 *TA*, *v*. **kjarr** 'brushwood', 'a marsh, bog'. HALL
CLOSE, 1841 *TA*, cf. *y*ᵉ *Haul Neatgang* c.1590, *the Hall neat gang*
1668, *y*ᵉ *Hall Neat Gang* 1679, *the* – 1686, – *Hall Neat-gang* 1706
all *Terrier*, *Hall* 1828 Bry, *v*. **hall**, with **nēat** 'cattle', **gang** 'a
track'. HOLME COTTAGE, cf. *y*ᵉ *holme* c.1590, *the great holmes*
1634, *Little Holm* 1686, *Little Holms Drain* 1706 all *Terrier*, *Holme
Field* 1841 *TA*, 'the higher ground amidst the marsh', *v*. **holmr**.
MANOR HO. MARSH FM, *in maresco de magna cotes* 1361
GrimsFC, *the marsh* 1634, – *Marsh* 1781, 1825 all *Terrier*, 1841
TA, self-explanatory, *v*. **mersc**. MARSH LANE, 1828 Bry.

MAWMBRIDGE DRAIN, 1824 O, 1831 *Monson, Malnebridg ditch* (sic) c.1590, *the Drain Mawm bridge* (sic) 1686, – *Maume brigge dreane* 1697, *Maum's bridge Drain* 1825 all *Terrier, Maumbridge Creek* 1828 Bry, *Malmbridge* 1841 *TA*, perhaps 'the bridge on sandy soil', from **malm** 'sand, sandy soil' and **brycg**; spellings in *Mawm-, Maum-* would then be the result of vocalisation of *-l-*. MOAT. THE NEDKINS (lost), 1828 Bry, obscure; this was an area of land north of Atkin's Fm. NEW CUT DRAIN. OLDFLEET DRAIN, *a drayne called Holefleete* 1613 *MinAcct*; for earlier forms and a discussion of the name, *v.* PN L **2**, 269. It means 'the stream, the creek in a hollow', *v.* **hol**[1], **flēot** and it forms the boundary between Great Coates and Stallingborough. PYEWIPE, – *Inn* 1828 Bry, *Pewet* – 1838 *Brace*; *pyewipe* and *pewet* are dial. terms for the lapwing, *Vanellus vanellus*, common in L. SWEEDALE CROFT DRAIN, cf. *Swetwell, Swittlecroft* c.1590, *the swith croft* 1634, *Swittle croft* 1668, 1679, – *Croft* 1686, 1706, *Swithle Croft* 1709, 1724 all *Terrier, Sweedale* – 1841 *TA*; the earliest form clearly suggests that the meaning of *Sweedale* is 'the sweet spring or well', *v.* **swēte**, **wella**. THREE DRAIN END PLANTATION, *Three Drain Plantation* 1841 *TA*. TOWN'S CROFT DRAIN, *v.* Cooks Lane *supra*. TOWN'S HOLT, *Towns Holt* 1841 *TA* and is apparently earlier *Car Holt* 1828 Bry, *v.* **kjarr**, **holt**. THE VICARAGE, *the personage* 1634, *ye Parsonage house* 1679, *the* – 1697, *(the) Parsonage house* 1709, 1724, *the Rectory House* 1825 all *Terrier, Parsonage* 1838 *Brace, Rectory House* 1841 *TA*. WADD FM. WOAD FM, *The Woads* 1824 O, *Taylors Woad F.* 1828 Bry, named from the family of Francis, Mathew and Thomas *Taylor* 1642 LPR; it must have been a farm where woad grew.

FIELD-NAMES

Undated forms are 1841 *TA* (Altered Apportionment). Forms dated 1227, 1281, 1297, 1492 are *FF*; 1318 *AD*; 1327, 1331 *SR*; 1361 *GrimsFC*; c.1590, 1634, 1668, 1679, 1686, 1697, 1706, 1709, 1724, 1781, 1825 *Terrier*; 1596 *Foster*; 1613 *MinAcct*.

(a) Arable Cl, – Fd, – Plot; Astrop Grove (from the family of John *Aystrop* 1785 *BT*); Aylesby Lane (cf. *Alesbiegate* c.1590, *Ailisbie gate* 1634 (from the neighbouring parish of Aylesby and **gata** 'a road'); Bank Cl (*v.* **banke** and cf. *the South acre Bank* in (b) *infra*); Bull Cl, – Garth (*v.* **garðr**); Bullneck; the Carr 1781, 1825, Carrs 1841 (*y*e *Car* c.1590, 1668, – *Great–Carre* 1668, – *Great Car* 1686, – *great Carr*, – *Little* – 1697, – *Great carr*, – *Little Carr* 1706, *Great* –, *Little Carr* 1709, *y*e *Great* –, – *little Carr* 1724, *v.* **kjarr**); Carr's Osier Grds (perhaps from the prec. n. or from the surn. *Carr*); Chapel Cottage garden and Croft; Church Cl, Church Yard, Church yard Close and Cottage and garden; Clarks Marsh; Clover Cl; Corn Cl (cf. *y*e *Cornefeild* c.1590); Corn Marsh; Cortis Marsh (named from the *Cortis* or *Curtis* family, cf. William *Curtis* 1629 *Inv*, Richard –, William *Curtisse* 1642 LPR); Cottage and Farm Buildings, Cottage(s) and garden(s), Cottage Fd, – Pasture, – Plot (cf. *Cottage Close* 1706); Cottagers Fd with road; the Cow Cl 1781, 1825; Cow Gate; Croft; The Eighteen Acres; Ewe Croft; Farm buildings Yard Rush & Long Cls; Fitty ground(s); (Old) Fox Covert; Freshney Bank; Garden, Garden and site of Old House; Gardens in Aylesby Lane; Great Groves ([*a marsh*] . . . *called the Groves*, *Groves bush*, *Groves yate* 1613, *the Groues* 1668, *the Groves* 1686, 1706, *the Neather Groves* 1697; *grove* is a dial. term for sites where digging (for turf) takes place, *v.* further PN L **2**, 155 and PN L **4**, 128); Great Marsh; Great Nooks Cl; Great Ox Pasture; Grimsby Plot 1825; Half Middle Ox Pasture; the Healing Plot 1825 (cf. *Heyling mere* 1318 (*v.* **(ge)mǣre** 'a boundary, boundary land'), *Heling hedge* 1668, *Healing hedge* 1668, – *Hedg* 1686, – *Hedge* 1706 (*v.* **hecg**, alluding to the neighbouring parish of Healing); High Dales; (the) Home Cl, – Plot; Horse Cl, – Marsh; House garden and Croft; Humber Bank Fd; Land and Cottages north of line (cf. Line of Railway *infra*); Land, buildings & Manure Works; Line of Railway; Little Nooks Cl; Little Pingle and garden (*v.* **pingel**); Lockings Cl (presumably named from the family of Judith *Lockin widow* 1670 *BT*); Mill Green (*Milnegrene* c.1590, *the Milne greene* 1634, *Mill green* 1668, *milne Greene* 1697, *Millgreen* 1706, *Mill Green* 1709, *y*e *far mill–green* 1724 (*v.* **grēne**[2]), Mill Holme (*Milneholme* c.1590, *the Milne holme* 1634, *Mill holme* 1668, *the Mill Holm* 1686, (*the*) *Milholme* 1697, *Millholm* 1706, *Mill Holme* 1709, *Mil–holme* 1724, *v.* **myln**, **holmr** and cf. "mill of" *Cotes* 1277); (Long) Neat Gang, Half – (*the Neategange* 1596, *the East* –, *the North Neat–Gang* 1668, – *Neat Gang* 1686, *y*e *Neatgang ditch* c.1590, *the Neatgang draught* 1706, 'the cattle walk, track', *v.* **nēat**, **gang** and cf. Hall Close *supra*); New Plantation next Railway; the North Fd (*in boriali campo* 1318, *the north feild*

1634, - *Northe field* 1668, *North feild* 1679, *The North Field* 1686, *the -* 1697, 1706 (*v.* **norð, feld**; one of the great fields of the parish, cf. the South Fd, *the west feild infra*); Ox Pasture (*the oxe pasture* 1634); Paddock, - and Plantn, Paddock North Fd and Holme Plot; Pingle Mdw (cf. *a peice of grounde . . . called a pingle* 1634, *v.* **pingel**); 2 Plantations rear of Waiting-room and platform; Private Rd; Public Rd; Rudforth; Semitry (sic, presumably for Cemetery); Part of Sheltons Wong (named from the *Shelton* family, cf. Thomas *Shelton* 1838, with **vangr**); Shipton Wong (*Shippen-wonge* 1634, *Sheepen Wong* 1706, *v.* **scypen, vangr** 'a garden, an in-field'); The Sixteen Acres; Skeddlecroft (c.1590, *Skettle croft* 1668, *v.* **croft**; Dr Insley writes "the first component may be a compound of ODan **skiūt* 'point, projection' and **hyll**, cf. the Danish p.n. *Skydebjerg* DaSN 14, 297. ODan **skiūt* would have given ME *skēt*, which would have later undergone shortening. The medial element **hyll** would have been reduced early as a result of weak stress arising from its medial position within the compound **Skēthilcroft*. The voicing of /t/-/d/ is attested in English dialects, *v.* EDGr paragraph 283, though it seems to be more common in the South-West than elsewhere."); The South Fd 1781, South Fd 1841 (*the South field* 1668, *- Feild* 1686, 1679, *South feild* 1679, *v.* **suð, feld**; one of the great fields of the parish, cf. the North Fd *supra*, *the west feild* in (b) *infra*); Stawn (sic) (*ye Strawne* c.1590); Stithy Green; Stock Fd (cf. *ye Stocke, long stocke* c.1590, *the long stocke* 1634, *- Stock* 1668, *- Stoke* 1686, *the Stock, Long Stock* 1706); Thorn Tree and Wash Dyke; Tidal land (presumably an area of rough grazing covered by the sea at high tide); Toft Marsh (cf. *Toft Wonge* c.1590, *v.* **toft** 'a messuage, a curtilage', **vangr**); Two Cottages and Land; Washing Dyke; Weather Neat Gang (from **weðer** 'a wether, a castrated ram' and **nēat, gang** (cf. Neat Gang *supra*), the sense of which extended to include sheep, cf. *Sheep gang wong* (b) *infra*); Wood Groves.

(b) *the South acre Bank* 1668, *Acre Bank* 1686, *the Acre bank* 1706 (*v.* **æcer, banke**, cf. Bank Fd(s) in (a) *supra*); *Appelderfeud* 1281 (*v.* **apuldor** 'an apple-tree', **feld**), *Appeltrefeld'* 1297 (*v.* **æppel-trēow, feld**) both (p)); *Bramores furlang* c.1590, *Bramer furlonge* 1634; *Bownam* c.1590, 1706; *Bul Marfrey* (sic) 1686, *Bull Marfrey* 1706 (*v.* **marfur** 'a boundary furrow'; *marfrey* is found frequently in north L as a variant of *marfur*); *ye Buttcloase* c.1590, *the butt close* 1634, *Butt close* 1706, *Butt-close Hedge* 1668, *But Close (Hedg)* 1686 (*v.* **butte**); *Cart Way* 1686, *the cart way* 1706; *ye Cheker* c.1590 (*v.* **cheker**); *ye Comon feildes* c.1590; *ye comon marfer* c.1590 (cf. *Bul Marfrey supra*); *the Commons* 1634; *the cony garts* (sic) 1634, *the Cony*

Garth 1706 (*v.* **coni, garðr**); *Cowburne* c.1590; *Cow–burn Hedge* 1668 (*v.* **cū, burna** and cf. *Gosburne infra*); *Cowsdurt* (sic) c.1590; *Crosegarth dale* c.1590 (*v.* **cros, garðr** with **deill**); *Croseheadland* c.1590 (*v.* **cros, hēafod–land**); *the Dove coat Marfrey* 1705 (*v.* **douve–cote, marfur**); *the east feild* 1634, *the East Field* 1706 (*v.* **ēast, feld**, perhaps a later addition to the great fields); *Easter Syke* c.1590, *the Easter sikes* 1634, *Easter Sykes* 1668, *– Sikes* 1686, 1697, *– sikes* 1706, *– siker* (sic) (perhaps from **eowestre** 'a sheepfold', with **sík**); *the fallow field* 1686, *the Fallow feild* 1697, *the Fallow Field* 1706, *ye Fallow field* 1709, *ye fallow –* 1724 (*v.* **falh**); *Furwell Hill* c.1590, *– hills* 1668, *– Hills* 1686; *goldinge* 1634 (*v.* **golde, eng**); *Gosburne* c.1590 (*v.* **gōs** 'goose', **burna** 'a stream' and cf. *Cowburne supra*); *greate Coates Clowe* 1613 (for *Clowe, v.* PN L **4**, xv); *ye Hale* c.1590, *the Hayle* 1668, *Hayle* 1686, *The hayle sid* (sic) 1634, *the Hail side* 1706 (*v.* **halh**); *ye headale* c.1590 (*v.* **hēafod, deill**); *High hill nook* 1706; *ad montem* 1327 (p), *del hill* 1332 (p) (*v.* **hyll**); *Inges* c.1590 (*v.* **eng** 'meadow, pasture'); *the little field* 1668, *– Field* 1686; *ye Lordshippe dale* c.1590 (*v.* **deill**); *Marhole* c.1590; *the milkin* 1634; *Neucroft* 1361, *Newcroft hawse* c.1590 (*v.* **croft**; *hawse* probably stands for ME *hawes* 'enclosures, curtilages', *v.* **haga**[1]); *ye owt marishe* c.1590 (*v.* **ūt, mersc** and cf. Marsh Fm *supra*); *ye Oxgangs* c.1590 (*v.* **ox–gang**); *the Salt marsh* 1668, *the Salt Marsh* 1706; *ye Seaditch* c.1590 (*v.* **sǣ, dīc**); *Sheep gang wong, Sheep–Gang Wong* 1668, *Sheep Gang Wong* 1686 (*v.* **scēp, gang** with **vangr**); *Shep head–Marfer* 1668, *Sheepherd Marfrey* 1706 (*v.* **marfur**); *Shortbutelease* c.1590 (*v.* **sceort, butte** with **lǣs**); *the short furlonge* 1634; *Skirwellcroft* 1361 ('the clear, bright spring', *v.* **wella**, with **croft**, the first el. being **scír** 'clear, bright' in a Scandinavianized form or the cognate ON **skírr** itself); *Southorne or great Coates groves* 1613 (cf. Great Groves *supra*); *Southurne* 1613, *v.* **sūð, hyrne** 'a corner'); *Stephen Wong* c.1590 (from the pers.n. or surn. *Stephen* and **vangr**); *the Vale* 1596; *le Warlotes, le Warlotstigt* 1318 (*v.* **warlot**, for a discussion of which, *v.* PN L **2**, 67, **stíg** 'a path', often occurring as ME *stigt*, ModE *stight* in north L); *the West–Dog–Marfer* 1668 (*v.* **marfur**); *the west feild* 1634, *– West field* 1668, *– Field* 1686, 1706, *– Feilde* 1697, *ye west feild* 1679 (*v.* **west, feld**; one of the great fields of the parish, cf. the South Fd, the North Fd *supra*); *Widdow–coat Marfer* 1668, *Wider Coates marfrey* 1686 (*v.* **marfur** and perhaps cf. *Mathew Coates Close* 1679); *Willow Mare* c.1590 (*v.* **(ge)mǣre**); *in le Wraa* 1327 SR (p) (*v.* **vrá**).

Little Coates

LITTLE COATES

Sudcotes (3x) 1086 DB
Sut Cotum c.1115 LS
Parva Cotes 1177 P, 1226–28, 1242–43 Fees, 1254 ValNor,
  1275 RH, 1303 FA, 1311 Orig, 1316, 1346, 1428, 1431
  FA, *parva* – 1291 Tax, *Parva Cotis* 1219 Fees, *Parua Cotes*
  1203 P, 1327, 1332 *SR*, 1381 Peace, *parua* – 1272 *Ass*,
  1320 *CottCh*, 1349 *Cor*, *Cotes Parva* 1313 Inqaqd, 1526
  Sub, – *parva* 1595, 1602, 1614 *BT*, *Cotts Parva* 1535 VE
  iv, *Coots* – 1539–40 Dugd iv, *Cootes parua* 1563 *BT*, *Cottes*
  parva 1570 *ib*, *Cotes* – 1640, 1743 *ib*, – *parva* 1822 *Terrier*
  "Little" *Cotes* 1227 Ch, 1258, 1260 Pat, 1266 Misc, 1278 Ch,
  1287, 1292 Ipm, 1306, 1309 Pat, 1314 Ipm *et passim* to
  1432 Pat
Littelcotes 1377, 1384 Fine, *Litel*– 1383, 1393, 1406 Pat, *Litill*
  Cotis 1493–1500 ECP, *Lyttle Cotts* 1535 VE iv, *Litle Cottes*
  1539 LP xi, *littyll coytes* 1546 *GrimsCB iii*, *lytell coottes*
  1566 *BT*, 1580 *Terrier*, *Little Cotes* 1610 Speed, 1828 Bry,
  – *Cootes* 1671, 1690 *BT*, – *Coates* 1674, 1679 *Terrier*,
  1691, 1724 *BT et freq*, –*coats* 1759 *BRA 1302*, *litlecotes*
  1612 *BT*, *Litlecoates* 1616 *ib*, – *Coats* 1627, 1632, 1668,
  1676 *ib*, – *Cotes* 1634 *Terrier*

The earliest spellings indicate that this is 'the cottages, the
sheds or shelters to the south', *v*. **sūð, cot**, and that at an early
date **sūð** was replaced by **lȳtel** 'little'. In both cases the description
is in relation to Great Coates immediately to the north. In contrast
to the latter only a single spelling has been noted reflecting the
dat.pl. form **cotum**.

R. FRESHNEY, *portu de Fresken* 1258 BC, *portum de Freskeney*
1275 RH, "water of" *Freshney* 1279–80 Inqaqd, *Freskene aqua*
1279–80 IpmR, "the water of" *Freskeney* 1280 Pat, – *Friskeneye*

1328-29 (1662) Imb, *Fresheney* 1569 *GrimsCB iv*, *Freshney Creek* 1731 *Td'E*, 'the river with fresh water', *v.* **fresc**, **ēa**, in the oblique case, (*æt*) *frescan ēa*.

BLOW WELLS, cf. *Blow Well Close* 1844 *TA*; for Blow Wells *v.* Blow Wells in Great Coates *supra*. COATES FEN (lost), *Cotes Fen* 1828 Bry; it was an area west of Blow Wells. DECOY PLANTATION (lost, approx. TA 237 084), *Decoy Pl^n.* 1828 Bry, cf. *Decoy* c.1759 *MapGrims*, the reference is no doubt to a duck decoy. GATE FIELD (lost), 1844 *TA*, *Gates field* c.1759 *MapGrims*, *the Gate Field* 1828 Bry; it was west of Little Coates Rd., in the southern part of the Golf Course. GREAT CHAPEL FIELD (lost), 1844 *TA*, *G.* – 1828 Bry, cf. *Chapel field* c.1759 *MapGrims*; it was part of the modern Golf Course. LITTLE COATES HALL, *Hall* 1828 Bry. TOOT HILL, 1824 O, 1831 *Monson*, *Toote* – 1825 Oliver, 1828 Bry, *Tout* – c.1757, c.1759 *MapGrims*, 'the look-out hill', *v.* **tōt–hyll**. The hill was levelled before the first World War. VICARAGE (lost), *the vicarage house* 1580, *a vicaridge* – 1634, *vickiridge* – 1662, *no Vicaridge House* 1762, *Vicarage House none* 1822 all *Terrier*.

FIELD-NAMES

Forms dated 1271 are *Ass*; 1279-80 (1662) Imb; 1343 Pat, 1537 *AOMB*; 1539 LP; 1580, 1612, 1634, 1662, 1668, 1674, 1762, 1822 *Terrier*; 1613 *MinAcct*; c.1757, c.1759 *MapGrims*; 1831 *Yarb*; 1832 *LindDep 19*; 1844 *TA*.

(a) Ash Garth c.1757, c.1759 (Mr Field suggests that this possibly alludes to a yard where ashes were heaped rather than to ash trees, *v.* **garðr**); Back Gares 1831 (*v.* **geiri**); Bartrams Carr c.1757, c.1759 (from the local surn. *Bartram*, cf. Richard *Bartram* 1642 LPR, with **kjarr**); Bean Fd c.1757, c.1759, 1832, 1844 (*v.* **bēan**); Broth Carr 1831 (*v.* **kjarr**; *Broth* is obscure); Car 1844 (*v.* **kjarr**); Cheesemans Fd c.1757, c.1759, Middle –, North –, South –, West Cheeseman Fd 1832, 1844 (from the surn. *Cheeseman*, cf. Samuel *Chesman* 1671 *BT*); Church Yd 1844; Coalman Platt 1831 (probably from the surn. *Coalman* or *Coleman* with **platt**); Common c.1757, c.1759, 1844; Common Car c.1757, c.1759, 1832, 1844 (*lytle cottis Car* 1537, *v.* **kjarr**); Cottage Garden 1844 (perhaps identical with *the Cottager plott* 1668, *Cotcher plot* 1674, *cotcher* being a common local form of *cottager* in north L); Far Marsh c.1757, c.1759; North –, South Fieldfare, North –, South Felfer c.1757, c.1759 (obscure); Fitty Land 1832; Garden; Gate Fd 1832; Gaunts Carr c.1575, Grants – c.1759 (from the surn. *Gaunt* or *Grant*); Grass Garth Cl 1831 (*v.* **garðr**); Great Marsh c.1757, c.1759, East –, South –, West Great Marsh 1844 (cf. *litle Cotes Marishes* c.1590 *Terrier* (Great Coates), *Little Coates marsh*, – *salt marsh* 1613, *Little Coates Marsh* 1703 *GrimsCB x* and cf. Little Marsh *infra*); Harpam Car c.1757, c.1759, *Harpan* –, *Harpens* – 1844 (probably from the surn. *Harpham*); High Fd c.1757, c.1759, East –, North –, South –, West High Fd 1832, 1844 (adjoins Laceby); Home Cl c.1757, c.1759, 1844, the – 1831 (there is a house marked in this field); Homestead c.1757, c.1759, 1844; Honey Hole 1831 (alluding to sticky soil); East –, West Ings c.1757, c.1759, 1832, 1844 (*v.* **eng**); Jackson ho. c.1757, c.1759, Jacksons Homestead 1832, 1844 (from the surn. *Jackson*, well-evidenced in the neighbouring parish of Great Coates, cf. John *Jackson* 1596 *BT*); the Little Cl 1831; Little fields c.1757, c.1759, East –, Middle –, North –, West Little Fd 1832, 1844; Little Marsh c.1757, c.1759, 1844 (cf. *Little Coates Marsh* 1703, – *coates marsh bridge* 1711 both *GrimsCB x*); Low Cl c.1757, c.1759; Middle Plat 1832 (*v.* **plat**); Mill Carr 1832, 1844 (*v.* **kjarr**), – Cl c.1757, c.1759, 1832, 1844, – fd c.1757, c.1759, – Fd 1844, Mill Field Plantn 1832, 1844, Mill Holm c.1757, 1759 (*v.* **holmr**, cf. *vnius modendini in parua Cotes iuxta Grymesby* 1271, *Mylnewelcryke* 1279–80, *Milnewell Creeke, Milnewelcryke* 1279–80 (1662), *v.* **myln, wella** with **crike**); (North) New Cl c.1757, c.1759, 1832, North –, South New Cl 1844; Newton Marsh 1844 (probably named from the family of John *Newton* 1606 *Inv*); Oak Plantn (in SW corner of M.F.) c.1757, c.1759; Olde Cl c.1757, c.1759, Old Close (Btm) 1832, 1844, East Old Cl 1844; Old Garth c.1757, c.1759, 1832, 1844 (*v.* **garðr**); Orchard 1832, 1844; Petty Green c.1757, c.1759, 1832, 1844 (probably from the surn. *Petty* with **grēne**[2]); Pingle c.1757, c.1759, 1844 (*v.* **pingel**); East –, Middle –, Road –, West platt c.1757, c.1759, East –, Middle –, Road Plat 1844 (*v.* **plat**, it adjoins Bradley); Plumb tree Carr c.1757, c.1759, East –, West Plumtree Car 1844 (*v.* **kjarr**), Close . . . called Poles 1831 (probably from the surn. *Pole*); Priest Moor 1831 (*v.* **prēost, mōr**); East –, Middle Ray c.1757, c.1759, 1832, 1844, North –, South Ray c.1757, c.1759, West Ray 1844; Rye Cl c.1757, c.1759, 1844, Rye Close Car 1844 (*v.* **kjarr**); Salt

Ings 1832 (*v.* **salt, eng** 'meadow, pasture'); Sand hill c.1757, c.1759, – hills 1832, 1844; Stripe 1832, 1844 ('the narrow piece of land', *v.* **strīp**); Sutton Esq^res Land c.1759; Thistle fd c.1757, c.1759, North –, South Thistle Fd 1832, 1844 (*v.* **þistel**); Thorn Hill 1831 (*v.* **þorn, hyll**); West Cl 1832, 1844; Win Green c.1757, c.1759, Winn – 1832, 1844 (named from the *Winn* family, cf. *Mr R. Winn* 1838 *Inv*, with **grēne**[2]).

(b) *pontem parve Coates* 1576 *GrimsChamb* (*v.* **brycg**); *Denesmylen* 1349 *Cor* (*v.* **myln**); *le Estfeld* 1343 (*v.* **ēast, feld**); *Martyn Hillyard's howse* 1539; *Wormedalle Carres* 1612 (*v.* **dalr, kjarr**; the first el. is **wyrm**, perhaps in the sense 'earthworm', rather than 'reptile, snake').

Great Grimsby

GREAT GRIMSBY

> *Grimesbi* (5x) 1086 DB, c.1115 LS, 1130 P, 1132 (1403) Pat, 1156, 1157, 1158 *et freq* to 1214 all P, 1177 Bly, 1179 RA i, 1185 Templar, lHy2 Dane, 1194 YCh iii, 1200 Cur, 1202 Ass, 1203 Cur, 1218 Ass, 1231 Memo, c.1250 Crone, 1268 Pat, 113 (e14) Havelok, 1392 Pap, *–bia* 1114–16, 1163 RA i, *–beia* 1153 RRAN, *Grimisbi* 1173 P, 1174 ChancR, 1179 P, *–bia* 1175 ib, 1178 ChancR, *–by* 1469 Pat
> *nova Grimesbi* 1155–58 Ch, "New" *Grimesby* Hy2 (1461) Pat
> *í grims bǽ miþivm* c.1120 (c.1300) Orkneyinga saga
> *Grimesby* 1155–56, 1156–57 RBE, 1190–96 (e14) YCh ii, 1192, 1194, 1200 P, 1201 Memo, 1201 ChR, 1202 FF, 1206 OblR, 1206 P, 1206 Ass, 1207 OblR, 1207 BC, 1207, 1208 ChR, 1211–12 RBE, 1216 *HarlCh*, 1217 Pat, 1223 Cur, 1225 ClR, 1225 Cur, 1226 FF, 1227 Ch, 1228 Pat, 1228 Lib, 1230 Cur *et freq* to 1499 HMCRep, *–bie* 1576 LER
> *Grymesby* c.1151 RA i, 1154–79 BC, 1155–58 (1334) Ch, Hy2 (1301) ib, 1252 Pat, 1256 (1318) Ch, 1275 Fine, 1285 Pat, 1291 Tax, 1300 Abbr, 1303 FA, 1305 Fine, 1305 Pat, 1305 Cl, 1308, 1314, 1317 Pat, 1319 Orig, 1322 *FF*, 1327 Pat,

1328 Banco, 1330 Cl, 1331 Pat, 1331 Ipm, 1336 Cl, 1338 Misc, 1341 Cl, 1341 Orig, 1343 Ipm, 1344 Fine, 1347 Pat, 1350 Cl *et freq* to 1560 Pat, *–bye* 1492 Fine, 1547, 1564 Pat *Grymysby* 1509 Ipm, *–be* 1534 LP vii

Grymmesby 1198 (1328) Ch, 1258 Cl, 1259 Pat, 1267 Cl, 1267 Lib, 1277 Pat, 1281 QW, 1293 Pat, 1296 Cl, 1297 Ass, 1309 Pat, 1312, 1318 Cl, 1319 Ch, 1322 Fine, 1323 Cl, 1326, 1335, 1338 Pat, 1342 Cl *et passim* to 1556 Pat, *Grymmysby* 1452 Fine, 1454 Cl, *–be* 1437 LP xii

Grimmesby 1217, 1218 Pat, 1226 Welles, 1228 Cl, 1230 Pat, 1255, 1258, 1264 Cl, 1266 Pat, 1268 Lib *et passim* to 1332 Pat, *–bi* 1224 ib, *Grimmisby* 1254 ValNor, 1260 Lib, 1261 Cl, 1262 Pat, *Grimmisbi* 1271 RRGr

Grimsby 1328 Cl, 1330 Pat, 1531 LP v *et passim*, *–bye* Saxton *Grymsby* 1434 Fine, 1461 Cl

magnam Grymesby 1293 *Ass, magna –* 1417 *GrimsCt*, 1480 Pap, 1541 *GrimsCB i*, 1546 *GrimsChamb, Magna Grymesbye* 1557 Pat, *magna grymsby* 1528 *GrimsCB i, – grymsbe* 1552 *ib*

Grymysby magna 1539 *GrimsCB iii, Grymesby Magna* 1543 *GrimsCB ii*, 1547 *ib iii*, 1553 Pat, *–bie –* 1574 *GrimsCB iv, –bye –* 1576 *ib iv, Grimesbie Magna* 1581 *ib i*, 1627 *ib, Grimsby Magna* 1676 *GrimsCB ix*, 1678 *Foster*, 1686, 1687 *GrimsCB ix*

mekill Grimesby 1481 *GrimsCB i*
mych Grymesby 1500 *GrimsCB i*
"Great" *Grimesby* 1319 ChancW, *– Grymesby* 1440, 1470 Pat, *– Grymysby* 1547 *ib*

Grete grimesby 1462 *GrimsCB i, Gret Grymesby* 1530 Wills iii, *grett Grymysby* 1540 *GrimsCB iii*

Great Grymesby 1508 Wills i, 1547 *GrimsCB iii*, 1563 Pat, 1615 *MiscDep 161*, 1658 HollesM, *–bie* 1625, 1634 *Terrier, –by* 1547 *GrimsCB iii*, 1681 *ib ix*

Great Grimsby 1557 Wills i, c.1600 *Dep*, 1692 *GrimsCt et passim, –bye* 1640 *GrimsCB viii, Greate Grimsbye* 1577 NCWills i, *– Grimesbie* 1612 *Td'E, – Grimsbie* 1654 *GrimsCB viii, – Greimisbye* 1658 *GrimsCB ix*

'Grim's village', *v.* **bȳ**. The first el. is the ON pers.n. *Grímr*, recorded independently several times in DB in L. That Grim was popularly regarded as the founder of Grimsby is seen in the appearance of *Gryem* on the earliest Seal of the borough and in the statement in *The Lay of Havelok the Dane* lines 744–49:

> And for þat Grim þat place aute
> Þe stede of Grim þe name laute,
> So þat Grimesbi it calle
> Þat þer–offe speken alle;
> And so schulen men calle it ay
> Bituene þis and Domesday. (l13 (e14))

The reference from *Orkneyinga saga* means "in the middle of Grimsby" and occurs in a poetic stanza which Dr Judith Jesch translates as "We have struggled through the mud–flats for five terrible weeks; there was no lack of mud when we were in the middle of Grimsby".

WELLOW

> *Welhou* 1155–58 (1334) Ch, Hy2 (1460) Pat, 1275 RH, 1303 Pat, 1316 Inqaqd *et passim* to 1442 Pap, *–howe* 1272 FF, 1305 Cl, 1328 Banco, 1332 *SR*, 1348, 1354, 1361 Pat, 1368 Ipm, 1373 Cl *et freq* to 1543 *GrimsExtent*, *–how* 1288, 1314 Ipm, 1450 LLD, 1471 *GrimsCB i*, 1508 Wills i, 1525 *GrimsCLeet*
> *Welhogh* 1314 Ipm
> *Wellehou* 1292 Ipm, 1293 Pat, 1293 RSu, 1345 Pat, 1349 Ipm, 1392 Pat, *–how* 1289 Ipm, *–howe* 1365, 1382 Cl
> *Wellehogh* 1314 Ipm
> *Wellou* 1322 Pat, 1326 Ipm, 1327 Cl, 1366 *GrimsCt*, *–owe* 1356 Pat, 1359 Misc, 1369 Pat, 1371 Cl, 1372 Misc, 1375 Fine, 1375 Peace, 1397 Pap *et freq* to 1581 HMCRep, *–ow* 1400 Pap, 1508 *GrimsCB ii*, 1511 *GrimsFC*, 1522 *GrimsCB i et freq*, – alias *Welhow* 1755 *NW*
> *Welho* 1477 Pat, *–hoo* 1517 ECB, 1519 DV, 1530 Wills ii, *Wello* 1477 Pat, 1537 *AOMB 209*, 1538 LP xiii, 1566 Pat, *–oo* 1535 VE iv, 1537 *AOMB 209*, 1548 Pat, 1552 FCP, 1553 Pat, 1613–15 *MinAcct*

'The spring by the hill–spur' or 'by the mound', *v*. **wella**, **hōh**, **haugr**. According to Watson 8, there was a mound here (in 1901) called Abbey Hill (*Abbey Hill* 1825 Oliver) with "a spring or well at the foot", which Oliver 30 himself describes. "The Abbey Hill measures ten acres, and is 2600 feet in length by 1600 feet in breadth and about 50 feet perpendicular". The feature is clearly shown on Fig. 17.1 in R.W. Ambler, "The historical development of Grimsby and Cleethorpes", *Historical Perspectives: a Region Through the Ages*, ed. S. Ellis and D.R. Crowther, 1990. Almost all the forms refer to the Augustinian abbey of Wellow and many are described as "by Grimsby". The name survives as that of a district in Great Grimsby.

MAJOR NAMES IN THE BOROUGH

ABBEY FM (lost), 1794 *GrimsCB xiv*, *The Abbay* c.1600 *GrimsMap (PRO)*, – *Abbey* 1642 *GrimsCB viii*, *Abbey farme* 1657 *ib*, 1660, 1677 *ib ix*, 1695 *GrimsChamb*, *Abby Farme* 1723 *GrimsCB xi*, *Abbey* 1801, c.1820 *GrimsMap*, *The –* 1851 *Census*, named from Wellow Abbey.

APPOLLO LODGE (lost), c.1820 *GrimsMap*, – *lodge* 1842 White; it was situated between the earlier Lower and Upper Burgess St., north of the "New Market Place". Dr Rod Ambler points out that in the 1851 Census of Religious Worship this was a Wesleyan Methodist Chapel and had earlier been a Masonic Hall.

AUSTIN FRIARS, "the Prior and Austin Friars of" *Grimesby* 1315 Pat *et passim* to 1390 *ib*, *oratorio prioris et fratrum ordinis heremitarum S. Augustini* 1307 Austin, *Austin freeres* 1565 *GrimsCB i*, *the white friers or Augustine friers* 1577 *GrimsFC*, *Augustine Friers* c.1600 *GrimsMap (PRO)*, *the White Friers* 1658 HollesM, *Cheife Messuage called the Augustine Fryers* 1691 *Td'E*, – *called Augustin Fryers* 1719 *ib*; founded in 1293, the site "lay between the present–day West Haven and Sanctuary Lane", *v*. Gillett 77.

BARGATES FM (lost), – *farme* 1652, 1657 *GrimsCB viii*, 1687 *GrimsFC*, 1695 *GrimsChamb*, – *Farme* 1677 *GrimsCB xi*, 1723 *ib*, – *farm house* 1731 *Td'E*, – *Farm* 1794 *GrimsCB xiv*, *Bargate farm* 1849 Hagar, *Messuage called Bargaites* 1565 *ib i*, named from Bargate *infra*.

THE BEADHOUSES (lost), *lez bedeshowses* 1580 *GrimsFC*, – *beadehowses* 1591 *ib*, *The beadhouses* 1665 *GrimsChamb*, *Beadhowse* 1667 *GrimsCLeet*, (*yᵉ*) *Beadhouse* 1679, 1683, 1695 *GrimsChamb*, *the Bead houses* 1707 *GrimsCLeet*, – *Beadhouses* 1680 *GrimsCB ix*, 1724 *Td'E*, *ye Bead houses* 1709 *GrimsCLeet*, cf. *Bead house Closes* 1700 *ib et passim* to 1842 *TA*, 'the prayer-house(s), chapel(s)', *v.* **bed-hūs**; there does not seem to be any indication of the site.

BEHINDBY (lost), *vico que vocatur Bihindeby* 13 (Ed1) *Newh*, *Behyndby* 1436 AD vi, *campo voc byhyndby* 1457 *TCC*, *Beindby* 1491 *Surv*, *Beindeby* 1492 *GrimsExtent*, *bei'nbye* 1543 *ib*, *Behinbie* c.1600 *GrimsMap* (*PRO*); this is apparently a unique name which means literally '(the place) behind, at the back of the town', from OE **behindan**, ME **bihinde(n)** and **bȳ**. The name suggests that ON **bȳ** was still a place-name forming el. in north L in the twelfth and thirteenth centuries. On the c.1600 map it is the name of a large area to the west of Bargate and Carter Gate. For a further example of **behindan**, *v.* PN L **3**, 28.

BLAKEMAN BEACON (lost), *signum* "called" *Blakeman* 1258 Ch, *arbor voc' Blakeman* 1395 *GrimsCt*, *Blakman Netstonde* 1444, 1450 *ib*; *Blakeman* is from the OE pers.n. *Blæcman*, ME *Blakeman* or the derived surn. In 1258 it is said to be a beacon, "erected in the port of Grimmesby, as a guide for fishermen and merchants coming to that port", in 1395 to be a tree and in 1444 to be a "net stand". This compound is not recorded in dictionaries.

BLOW WELLS, 1820 *GrimsCB xv*, c.182O *GrimsMap*, *blowe welles* 1571 *GrimsCB iv*, *the Blow wells* 1676 *GrimsCLeet*, cf. *North* –, *So. Blo Wells* c.1775 *GrimsMap*; for Blow Wells, *v.*

Blow Wells in Great Coates *supra*. The earliest reference here to *blow-well* predates that in NED (1799) by over 200 years.

BLUE STONE (lost), 1707 *GrimsCLeet*, 1822 *GrimsCB xv*, 1831 *Monson*, 1838 *Brace*, 1840 *EnclA*, *the blew stone* 1639 *GrimsCB viii*, *y[e] blewstone* 1656 *ib*, – *blew Stone* 1694 *GrimsCLeet*; this was the name of an erratic, often called a Blue Stone in L, and shown on maps as being on the extreme eastern boundary of the town on the coast just north of the old Race Ground and actually now in Cleethorpes parish, *infra*. It is possible that some of the 17th century forms refer to *Havelock Stone infra*.

BRIDGE DYKE (lost), *le Bryghdik'* 1390 *GrimsCt*, *brygdyk'* 1518 *GrimsCLeet*, *v.* **brycg** (in a Scandinavianized form), **dík**; its site is unknown.

BRIGHOW (lost), *Brighov* 1387 *GrimsFC*, *Bryghowe* 1403 *GrimsCt*, 1494 *GrimsCB i*, 1543 *GrimsExtent*, *Brig-* 1491 *Surv*, 1492 *GrimsExtent*, 1500 *GrimsChamb*, 'the bridge by the spur of land' or 'by the mound', *v.* **brycg** (in a Scandinavianized form), **hōh** or **haugr**. It gave name to Brighowgate *infra*.

BULL RING, *(the)* – 1717 *GrimsCB x*, 1800, 1806, 1812 *ib xiv et freq*, *le bullringe* 1576 *GrimsFC*, *le Bullringe* 1580 *ib*, *le bulringe* 1587, 1595 *GrimsFC*, *the bullringe* 1625 *GrimsCLeet*, – *bull ringe* 1636 *GrimsCB viii*, – *Bullring* 1625 Heneage, 1645 *GrimsCB viii*, 1665 *GrimsCLeet et freq*, self-explanatory.

BURDIKE (lost), *le Burghdik'* 1349 *GrimsFC*, – *burghdike* 1374 *ib*, – *Burghdyke* 1425 *GrimsCt*, *Burghdik'* 1364 *GrimsFC*, 1390 *GrimsCt*, *le Bourdyk'* 1392 *GrimsCt*, – *Burdike* 1396 *GrimsFC*, –*dyk(e)* 1402, 1403 *GrimsCt*, – *Burghdyke* 1457 *TCC*, *(le) Burdyke* 1511, 1532 *GrimsFC*, 1607 *GrimsCB vii*, *sewer voc' Burdyk* 1508 *ib ii*, *Burghedyke* 1563 *TCC*, *Burdike* 1576, 1593 *GrimsFC*, *quandam suram anglice a burdike* 1599 *ib*, *the Dike called Burdike* 1653 *GrimsCLeet*, 'the town dyke', *v.* **burh**, **dík**; as Gillett 13 states it was "no doubt originally constructed as a defence for the inner, built up part of the town".

BURNCRIKE (lost), *Burncryke* 1402 *GrimsCt*, 1457 *TCC*, 1492 *GrimsExtent*, 1499 *GrimsCB i*, *Bourn-* 1422 *GrimsCt*, apparently 'the stream creek', *v.* **burna**, **crike** (ON **kriki**). According to Gillett 1, "between these two bridges [i.e. Stone Bridge and Carter Bridge] the stream was called Burncreek and was probably a good source of fresh water, since no one was allowed to wash clothes in it".

CANONBIG (lost), 1372, *-byg* 1372 both Misc, *Cannonbygh* 1362 AD vi, *Canonbig'* 1390 *GrimsCt*, *-bigge* 1514 *GrimsCB i*, (and cf. *Canonbig Lane infra* where a later form is given); probably from **canoun** 'a canon', presumably a reference to the Canons of Wellow Abbey, and an unrecorded ME ***big** 'a building'. The noun would then be derived from the ME verb *biggen* (ON *byggja* 'to build'), cf. ME **bigging** 'a building' which is found in *Newbigging* in Great Grimsby *infra*. This is the first example of ME ***big** so far noted in the Survey though another is Newbig in Haxey, LWR, *Neubug* m13, *Le Neubygfeld* 1328, *campo de Neubyges* 1378 all *AD*. However, it should be pointed out that the surn. *Canon* is found in medieval Grimsby, cf. John *Canon* 1339 Pat and it is therefore possible that *Canonbig* is the tenement recorded in *vno t. quondam Johannis Canon* 1492 *GrimsExtent*. It was situated "near the abbey gate", Gillett 7. CANON BRIDGE (lost), *canonbrig* 1512 *GrimsCt*, *Canon brygge in wellowe gate* 1569 *GrimsCB v*, *Cannon bridge* 1638 *GrimsMiscD*, *v.* **brycg** and cf. *Canonbig supra*.

CARTER BRIDGE (lost), *Carterbrygge* 1424 *GrimsChamb*, *le –* 1457 *TCC*, *-brige* 1441 *ib*, *-brigge* 1448 *GrimsCt*, *-brigg* 1492 *GrimsExtent*, *– bryge* 1495 *GrimsCB i*, from the occupational name or derived surn. *Carter* and **brycg** in a Scandinavianized form, cf. Gilbert *Carter* 1339 Pat and cf. also Carter Gate *infra*. This bridge crossed the West Haven to the west of Stone Bridge, *v.* Gillett 1 and 3 and cf. *Mill Bridge infra*.

CASTLE (lost), *castelli de Grimesbi* 1200, 1201, 1203 P, *– Grymesby* 1200 OblR. "In 1200 Ralph of Bradley received £80 to provide materials for a castle for the king at Grimsby. Work was in fact started but no trace of a castle has ever been discovered and all that can be determined as to its position is that it was on land which later belonged to the Templars", Gillett 10 and *v.* further Rigby 39.

THE CHANTRY (lost), 1676 *GrimsChamb*, 1691 *GrimsCB x*, 1691 *GrimsCLeet*, 1737 *GrimsChamb et passim* to 1792 *Yarb*, *the Chauntery in Denesgate* 1514 *GrimsCB i*, *y*ᵉ *chantre* 1527 *ib ii*, *the chavntre* 1547 *GrimsCLeet*, *the Chauntre* 1553 *GrimsChamb*, – *chaunterye* 1564 *GrimsCB iv*, – *chauntry* 1565 *ib*, 1632, 1692 *GrimsCLeet*, *Chantery* 1670, 1687, 1695 *GrimsChamb*, 1707, 1712 *GrimsCLeet*, *le chauntrie howse* 1582 *GrimsChamb*, *the Chauntry howse* 1652 *GrimsCB viii*, *Chantry Farme* 1677 *ib ix*, *Chauntry farm* 1695 *GrimsChamb*, *(the) Chantry Farm* 1718 *GrimsCB x*, 1777 *ib xiii*, 1787, 1797, 1800, 1809 *ib xiv*. This refers to property belonging to the Chantry of Holy Trinity in St James Church founded in 1344 by Edward de Grimsby for his soul and those of members of his family and apparently those of John *Reyner*, for it was known as *Rayner Chauntre* 1344 *GrimsCB i*, *cantaria vocat' Rayner Chanterye* 1387 *GrimsFC*, *Cantar' vocata Reyner Chantery* 1390 *ib*, *Raynerschauntr'* 1409 *GrimsChamb*, *Raynerchantre* 1492 *GrimsExtent et freq* to *Rainarde Chauntrie* 1576 *GrimsChamb*, *Raynyard Chauntrie* 1585 *GrimsFC*, *v.* also Gillett 3 and 83. There are a number of other references to property belonging to the Chantry, e.g. *ter' Cantar' voc' Rayner chauntr, Chauntredayle* (*v.* **deill** 'a share of land'), –*landes* 1457 *TCC*, *the shoppys of Rayner Chantre* 1480 *GrimsMiscD*, *terre cantarie Reyner* 1513 *GrimsChamb*, *terr' nuper pertin' cantarie voc' Raner Chauntrie* 1562 *ib*, *Grimsby Chantry Lands* 1694 *GrimsQR*, and *Chauntr'milln'* 1397 *GrimsCt*. Cf. Chantry Lane *infra*.

COLLEGE HO (lost), *the colledge howse & groundes in Sostangate* 1587, *Colledge land* 1634, *ye Colledge ground* 1651, *the Collige ground* 1662, *(apud) le Colledge*, *y*ᵉ *Colledg ground* 1679 all *GrimsCLeet*; the significance of the name has not been discovered,

but it may perhaps relate to Trinity College Cambridge which held
land in Grimsby.

CORN FIELDS (lost), *the corn Felde* 1500 *GrimsCB i*, – *Corne feld*
1528 *GrimsBCB*, – *cornfelld* c.1540 *GrimsCLeet, Corne feldes*
c.1600 *GrimsMap (PRO)*, *the corne feilde* 1639 *GrimsCB viii*, –
Corne Feilds 1651 *GrimsCLeet*, – *feild* 1687 *ib*, *y^e* – 1698 *ib*, *the*
Corne Feild 1723 *GrimsCB xi*, self–explanatory. "The corn field
lay at the south end of the town and contained some 640 acres",
Gillett 4.

CORNMARKET (lost), *la* – 1400 *GrimsFC*, *le* – 1487 *GrimsCt*, –
cornmarket 1469 AD i, *Corn'm'* 1492 *GrimsExtent*, *marcato*
blador' siue granor' 1576 *GrimsFC*, self–explanatory, *v*. **corn**,
market.

CUCKSTOOL PIT (lost), *le Kucstoleput* 1394 *GrimsChamb*,
Cokstolepitte 1470 *ib*, *Coke–* 1468 *GrimsCB i*, *–pytt* 1478
GrimsChamb, *Cukstolepitt* 1500 *ib*, *cokstoll pytt* 1511 *GrimsCB i*,
Cukstoll pitt 1513 *GrimsChamb*, *Cukstallpit* 1541 *ib*, *Kockestoole*
pytt m16 *GrimsCLeet*, *Cuckstolepytt* 1564 *GrimsFC*, *Cooke stoole*
pitt 1576 *GrimsChamb*, *Coukstoole* (sic) 1638 *GrimsCB viii* and
cf. *cookstoolepithouse* 1570 *GrimsChamb*, *Cookstollepithouse*
1573 *ib*, *cowkstoule pitthowse* 1585 *ib*, 'the ducking–stool', *v*.
cukstōl, with **pytt**; according to Gillett 5n, this was "in the
market".

CUSTOM HOUSE, c.1820 *GrimsMap*, 1851 *Census*, *ye Custom–*
house 1691 *Cragg*, *Custom house* 1816 *Td'E*, *the Custom House*
1831 *Monson*; the 1816 document concerns a toft on which to
build a Custom House.

DOCK HEADS, *the* – 1764 *Td'E*, *Dockheads* 1670, 1676, 1681,
1695 all *GrimsChamb*, *Dochheads* (sic) 1719 *Td'E*, *Dockheades*
1766, 1777 *GrimsCB xiii*, *Dock Head* 1809 *ib xiv*.

EAST CLOUGH (lost), *the* – 1780 *GrimsCB xiii*.

EAST MARSH, (*the*) – 1625 Heneage, 1660 *GrimsCB ix*, 1665 *GrimsCLeet*, 1707 *ib et freq*, – *upon which the New Town is built, was an open field* 1831 *Monson*, – *the Estmarsh* 1471 *GrimsCB i*, *orient' marisco* 1500 *GrimsChamb*, *orientale marisco* 1582 *ib*, *le orien' Marisc* (sic) 1630 *GrimsCLeet*, *the marshes on thestside the haven* 1587 *ib*, *the East marshe* 1607 *GrimsCB vii*, – *east marshe* 1669 *ib ix*, (*the*) *East Marshes* c.1600 *GrimsMap* (*PRO*), 1678 *GrimsCLeet et passim* to 1832 *GrimsCB xvi*, *yᵉ east Marshes* 1648 *ib viii*, self–explanatory, *v.* ēast, mersc. Cf. *the east marsh bankes* 1656 *ib*, *East Marsh banks* 1697 *ib x*, – *Banke* 1720 *ib xi*, – *Bridge* 1679 *GrimsChamb*, – *Common* 1795 *GrimsCB xiv*, *the East marsh dicke* 1707 *GrimsCLeet*, *East Marsh Drain* 1812 *GrimsCB xiv*, – *Gate* 1800 *ib*, – *Lots* 1799 *ib* and West Marsh *infra*.

FISH PONDS (lost), – *pondes* c.1600 *GrimsMap* (*PRO*), *the Fish Ponds* 1719 *Td'E*, *the fishponds Saint Mary Lane* (sic) 1723 *GrimsCB xi*, – *fish ponds* 1723 *Td'E*, – *Ponds* 1831 *GrimsCB xvi*, cf. *the fishpond close* 1666 *GrimsCLeet*; the ponds are shown on the c.1600 map between the old Flottergate and the Haven near to the sea.

FISH SHAMBLES (lost), *le fyshe shambles* 1583 *GrimsFC*, cf. *Fish Market* 1815 *GrimsCB xv*, *v.* sceamol 'a bench, a stall' in this case for displaying fish.

THE FITTIES, 1612 *Shaw*, 1695 *GrimsChamb*, 1840 *EnclA*, *the Fytthes* (sic) 1537 *GrimsCLeet*, *the Fyttes* (sic) 1553 *GrimsChamb*, – *Fytties* 1569 *GrimsCB iv*, *Fytties* 1573 *GrimsChamb*, *the fittys* 1665 *GrimsCLeet*, *fitties* 1676 *GrimsChamb*, *fittyes* 1694 *ib*, *le Fittes* 1683 *ib*, *the Fittys* 1697 *Td'E*, – *Fittees* 1723 *ib*, and cf. *East Fitties* c.1600 *GrimsMap* (*PRO*), 1830 *GrimsCB xvi*, *le west fittyes* 1626 *GrimsCLeet*, *west Fitties* 1679 *GrimsChamb*, *the West Fittis* 1684 *GrimsCB ix*, – *Fittyes* 1731 *Td'E*; this is a common name in north L coastal parishes meaning 'the outer marsh', dial. *fitty*, *fitties*, a derivative of ON fit 'grassland on the bank of a river', *v.* The Fitties, PN L 4, 116–17. The 1537 reference above is the earliest so far noted for this word.

FLEET BRIDGE (lost), *Flete brigg, – brygge* 1492 *GrimsExtent, fletebryge*1543 *ib, v.* **flēot, brycg** in a Scandinavianized form and cf. *Fleet Gate infra.*

THE FOLD (lost), *the Commom fould* 1565 *GrimsCLeet, comon fold* a1600, 1707 *ib, Common Fold* 1698 *ib, – fold* 1703, 1707 *ib, – fould* 1723 *ib, the towne folde* 1648 *GrimsCB viii, fold* 1707 *GrimsCLeet, (the) fould* 1725, 1735 *ib, v.* **fald** 'a small enclosure for animals' and cf. Pound *infra.*

FRAUNKS CHANTRY (lost), *Frankeschauntrie* 1396 *GrimsFC*; only a single reference has been noted and nothing further appears to be known about the Chantry. It must have been named from the family of John, Philip and William *Fraunk* 1285 Pat.

FRESH INGS (lost), 1651 *GrimsCtLeet*, 1686, 1697 *Terrier, Fresshenges* 1457 *TCC, le Freschynges* 1518 *GrimsFC, Freshyngis* 1540 *AOMB 212, the Freshe ynges* c.1560 *GrimsCLeet, – Fresh inges* 1579 *Terrier, Fresh Inges* c.1600 *GrimsMap (PRO), the fresh Inggs* 1601 *Terrier, – inges* 1625 *ib, – Inges* 1634 *ib,* 'the fresh (i.e without salt) meadows, pastures', *v.* **fersc, eng** in the pl., in contrast to *Salt Ings Ho infra.*

FRESHWATER HAVEN, *ye freshwatter haven* p1600 *GrimsCLeet, the Freshwater haven* 1639 *GrimsCB viii,* 1671 *GrimsCLeet, – fresh water haven* 1649 *GrimsCB viii, – freshewater haven* 1655 *ib,* 1692 *GrimsCLeet, ye Freshwater Haven* 1685 *Td'E, freshwater haven late Gannocks* 1692 *GrimsChamb, the Freshwater Haven* 1719, 1765 *Td'E, the freshwater – 1794 ib,* self–explanatory, cf. *Gannocks infra.*

GANNOCKS (lost), 1683, 1692 *GrimsChamb,* 1801, c.1820 *GrimsMap,* 1842 *TA, the – 1795 LindDep Plans,* 1798 *Hill,* cf. *Gannock land* 1691 *GrimsChamb, Gannooks – 1692 ib, Ganacks Closes* 1712 *GrimsCLeet*; this is an obscure name which Mr Field has suggested may allude to an outlying pig–farm, *v.* PN L **2**, 61. The problem, however, is complicated here by the presence in

Grimsby of a family called *Gannock(s)*, cf. *Mrs Gannocks* 1676 *GrimsChamb*, John *Gannok* 1691 *GrimsMiscD* and so must be left unresolved. It was the name of a piece of land west of the old *Ropery Lane*.

GOOSEGATES (lost), *goosgates* 1692 *GrimsChamb*, *ye Goosegates* 1737 *GrimsCB xi*, *Goosegates* 1754 *ib xii*, 1782 *ib xiii et passim* to 1832 *ib xvi*, cf. – *Bridge* 1782 *ib xiii*, *Freemen's Gosegates* 1710 *Td'E*, *Fat pasture commonly called Twelveman's Goose gates* 1710 *Td'E*, *Twelvemans* – 1716 *ib*; from the pl. of *goose–gate* 'the right of pasture, pasturage for a goose', *v.* NED s.v., comparable to the common L **shep–gate**. It is recorded here some forty years earlier than in NED. Cf. also *Swangates* in f.ns. (b) *infra*. The twelvemen were the members of the mayor's council, *v.* Rigby 106–8.

GRAMMAR SCHOOL (lost), *Scola grammaticalis* 1547 *NELA*, *the scholehouse* 1571 *GrimsChamb*, *grammatic' schole* 1586 *GrimsFC*, *scole gramatice* 1594 *GrimsMiscD*, *ye Schoole house* p1600 *GrimsCLeet*, – *free Gramer scoole* 1647 *GrimsCB viii*, *the Gramar Schole* 1658 HollesM, *schoolhouse* 1676 *GrimsChamb*, *le Schoole house* 1682 *GrimsCLeet*, *Gramar Schoole* 1695 *GrimsChamb*, *the Free Grammar School* 1708 *GrimsCB x*, *free* – 1713 *ib*, *(the) Grammar School* 1750 *ib xii et passim*; for the history of the school, *v.* Gillett 308.

THE GREEN (lost), *le Grene* 1576 *GrimsCB v*, *le Greene* 1677 *GrimsCLeet*, *ye Green* 1697, 1712, 1722 *ib*, *the* – 1767 *Td'E*, 1795 *LindDep Plans*, 1816 *Td'E*, – *Greens* 1798 *Hill*, 1801 *GrimsMap*, 1824 *Td'E*, 1842 *TA*, *Lands called* – 1833 *Td'E*, cf. *Atte Grene* 1327 *SR*, *atte* – 1332 *ib*, 1382 *GrimsCt*, *de* – 1339, 1373 Pat, 1393 *GrimsCt*, *del* – 1391 *ib* all (p), 'the green', *v.* **grēne**^{2}; it was situated west and north of the present–day Lock Hill.

GREY FRIARS, *Fratres Minores (in Grymesby)* 1406 *GrimsLeases*, 1492 *GrimsExtent*, "a house called" *le Graye Freres* 1547 Pat, *the gray freeres* 1565 *GrimsCB i*, *fratres minor als dict le graiefriers*

1577 *GrimsFC*, *fratres minores* 1585 *ib*, *the gray Fryers* c.1600 *Dep*, *friers miner* c.1600 *GrimsMap* (*PRO*), *Gray Fryers* 1657 *GrimsFC*, *messuages vocat the Lesser Fryers alt Gray Fryers* 1662 *ib*, *the friers* 1588 *GrimsCLeet*, *le freres* 1628 *ib*, (*dwelling house called*) *the Fryers* 1639 *GrimsCB viii*, 1774 *Yarb*, *The Friary* 1851 *Census*, founded already in 1240, the "site . . . was west of St. James's church, on the north–west side of Cartergate, near the level crossing called Friargate, a place–name of no greater antiquity than the railway itself", Gillett 76.

GREYFRIARS BRIDGE (lost), *Gray Fryers bridge* c.1600 *Dep*, probably the same as *Fryers brigge* 1651 *GrimsCB viii*, *the fryars brigg* 1655 *ib*, *Freer bridge* 1679 *ib ix*, *ye friers bridge* 1681 *GrimsChamb*, *v.* prec.

GRIMSBY FM (lost), 1718, 1724, 1788 all *Terrier*, *Grimsby farme* c.1634, 1662, 1697 all *ib*, 1698 *GrimsCLeet*, *Grymsbye Farme* 1644 *GrimsCB xiii*. Gillett 62n, comments "In the seventeenth century we begin to hear of Grimsby Farm, which may have been the local seat of this family [i.e. of Sir William Grimsby]. Its site is now occupied by the house . . . called the *Cedars*". He further notes that "there had been a family of this name in the town since the fourteenth century".

GRIMSBY HO (lost), 1670, 1679, 1694, – *house* 1682, 1694, 1695 all *GrimsChamb*; the significance of the name has not been discovered.

GROVE HO (lost), 1842 White, 1849 Hagar, *Grove* 1826 White.

HAVELOCK STONE (lost), 1687, 1694, *GrimsChamb*, *havelokeston'* 1521 *GrimsCB*, *Halocke stone* (sic) 1565 *GrimsCLeet*, *havelockstoune* 1585 *GrimsChamb*, *Havelockston* 1589 *GrimsFC*, *Hauelock stone* 1631 *GrimsCLeet*, *Havelocke Stone* 1662 *ib*, *the blew stone in Welowgate* 1637 *GrimsCB viii*, *The street leading to Welowgate nigh the blewstone* 1656 HMCRep, *the blue stone in Wellow* 1698 *GrimsCLeet*, an erratic commemorating Havelock the hero of the late 13th century poem *Havelok the Dane* and note *that Havelocke did some tyme reside in Grimsby may be gathered from a great blew Boundry-Stone lying at ye East-ende Of Briggow-gate, which retaines ye name of Havelocks Stone to this day* 1634 Holles.

THE HAVEN, *portum de Grymesby* 1154–79 BC, Hy2 (1301) Ch, 1335 Fine, 1389 *GrimsCt*, 1537 *AOMB 207*, *portus de Grimesby* 1230 Cl, – *grimesbie* (sic) 113 *AD*, *portum de Grimmesby* 1276 RH, – *Grimesby* 1301 LRCh, 1307 Austin, – *Grimsbie* 1577 *GrimsFC*, *litus port'* 1392 *ib*, *portum maris* 1492 *GrimsExtent*, *portum* 1522 *GrimsCB i*, 1543 *GrimsExtent*, 1591 *GrimsFC*, *la havene* 1359 Misc, – *Havene* 1359–60 ImpR, *del Hauen* 1392 *GrimsCt* (p), *atte Hauen'* 1401 *GrimsCt* (p), *the havyn* 1471 *GrimsCB i*, 1537 *GrimsCLeet*, *le* – 1531 *GrimsCB i*, – *haven de magna grymesby* 1547 *ib iii*, *the haven* 1582, 1590, 1627 *GrimsCLeet et passim* to 1735 *ib*, *ye Haven* 1645 *GrimsCB viii*, *the* – 1641 LNQ i, 1649 *GrimsCLeet et freq*, – *or Wet Dock* 1803 *GrimsCB xiv*, 1833 *Td'E*, *(The) Old Haven* 1801 *GrimsMap*, 1811 *GrimsCB xv*, 1815 *ib*, 'the haven, the harbour', *v*. **hæfen**, **hafn**. It is called *the harbour* a1600 *GrimsCLeet*, 1753 *GrimsCB xii*, *ye Creeke, or Harbour* 1660 *ib ix*, *Grimsby Creek* 1666 SP (*v*. **crike** (ON **kriki**)).

WEST HAVEN, 1640 *GrimsMiscD*, 1789 *GrimsCB xiv et passim*, *the West haven* 1582 *GrimsCLeet*, *iuxta occidentem portum* 1583 *GrimsFC*, *portus occidental* 1591 *ib*, "the West Haven . . . the only part of the medieval harbour which is still substantially intact", Gillett 21.

EAST HAVEN (lost), *Old East Haven* c.1800 *GrimsMap*.

HAVEN BRIDGE (lost), 1869 *LindDep Plans*, *pontem portus* (sic) 1566 *GrimsCB iv*, – *port'* 1566 *ib*, *haven bridge* 1651 *ib viii*, *Haven bridge* 1781 *ib xiii*; in 1573 *GrimsMiscD* a grant was made *for makinge of a bridge . . . ouer our Haven*.

HAVEN MILL (lost), *the Havyn mylne* c.1560 *GrimsCLeet*, – *havenmilne* a1600 *ib*, *le haven iuxta le milne* 1628 *ib*, *haven bridge by tholde Milne* 1651 *GrimsCB viii*.

HELL HILL (lost), 1686 *Terrier*, c.1832 *Yarb*, *hell hyll* 1547 *GrimsCLeet*, *Hell hill* c.1600 *GrimsMap (PRO)*, *hellhill* 1634 *Terrier*, *Ellyll Hills* (sic) a1825 Oliver (Plan), perhaps cf. *Helle* 1457 *TCC*; presumably a derogatory name; according to Oliver 29 (1825) "The three mounds at Ellyll contain together about three acres – each being about 800 feet long by 600 feet broad; the perpendicular height being not more than six feet".

HERRING BRIDGE (lost), *del Heryngbrigg* 1417 *GrimsChamb*, from OE *hæring* 'a herring' and **brycg** (in a Scandinavianized form), presumably denoting a bridge where herring was sold.

HIGH BRIDGE (lost), y^e *hye brigge other Wyse callyd Holme brigge* 1471 *GrimsCB i*, *the high bridge otherwise Holme bridge* c.1581 *GrimsCt*, *the high bryge* 1500 *GrimsCB i*, – *hygh bryg* 1541 *GrimsChamb*, – *highe brigge* a1600 *GrimsCLeet*, *high bridge* 1636 *GrimsCB viii*, 1681 *GrimsCLeet*, *High brig* 1691 *GrimsChamb*, – *brigg* 1710 *Td'E*, *Highbriggs* 1736 *GrimsCB xi et freq* to 1832 *ib xvi*, *High Briggs* 1763 *Td'E*, 1811 *GrimsCB xiv*. cf. *de Ponte de Grimmesby* 1239 Cl, *de Ponte* 1276 RH, 1327, 1332 *SR*, *atte Brigg* 1330 Cl, *de Brygge* 1399, 1402 *GrimsCt* all (p), *v*. **hēah**, **brycg** (with the majority of forms Scandinavianized). OE **hēah** has the sense here of 'chief, important'. The alternative name HOLME BRIDGE (lost) is *holmbriges* 1393, *le holmbriges* 1409, *holme bridge* 1585 all *GrimsChamb*, 'the bridge leading to Holme Hill (in Cleethorpes parish *supra*)', *v*. **brycg**, again in a Scandinavianized form. Gillett 1 states that Holme Bridge crossed the older branch of the haven which formed the eastern boundary of the built-up area of the borough.

HILL DOCK (lost), *hill dock* 1849 Hagar.

HORSE BRIDGE (lost), *the horse bridge* 1695 *GrimsChamb*, self-explanatory.

HORSE FAIR (lost), *the hors Fayr stede* 1507 *GrimsCB i*, *v.* **stede** 'a place', a name not included in Sandred.

HORSE MARKET, *Horsmarket* 1392 *GrimsCt*, self-explanatory, *v.* **market**.

HOUSE OF INDUSTRY (lost), 1802 *GrimsCB xiv*, c.1820 *GrimsMap*, 1831 *Monson*. "Nothing of the original house of industry now remains, but some of the houses built as an extension to it prior to 1837 can be seen as the row now called Alfred Terrace in Brighowgate", Gillett 186.

LATHEGARTHS (lost), *Lathegarthes* 1372 Misc, *lathgarthis* 1492 *GrimsExtent*, *laythgarthe* 1517 *GrimsCB i*, *Lath Garthys in the parish of St Augustyn and St Olyff next Grymesby* 1531 Wills iii, *layth garthe* 1543 *GrimsExtent*, *layth garthes* 1557 *Inv*, 'the enclosures by the barn', *v.* **hlaða, garðr**. In 1372 it is said to be a manor adjoining the Abbey.

LIME HO (lost), *le lime howse* 1680, *the Lime House* 1700, – *Limehouse* 1719 all *Td'E*.

LITTLEFIELD, *Lytelfelde* 1457 *TCC*, *Litelfeld* 1464, 1467 Fine, *the litle felde* 1483 *GrimsCB i*, *lee littel Feld* 1500 *GrimsChamb*, *littil* – 1501 *GrimsCB i*, *the Litle felde* 1505 *ib*, *paruo campo vocat lyttyll feld* 1511–12 *GrimsCt*, *parvo campo* 1541 *GrimsCB iii*, *paruo Feld* 1544 *ib*, – *campo* 1569 *GrimsCB iv*, 1571 *ib*, 1585 *GrimsChamb*, 1634, 1649, 1684 *GrimsCLeet*, *ye lytyll feld* 1522, 1557 *GrimsCB i*, *the littyll feylde* 1524 *ib*, *litelfelde* 1537 *AOMB 209*, *Lyttlefeld* 1547 Pat, *lytyll felld* 1547 *GrimsCB iii* 1553 *GrimsChamb*, *the Lyttle fyld* 1565 *GrimsCLeet*, (*the*) *litle feild* 1571 *GrimsChamb*, 1626 *GrimsCLeet et freq* to *Little* – 1681 *GrimsCB viii*, *the little felde* 1688 *GrimsCLeet*, (*the*) *little field* 1625 Heneage *et passim* to (*y^e*) – 1696 *GrimsCLeet*, (*the*) *Little*

Field 1719 *Td'E et freq*, self–explanatory, *v.* **lȳtel, feld**; the importance of this field may be judged by the wealth of reference to it and by the fact that it gave rise to the name of a lane. It is now the name of a district in the borough.

MALT KILN COTTAGE (lost), 1851 *Census*, cf. *Malt Kiln* 1798 *Hill, Kylne Close* 1540 *AOMB 212, Kiln Close* 1798, *– Garden* 1798 *Hill, – garth* 1692 *GrimsCLeet, Kilne Garth* 1698 *ib, Kiln –* 1798 *Hill,* 1823 *Td'E,* 1842 *TA, le Kilne yard* 1681 *GrimsCLeet, the –* 1699 *ib, ye kill yard* 1702 *ib, the –* 1712 *ib* and *a Malte Kilne* 1723 *GrimsCB xi.* It is uncertain whether these all refer to the same kiln but at least the occurrence of the two cognate words, **garðr** and **geard**, is noteworthy.

MALT MARKET (lost), *The malte Markett* 1594 *GrimsFC.*

MARKET PLACE, *foro de Grymesby* 1390, 1468 *GrimsCt, in foro* 1392, 1395 *ib, – (super cornere de Southsaintmarigate)* 1397 *ib, (– de Grimsby)* 1441 *ib et passim* to 1598 *ib, in commune' marcat' siue foro* 1591 *ib, le Marketstrete* 1393 *ib, marketstede* 1487 *ib, ye markitsted* 1511 *GrimsCB i, the marketsted* 1515 *ib, – sted* 1522 *ib ii et passim* to *market stead* a1600 *GrimsCLeet, markett Square* a1600 *ib,* 1804 *GrimsCB xiv, the Market place* 1480 *GrimsMiscD,* 1743 *Td'E et passim* to 1826 White, *the market place* 1525 *GrimsCB i,* 1546, 1557 *GrimsCLeet et freq* to 1712 *ib, – markett place* 1566 *GrimsCB iv,* 1582 *GrimsCLeet,* 1650 *Td'E, – markitt place* 1664 *GrimsCB ix,* 1728 *Td'E, ye Markett place* 1667 *GrimsCLeet,* 1695 *GrimsCB x,* 1708 *Td'E, (the) Market Place* 1797 *ib et passim* to 1851 *Census, New Market Place* 1800 *GrimsCB xiv,* 1801 *GrimsMap et passim.* Gillett 140 comments, "The market was held in the streets, as there was no proper market place" and 140n, "The present–day Old Market Place did not exist except as a topographical expression". Cf. *Newbigging infra.*

MARKET CROSS (lost), *the cros in the marketsted* 1515 *GrimsCB i, market Cross* a1600 *GrimsCLeet, the Market Crose* 1712 *Td'E, the Cross* 1739 *GrimsCB xii.*

MARKET WELL (lost), *ye market well* 1679 *GrimsChamb*.

MIDMARKET (lost), *le midmarket* 1394 *GrimsFC*, presumably 'the middle market'.

MILL BRIDGE (lost), 1679 *GrimsChamb*, 1688 *GrimsCLeet*, *Milnebrigge* 1448 *GrimsCt*, *Mill brige* p1600 *GrimsCLeet*, *ye milne brigg* 1678 *ib*, *Mill brigg*, *le Mill brige* 1679 *ib*. "When the new mills were made either side of the West Haven they were linked by a new bridge called Milnebrigge which probably took the place of the old Carterbrigge", Gillett 3.

MILLFIELDS HO, *Mills Field House* 1851 *Census* and is *Davy's Mill* c.1820 *GrimsMap*, named from the family of William *Davy* 1807 PRStJ. Dr Rod Ambler points out that this is today the name of an hotel.

MILL HILL (lost), *Mylnehyll* 1457 *TCC*, *Mill Hill* 1670, 1683, 1691 *GrimsChamb*, 1719 *Td'E*, 1766 *GrimsCB xiii*, *(the)* – 1788 *Heneage*, cf. *mylne hyll furlonge* 1540 *AOMB 212*, self-explanatory.

NEWBIGGING (lost), *la Neubigg'* 1394 *GrimsChamb*, *Newe–* 1403 *GrimsCt*, *neubigging iuxta portu' in Grymesby* 1396 *GrimsFC*, *Newebiggyng* 1401 *GrimsFC*, *(la)* – 1409 *GrimsChamb*, *(– iuxta portum)* 1496 *GrimsCB i*, *–biggynge* 1499 *ib*, *– beggyng* 1521 *ib ii*, *the new Biggen otherwise called the Market Place* 1563 *TCC*, *Newebyggynge iuxta portum* 1581 *GrimsFC*, *the newe byggynge near the haven* 1582 *GrimsCLeet*, *Newebigginge* 1584, 1590 *GrimsFC*, *lee Newbigynge* 1498 *GrimsCB i*, *Newbiggynge* 1500 *GrimsChamb*, *newbyggyng* 1522 *GrimsCB i*, *the new buldyng* (sic) 1565 *ib*, *newbigginge* 1569 *ib*, 1581 *GrimsFC*, *(le)* – 1577, 1595 *ib*, *Newbigging* 1678, 1681 *ib*, *quodam vico vocat' le* – 1650 *Td'E*, *– . . . vocat le Newbigging* 1680 *ib*, *a Certaine Street . . . Called New Bigging* 1685 *ib*, *– the Newbigging* 1700 *ib*, *a Street called –* 1719 *ib*, *– Newbiggin* 1765 *ib*, 1801 *GrimsMap*, *New Biggin* 1851 *Census*, 'the new building', *v.* **nīwe**, **bigging** and note the 1565 form, which seems to suggest that the meaning of ME **bigging** was still understood. Gillett 21 notes that after the construction of West Haven most of the southern portion of the common pasture cut by the new dock "was filled up by building called 'Newbyggyng'". The name has been revived as that of a Mall on the Plan of Freshney Place Shopping Centre.

NEW LOT (lost), 1842 White, 1849 Hagar.

NUNS CORNER, cf. *mes' voc' le nonnes* 1574–5 *MinAcct, mesuag' voc' le Nonnes* 1594–96 *ib, The Nonns* c.1600 *GrimsMap (PRO), (the) Nuns* 1641 *GrimsCB viii,* 1671 *ib ix et passim* to 1840 *EnclA, the Nunnes* 1679 *GrimsCLeet, the Nunnes house close* 1634 *Terrier, yᵉ Nuns house* 1668 *ib, – Nonnes –* 1679 *ib, Nunns farme* 1657 *GrimsCB viii, Nunns Farme* 1677 *ib ix, nuns farme* 1695 *GrimsChamb, (the) Nuns Farme* 1762 *Terrier, Nuns Farm* 1774 *Yarb et passim* to 1851 *Census, the Nuns farm house* 1731 *Td'E* and *Nunhill'* 1404 *GrimsCt, Nonehill* 1425 *ib, Nonhyll* 1457 *TCC,* named from the Augustinian Nunnery of St Leonard.

NUNSTHORPE, a modern district about which Gillett 295 comments, "by 1939 the corporation . . . had built 714 houses on the new Nunsthorpe estate".

OLD CHURCH YARD (lost), *yᵉ old churche yard* 1600 *TCC, The ould Church yarde* c.1600 *GrimsMap (PRO), the old Church yeard* 1620 *GrimsCLeet, – Old Churchyard* 1626 *Td'E, vetero Cemeterio* 1634 *GrimsCLeet, The ould Church Yard* 1649 *ib, owld Churchyard* 1694 *ib, (the) Old Church Yard* 1697 *GrimsFC,* 1731 *Td'E et passim, – yard* 1699 *GrimsCLeet, S. Mary's Church Y.* 1801 *GrimsMap, St. Mary's Church Yard* c.1820 *ib, Old Churchyard* 1842 *TA,* the churchyard of the demolished church of St Mary *infra.*

PEARTREE HO (lost), *– house* 1691 *GrimsChamb,* 1721 *GrimsCLeet, peartre house* 1670 *GrimsChamb, Peare Tree House* 1679 *ib, Peargarthhowse* 1682 *GrimsFC, pear tree house* 1777

GrimsCB xiii, cf. *the peartree garth* 1698 *GrimsCLeet*, v. **garðr** 'an enclosure'.

PIG MARKET (lost), 1812 *GrimsCB xiv*, 1816 *ib xv*; it was in the Bull Ring.

PINCUSHION GREEN (lost), 1851 *Census*; Mrs Bettie Watkinson points out that the name survived as *Pincushion Square* in 1871 Gait.

PIPER CREEK, 1779 *GrimsCB xiii*, 1795 *LindDep Plans*, *piper Crike* 1684 *GrimsCB ix*, 1697 *GrimsCLeet*, – *Creeke* 1696 *ib*, *Piper Crike* 1752 *GrimsCB xii*, probably from the surn. *Piper* and **crike** (ON **kriki**). It formed in part the boundary between Grimsby and Little Coates.

POUND (lost), 1840 *GrimsMap*, *del Pund* 1272 *Ass* (p), *le Comyn pounde* 1521 *GrimsCB i*, *Common pound* 1703 *GrimsCLeet*, 1732 *ib xi*, 1789 *GrimsCB xiv*, v. **pund**; it is shown on 1840 *GrimsMap* at the south end of Wellowgate. Cf. The Fold *supra*.

THE PUMP (lost), *the Towne's Pump* 1736 *GrimsChamb*, *the Pump* 1786 *GrimsCB xiii*, – *in the Bull Ring* 1818 *ib xv*.

RAFF YARD (lost), *le Raffe yard* 1680 *Td'E*, *the –* 1700 *ib*, *Raff Yards* c.1820 *GrimsMap*, cf. *yᵉ Raffe howse side* 1681 *GrimsCLeet*, *Mr Popples Raffe House* 1684 *GrimsCB ix* and cf. *one wessell of Raffe* 1655 *ib viii*, from *raff* NED sb. 3. 'foreign timber, usually in the form of deals'; note that *raff–yard* is not recorded in NED until 1840.

RED HILL (lost), – *hill* 1849 Hagar.

RIVER HEAD, 1851 *Census*, – *head* 1849 Hagar.

ROYAL DOCK, 1852 White and is *Harbour or New Dock* c.1820 *GrimsMap*.

ST JOHN A BOWER HO (lost), *t' quondam Mr Johanne Bowere* 1492 *GrimsExtent, tent' jacens . . . oppsit' portum voc Saynt John' bower house* 1441 *GrimsCB i, Tenementum appellat St John a bowers howse* 1598 *GrimsFC, uni messuage vocat St. John a Bowers' house* 1614 *ib, One platt of Ground . . . of old Called John of Bowers* 1685 *Td'E, one Plot of Ground . . . formerly called John of Bowers* 1765 *ib, a Plot of Ground . . . commonly called John of Bowers* 1794 *ib*; "the guild called 'of Holy John of Bower' which may have had its altar in St. James's, and the guild hall, often called St. John a Bower house, was on the south bank of the West Haven", Gillett 84 and "At the beginning of the sixteenth century the town had its own play of 'Holy John of Bower'", ib. 117. Nothing is apparently known of the identity of *John a Bower*.

ST MARY BRIDGE (lost), *la havene de Seynt Mariebrigge* 1359 *Misc, la Havene de Seint Marie brigge* 1359-60 *IpmR, sayntmarybrigg* 1390 *GrimsChamb*, named from the later demolished church of St Mary. Gillett 18 comments, "Part of the haven known as the haven of St. Marybrigg lay inside St. Mary's parish, and corpses found there were buried in St. Mary's churchyard".

SALT INGS HO (lost), 1851 *Census*, cf. *Saltenges* 1457 *TCC, -ynges* 1518 *GrimsFC, the Salte ynges* 1537 *GrimsCLeet, Saltinges* 1571 *GrimsCB iv*, 1638 *ib viii, - Inges* c.1600 *GrimsMap (PRO)*, 1627 *GrimsCLeet*, 1684 *GrimsCB ix, - inges* 1634 *Terrier*, 1651 *GrimsCLeet, -ings* 1686 *Terrier*, 1688 *GrimsCLeet, (a marsh called) -* 1719 *Td'E*, 1823 *GrimsCB xv, - Ings* p1600, 1670 *GrimsCLeet et freq* to c.1820 *GrimsMap, the -* 1840 *EnclA, Grimsby -* 1792 *Yarb*, cf, also *le salt Inges brigges* 1576 *GrimsChamb, Salt Ings brigge* 1663 *GrimsCLeet, - Bridges* 1700 *ib* and *Salt Inggs Dike* 1742 *GrimsCB xii, - Ings Dike* 1792 *Yarb*, 'the salty meadows, pastures', *v.* **salt, eng** and note the use of the compound as an appellative in *a saltinge* 116 *GrimsCLeet*. This was an area which, at extraordinary spring tides, was liable to flooding, *v.* Gillett 109–10. Cf. *Fresh Ings supra*.

SALTWATER HAVEN (lost), *the salt water haven* 1639 *GrimsCB viii*, – *Saltwater Haven* 1663 *GrimsCLeet*, – *saltwater Haven* 1695 *GrimsCB x*, self-explanatory.

SEA DYKE (lost), *la Seedyk* 1409 *GrimsChamb*, *le Sedik* 1508 *GrimsCB ii*, – *Seedyke* 1538 *ib iii*, *les Seadick'* (sic) 1569 *ib iv*, *the Seadike at Fletergate* (sic) 1571 *GrimsChamb*, – *sea dyke* 1581 *GrimsCt*, *le seadickes* 1582 *GrimsChamb*, *the Seadicke* 1590 *GrimsCLeet*, and cf. *Westsedyke gote* 1471 *GrimsCB i* (*v.* **gotu** 'a sluice'), self-explanatory, *v.* **sǣ**, **dík**; in 1571 it is said to be "at Flottergate" *infra*.

THE SHAMBLES (lost), *le Shamles* 1394 *GrimsChamb*, *lee shamillis* 1527 *ib*, *yᵉ shambles* 1679 *ib*, 1709 *GrimsCLeet*, *the* – 1691 *GrimsChamb*, 1695 *ib*, 1712, 1714 *GrimsCLeet*, cf. *Fisshameles* 1409 *GrimsChamb*, *le fyshe shamelles* 1580 *ib* and *les Flesshameles* 1409 *ib*, 'the stalls for displaying goods for sale' *v.* **sceamol**, in the last three forms for fish and meat respectively.

SIMWHITE BRIDGE, *Symewhytebrigg* 1492 *GrimsExtent*, *symwhytbrige* 1500 *GrimsChamb*, – *whyt bryg* 1525 *ib*, *Symwhitbrig* 1514 *GrimsCB i*, 1518 *ib ii*, – *bryg* 1546 *GrimsChamb*, – *bridge* 1590 *GrimsCLeet*, – *brigge* a1600 *ib*, –*whyte bryg* 1533 *GrimsCB ii*, – *White brygg* 1537 *GrimsCLeet*, –*white brigge* 1573 *GrimsChamb*, 1591 *GrimsFC*, *Syme Whyte brygges* 1538 *GrimsCB iii*, *Simwhit bryg* 1628 *GrimsCLeet*, *Simwhite bridge* 1664 *ib*, *Symon white Brigg* 1640 *GrimsCB viii*, *Symmon white bridge* 1664 *GrimsCLeet*, *Symon White Bridge* 1685 *GrimsChamb*, 1697 *GrimsCLeet*, – *bridge* 1707 *ib*, *Seaman white bridge* 1683 *GrimsChamb*, *Seman* – 1707 *GrimsCLeet*, *Seymor White Bridge* 1695 *GrimsChamb*, *Seamor* – 1696 *Td'E*, *Seymour* – 1709 *GrimsCB x*, *Seamore white* – 1714 *ib*, – *White Bridge* 1799 *ib xiv*, named from Simon *White* 1392, 1401 *GrimsCt* or a later member of the family with the same forename and **brycg** with the majority of forms Scandinavianized. Gillett 1 comments, "The older branch of the haven formed the eastern boundary of the built-up area and was crossed by Simwhite-bridge, where the

River–head now is". The name has been reintroduced with the building of a new bridge there.

THE STAITH (lost), *le Comunstathe* 1409 *GrimsChamb*, *le Stayes* 1559 *ib*, *cōem le* – (sic) 1581 *GrimsFC*, *the coe' stayes iuxta portum* 1595 *ib*, *staythes* a1600 *GrimsCLeet*, *le coem Stayhes* 1627 *ib*, *le Staith iuxta simwhit bryg* 1628 *ib*, *Staiths* 1804 *GrimsCB xiv*, *v.* **stæð** in its later sense 'a landing–place'.

STONE BRIDGE (lost), c.1600 *GrimsMap* (*PRO*), 1634, 1665 *GrimsCLeet*, 1737 *GrimsChamb*, *Stanebrygge* 1423 *GrimsCt*, 1424 *GrimsChamb*, *apud pontem lapidem* 1476 *GrimsCB i*, – *lapideum* 1491 *Surv*, – *Lapideum* 1492 *GrimsExtent*, *ultra* – 1518 *GrimsFC*, – *lapidarorum* 1529 *GrimsCB ii*, *iuxta pontem lapideu'* 1543 *GrimsExtent*, – *lapedum'* 1583 *GrimsFC*, *the stone bryg* 1517 *GrimsCB ii*, – *bryge* 1565 *GrimsCLeet*, – *brigge* a1600 *ib*, – *bridge* c.1600 *GrimsMap* (*PRO*), 1676, *GrimsCLeet*, 1681 *GrimsChamb*, – *brigg* 1692 *GrimsCLeet*, – *ston bryg* 1546, 1556 *ib*, – *stoune bridge* 1642 *GrimsCB viii*, *New Bridge or Stone Bridge* 1723 *ib xi*, self–explanatory. Gillett 1 notes that the West Haven "was crossed by the Stone–bridge in Flottergate" (*infra*). Dr Rod Ambler comments that "there is still evidence of its stone construction in the foundations of the bridge which crosses the old West Haven in what was formerly Flottergate".

SWAIN BRIDGE (lost), *Swaynbrigg, Ponte dicit Swaynbrygt* (sic) 1492 *GrimsExtent*, *Swan bryg* (sic) 1543 *ib*; the first el. appears to be **sveinn** 'a young man, a servant', and cf. *Swan Lane infra* in which the three earliest forms are also *Swain–* and *Swayne–*.

THORNTON HO (lost), *Thorntonhous* 1344 Pat, 1374, 1379, 1382 all (p), –*huses* 1344 (p), – *hous* 1345 (p), –*house* 1364 all *GrimsCt*, cf. *terr' abbat' de Thornton* 1531 *GrimsCB i*, *Lande called Thornton grounde* 1565 *ib*; as is indicated by the 1531 form, this was a house and land owned by Thornton Abbey.

TOWN HALL, 1788 *GrimsCB et passim*, *coī Aula* 1389 *GrimsCt*, 1433 *MiscDon 302*, *aula com'* 1393 *GrimsCt*, 1490 *GrimsCB i*, *coēm aulam* 1518 *ib*, *coem Howlem Burgi* (sic) 1578 *GrimsFC*, *Guyhalda* 1469 *GrimsCB i*, *comen hall* 1482 *ib*, *yᵉ comon'* – 1507 *ib*, *the Comone Hawlle* 1524 *ib*, *the townes hall* 1637 *GrimsCB viii*, – *Townes Hall* 1683 *ib ix*, – *Towns Hall* 1694 *GrimsChamb et passim* to 1831 *GrimsCB xvi*, – *Towne Hall* 1664 *ib ix*, *the Towns* – 1695 *ib*, 1719 *Td'E* and cf. *le Moytehall' burgh'* 1539 *GrimsBCB* (*v*. **mōt** 'a meeting', **hall**); Gillett 2 notes that the Town Hall stood in the Market Place, that a new hall was completed by 1395 and that "On rare occasions the town hall was called the Guildhall", *v*. **gild–hall**.

TURRET HALL (lost), *the* – 1730 *Td'E*, – *Turritt Hall* 1732 *ib*; Gillett 155–56n quotes Hocken that ". . . Torret Hall, which was converted into a house of industry and afterwards into the present (1839) Granby inn, and the town's court house", *v*. The Granby Inn *infra*.

THE VICARAGE, 1851 Census, *the vicarige house* 1639 *GrimsCB viii*, *viccaridge house* 1670, 1679 *GrimsChamb*, *the Vicaridge* 1679 *GrimsCLeet*, *le Vickridge* 1684 *ib*, *the Vicckirridg* c.1700 *ib*, *Vicarage house* 1777 *GrimsCB xiii*, 1841 *TA*, cf. *viccaridge Closse* 1630 *GrimsCLeet*. Dr Rod Ambler points out that the present Old Rectory on Bargate was built in 1848 as the Vicarage to replace the buildings referred to here. It was known as the Vicarage until a Rectorial benefice was created in Grimsby.

WALK MILL (lost), *Walkmyln'* 1441 *GrimsChamb*, 'the fulling mill' *v*. **walc**, **myln**.

WASTLE BRIDGE (lost), *Wastelbrygge* 1518 *GrimsFC*; the first el. appears to be ME *wastel* 'bread made from the finest flour', but the significance of 'wastle bridge' is unclear, unless it was where such bread was sold.

WATER MILL (lost), *molendinum ad aquam quod sedet in antiquo portu* 1201 ChR, *molendinum aquat'* 1465 *GrimsChamb*, - *aquatic'* 1519 *GrimsCB ii*, *firma molendini aquatici* 1546, 1559 *GrimsChamb*, - *Aquatico* 1576 *ib*, *molend' aquatico* 1585 *ib*, *the Water myln in the Kynges streme* 1495 *GrimsCB i*, *Watur milne* 1517 *ib*, *the watter myln* 1546 *GrimsCLeet*, *the towns Watter mylln* 1547 *ib*, *the water mylne* 1582, 1590 *ib*, *-milne* 1649 *GrimsCB viii*, self-explanatory; in 1495 it is said to be near *Carter Bridge*.

WELLOW MILL (lost), 1662, 1671, 1697, 1706, 1718 *Terrier*, 1735 *GrimsCB xi*, 1801 *ib xiv*, - *House* 1851 *Census*, *the watter milne of the said Abby* 1471 *GrimsCB i*, *y*[e] *Abbey mylln* 1481 *ib*, *molend de Wellow ib ii*, *Welloo myln* 1535-46 *MinAcct*, - *Mille* 1537 *AOMB 209*, *Welhow myll* c.1581 *GrimsCt*, *a water mill called Welhow Mill* 1625 Heneage, *Wellow Milne* 1638 *GrimsMiscD* and cf. *Wellow Mill Lane infra*; it belonged to Wellow Abbey. According to Gillett the mill was erected on waste land on the west side of the Haven. Dr Rod Ambler queries whether this is the water mill shown at the head of the Haven on c.1600 *GrimsMap* (*PRO*).

WEST BRIDGE (lost), (*the*) - 1782 *GrimsCB xiii*, 1799 *ib xiv*.

WEST MARSH, 1692, 1702 *GrimsCB x*, 1795 *LindDep Plans*, 1801 *GrimsMap et passim*, *the west marshe* 1528 *GrimsCB i*, *le west marssche* 1537 *ib iii*, *the west marsh* 1632 *GrimsCLeet*, - *marshes* 1648 *GrimsCB viii*, - *Marshes* 1662 *GrimsLeases*, *West Marshes* 1678 *GrimsCLeet et freq* to 1840 *EnclA*, *westmarshe* 1664 *GrimsCB ix*, *in marisco occident'* 1582 *GrimsChamb*, *in occidentali marisco* 1670 *GrimsCLeet*, *Occident' Marisc' de Grimsby* 1691 *Td'E*, *unum mariscum* 1201 ChR, cf. *comēn mariscum* 1366 *GrimsFC*, *le Marsch* 1457 *TCC*, *in marisco* 1492 *GrimsExtent*, *Marschys* 1537 *GrimsCLeet*, self-explanatory, *v*. **west**, **mersc** and cf. East Marsh *supra*.

WEST SLUICE BRIDGE (lost), 1798 *LindDep Plans*, *Sluice Bridge* 1799 *GrimsCB xiv*.

WHIPPING POST (lost), *ye whipping poast* 1660 *GrimsCB ix*, *(ye) Common Whipping post* 1709, 1714 *ib x*, 1735 *ib xi*, *the whipping post* 1711 *ib x*.

WILLOW BRIDGE (lost), *Willughbrygfurlanges* 1457 *TCC*, *Willoigh' brigges* 1540 *AOMB 212*, *willowbrigges* 1601, *–brigs* 1625, *willow–brigg* 1634, *Willow Brigges* 1671, *– brigges* 1706, *– briggs* 1690, *– Briggs* 1697 all *Terrier*, cf. *Willow Bridge wong* 1792 *Yarb* (*v.* **vangr** 'a garden, an in–field'), presumably a bridge by which willows grow, *v.* **wilig**, **brycg**.

WINDMILL (lost), *molendinum ad ventum* 1201 ChR, *situ molend' ventrit'* 1441 *GrimsChamb*, *molendin' ventritic'* 1470 *ib*, *molendini Ventritic'* 1513 *ib*, *Un' molend' ventrit'* 1539–40 Dugd iv, *vnius mont' molendini ventritici voc' tulhilles* 1559 *GrimsChamb*, *monte molend' ventritic'* 1585 *ib*, *the Wyndmyln'* c.1540 *GrimsCLeet*, *Wind mill hill* 1565 *GrimsChamb*, *wyndmylnehill* 1573 *ib*, *montis molendini ventritici iuxta tulie hilles* 1580 *GrimsFC*, *Wind Mill Hill* 1842 *TA*; for *tulhilles*, *v. Le Tollehilles* in f.ns. (b) *infra*.

WRAYES BRIDGE (lost), *the Wrayes bridg* 1654 *GrimsCB viii*; probably named from an ancestor of Miles *Wray* 1726 PRStJ.

STREET–NAMES

The street–names in the following list are chiefly those in the old borough and for the most part include only those found up to and including the 1851 *Census*.

ABBEY PARK RD, 1851 *Census*, ABBEY RD, 1851 *ib*, cf. *venell que ducit versus Abbiam*, *venell' versus Abbathium* 1492 *GrimsExtent*, *ye Abby Laine* 1667 *GrimsCLeet*, *the abby lane* 1714 *ib*, *Abbey Way* 1801 *GrimsMap*, both named from Wellow Abbey. ALBERT ST., *– St.* 1851 *Census*. ALFRED TERRACE, 1851 *ib*. APPLEBY LANE (lost), *ye est sid of Bryghowgate next appulbe layne* 1513 *GrimsCB i*, named from the family of John *Appelby* 1394

GrimsCt. AUGUSTA ST., 1851 *Census*. AUSTRALIAN PLACE (lost), – *Pla*. 1851 *ib*.

BACK LANE (lost), 1713, 1724 *GrimsCLeet*, 1840 *GrimsMap*, *the baklayn'* 1555 *GrimsCLeet*, *bake Layne* (sic) 1561 *GrimsFC*, *the back layne* 1582, 1590 *GrimsCLeet*, 1649 *GrimsCB viii*, (*the*) *back lane* 1582, 1633 *GrimsFC*, 1663 *GrimsCLeet et passim* to 1762 *Terrier*, *quandam venellam anglia a backlayne* (sic) 1587 *GrimsFC*, *back laine* 1620 *GrimsCLeet*, *the back laine goinge to the hauen* 1636 *GrimsCB viii et passim* to – *going to Wellow* 1707 *ib*, *Backlaine* 1637, 1649 *ib*, *backlaines* 1627 *ib*, *–laines* 1681, c.1700, 1701 *ib*, self–explanatory; it is likely that more than one back lane is referred to here. BACK ST. (lost), 1840 *GrimsMap*. BARGATE, 1404 *GrimsCt*, 1409 *GrimsChamb*, 1801 *GrimsMap*, 1842 White, *le Baryates* 1392 *GrimsFC*, *Barʒates* 1393 *GrimsCt*, *le* – 1402 *ib*, *baryattes* 1547 *GrimsCLeet*, *barre yates* Eliz *GrimsCt*, *bargaite* 1565 *GrimsCB i*, *le Bargates* 1393 *GrimsChamb*, (*the*) *Bargates* 1587, 1634 *GrimsCLeet et passim* to 1788 *Terrier*, *le barre gates* 1542 *GrimsCB iii*, *yᵉ* – c.1560 *GrimsCLeet*, *Barrgates* 1639 *GrimsCB viii*, 1688 *GrimsCLeet*, cf. *Bar Gates Gate* 1792 *Yarb*. The earliest spellings in *–ʒ–* and *–y–* suggest that this is 'the gate(s) with a bar', *v*. **barre**, **geat**, an entrance to the borough and the main street leading into the town. BATH ST., 1851 *Census*. BAXTERGATE (lost), *Bakestergate* 1364, 1392 *GrimsFC*, *Bakster–* 1397, 1399, 1403, 1419, 1426 *ib*, *Baxtergate* 1391 *ib*, 1414 *GrimsCt*, 1474 *GrimsCB i*, 1495 *GrimsFC et freq* to 1842 White, *Baxstergate* 1457 *TCC*, *baxter–* 1554, 1588, 1590 *GrimsFC*, *Baxter gayte* 1535, 1565 *GrimsCB i*, m16 *GrimsCLeet*, *Baxstergate street* 1563 *TCC*, *a certain Street . . . formerly called High Street but now called Baxtergate* 1801 *Td'E*, either 'the street of the bakers' *v*. **bæcestre**, **gata**, or from a family with the occupational surn. *Baxter*, cf. John *bakester* 1378 *GrimsCt*, Robert *Bakester* 1390 *ib*. The name has been revived as that of a Mall on the plan of Freshney Place Shopping Centre. BENNET LANE (lost), *bennitt Lane* 1689 *GrimsCLeet*, from the family name *Bennet*, cf. *Jhon Bennet* (sic) 1540 PRStJ. BETHLEHEM ST., 1762 Gillett, 1851 *Census*, *Bethlem street* 1842

White, cf. *the New Buildings where Beddlam stood* 1779 *Yarb*, *Bethlem* 1801 *GrimsMap*, 1826 White, a transferred name from the well-known Royal Bethlem Hosital in London. BICHELL LANE (lost), *venell' que ducit versus Bichell* 1492 *GrimsExtent*, – *bichell'* 1543 *ib*, obscure. BLACKFRIARGATE LANE (lost), *Blakfreregatelane* 1464 Fine, *Blakeffreregatelane* 1468, 1475 ib, *Blakefrerellane* (sic) 1466 ib; nothing seems to be known of the Black Friars in Grimsby, except a single reference to *close before the blacke fryers* 1639 *GrimsCB viii*. BOY LANE (lost), 1736 *Td'E*, 1737 *GrimsChamb*, *boylane* 1492 *GrimsExtent*, Eliz *GrimsCt*, – *lane* 1692, 1705 *GrimsCLeet*, *Boylane* 1491 *Surv*, 1501 *GrimsCB i*, –*layn* 1505 *ib*, – *layn* 1515 *GrimsChamb*, *Boyelane* 1543 *GrimsExtent*, *Boie-* 1576 *GrimsChamb*, *boy laine* 1664, 1676 *GrimsCLeet*, *Boy* – 1678 *ib*, 1736 *GrimsCB xi*, cf. *boys lan end* (sic) 1547 *GrimsCLeet*, *boye laine end* 1571 *GrimsChamb*, *ye boy laine end* 1651 *GrimsCB viii*; the significance of ME **boie** 'a boy, a servant' is uncertain and no plausible explanation can be offered. BRADERGATE (lost), *le Bradergatte* 1543 *GrimsExtent*, cf. *braderthyng* 1543 *ib*; no doubt named from the family of Richard *Brader* 1570 *GrimsQR* with **gata** and **þing** 'property, possessions'. BRADLEY RD, 1792 *Yarb*, cf. *Bradleygate* 1457 *TCC*, *bradlye gate* 1601, *Bradley* – 1625, 1634, – *Gate* 1686, 1690, *Braidley gait* 1706 all *Terrier*, 'the road to Bradley' *v.* **gata**. BRAYLANE (lost), *Braylanende* 1393 *GrimsChamb*; with a single form no certainty is possible but it may be 'the broad lane', *v.* **breiðr, lane**, with the loss of –*th*–. BRIGHOWGATE, 1518, 1532, 1589 *GrimsFC*, 1630 AASR xl *et passim*, *Brighou-* 1364, 1390 *GrimsFC*, 1389 *GrimsCt*, 1390 Cl, 1390 Misc, 1401, 1417 *GrimsCt*, 1421–23 *MinAcct*, 1516 *GrimsCB i*, *Brighov-* 1387 *GrimsFC*, *Bryghow-* 1391, 1403, 1422 *GrimsCt*, 1457 *TCC*, 1477, 1490 *GrimsCB i et passim* to 1599 *GrimsFC*, *Brigowe-* 1470 *GrimsChamb*, *Brigou-* 1474 *GrimsCB i*, *Brigow-* 1500 *GrimsFC*, 1801 *GrimsCB xiv*, *Bryghowegayte* 1536 *ib i*, 1585 *GrimsFC*, *brigghow-* 1543, 1649 *GrimsCB i et passim* to 1788 *Terrier*, *Bryghogayte* 1553 *GrimsChamb*, *bryga-* (sic) 1559 *ib*, 1694 *GrimsCLeet*, *Briggo-* 1567 *GrimsCB iv*, 1663 *GrimsCLeet*, 1676 *Td'E*, –*gaite* 1580 *GrimsFC*, a1600 *GrimsCLeet*, *Briggowgate* 1593 *GrimsFC*, 1718

Td'E, *Briggoe–* 1639, 1652 *GrimsCB viii*, 1719 *Td'E*, 'the street leading to *Brighow* (*supra*)', *v.* **gata**; note however there is reference to a gate in *portam de Bryghowe* 1491 *Surv*, 1535 *GrimsExtent*, to bars in *barras de Brigougate* 1476 *GrimsCB* and also to a lane and a street in *venell' de Brighowe* 1396–97 *GrimsChamb* and *alte vie de Brighowe* 1491 *Surv*. BULL LANE (lost), *bullayne* 1508 *GrimsCB ii*. BULL RING LANE, 1801 *GrimsMap*, 1851 *Census*, *–ring Lane* 1769 *LincsD*, *v.* Bull Ring *supra*. LOWER, UPPER BURGESS ST., *Lower Burgess Street* 1800 *GrimsCB xiv*, 1801 *GrimsMap et passim*, *Upper –* 1801 *ib et passim*. BUTCHER LANE (lost), *Butcther Lane* (sic) 1697, *butcher Lane* 1698, *Butchers laine* 1701, *ye Butcher lane* 1705 all *GrimsCLeet*. BUTCHERY LANE (lost), 1765 *GrimsCB xiii*, 1801 *GrimsMap*, 1831 *Td'E*, *– lane* 1842 White, 1849 Hagar.

CAISTOR RD, *Caystergate* 1405 *GrimsCt*, *Castergate* 1492 *GrimsExtent*, *lee castorgayt* (sic) 1543 *ib*, *Caster –* 1625, 1686, *–gate* 1718, 1724, *Caistor –* 1634, *– Gate* 1762, *Castor gate* 1662, *– Gate* 1690, 1788 all *Terrier*, 'the road to Caistor', *v.* **gata**. CANDLE HOUSE LANE, 1840 *GrimsMap*. CANONBIG LANE (lost), *Canonbigge layne* 1586 *GrimsFC*, *v. Canonbig supra*. CARPENTERS WAYS (lost), 1831 *GrimsCB xvi*. CARTER GATE, *le Cartergate* 1390 *GrimsCt*, 1411 LAAS vi, 1492 *GrimsExtent*, *Cartergate* 1406 *GrimsLeases*, 1409 *GrimsChamb*, 1411 LAAS vi, 1436 AD vi, 1492 *GrimsExtent*, 1501, 1515 *GrimsCB i et freq*, *– gaytt* 1524 *ib*, *–gayett* 1543 *GrimsExtent*, *– gayte* 1565 *GrimsCB i*, *–gait* 1578 *GrimsFC*, and cf. *Carter laine* 1639 *GrimsCB viii*, 'the street of the carters' from ME **carter** and **gata**. THE CAUSEWAY (lost), 1681, 1707 *GrimsCLeet*, *the Cawsie* 1585 *Shaw*, *Causey* 1634 *GrimsCLeet*, self–explanatory, *v.* **caucie**. CHANTRY LANE, 1801, c.1820 *GrimsMap et passim*, *the Chantre layn* 1522 *GrimsCB ii*, *vennelle voc' Chantre layne* 1538 *ib iii*, *the chantrey layns* (sic) *GrimsChamb*, *ye Chantre lane* 1544 *GrimsCB i*, *Chauntre layn* 1549 *ib ii*; Gillett 83 suggests that the situation of the house of the priest of the Rayner Chantry "seems to have been the origin of Chantry Lane", cf. *The Chantry supra*. CHAPEL LANE (lost), 1799 *GrimsCB xiv*, *– lane* 1816, 1842 White, 1849

Hagar, *Chappel* – 1788 *Terrier*, perhaps named from the family of Stephen *Chappell* 1577 *GrimsCB v*, but of course it may have been named from a *chapel*. CHURCH LANE, 1851 *Census, the Church lane* 1692 *GrimsCB x*. CHURCH ST., 1851 *Census*, cf. *Old Church Street* 1840 *GrimsMap*. CLEE RD, 1792 *Yarb*. CLEETHORPES RD, *Cleethorpes road* 1849 Hagar. COBSEY LANE (lost), – *Laine* 1665 *GrimsCLeet*, *-laine* 1673 *ib*, cf. – *house* 1670, 1679 *GrimsChamb*, *Cobse howse & Close* 1682 *GrimsCLeet*, named from the family of John *Cobsey* 1682 *GrimsCB ix*. COLEHILL LANE (lost), *colehill lane* 1690 *GrimsCLeet*, cf. *(the) Coal Hill* 1679 *GrimsChamb*, 1795 *LindDep Plans et passim* to c.1820 *GrimsMap*, – *Cole hills* 1691, 1700 *GrimsCLeet*, perhaps 'the hill where charcoal is burnt' *v*. **col**[1], **hyll**. CONTRACTORS ROW (lost), 1851 *Census*; Dr Rod Ambler points out that this refers to buildings, later demolished, where navvies and other workers involved in the construction of the new dock were living in 1851. *Irish Green infra* is similarly to be explained. CRESSY ST., 1851 *ib*, named from the family of John *Cressy* 1754 PRStJ. CROMWELL RD, 1851 *Census*. CROSS LANE, 1800 *GrimsCB xiv*, *Lower* – 1800 *ib*, *the Upper or South* – 1801 *Td'E*. CROSS ST., 1800 *GrimsCB xiv*. CUXWOLD LANE, *Cokewaldelane* 1392 *GrimsCt*, no doubt from a surn. derived from Cuxwold, PN L **4**, 63.

DEANSGATE, *Danegate* c.1220 de l'Isle, 1401 *GrimsChamb*, *Danes*– 1395 *GrimsCt*, 1457 *TCC*, *GrimsCB i*, e17 *GrimsCLeet*, *danys*– 1520 *GrimsCB i*, *Denesgate* 1392, 1403 *GrimsCt*, 1409, 1417 *GrimsChamb*, 1436 AD vi, 1469 *ib* i, 1492 *GrimsExtent et freq* to 1622 *GrimsMiscD*, *denesgate siue finkelstreete* 1587 *GrimsFC* (*v. Finkle St. infra*), *Denesgatte* 1396 *GrimsFC*, *-gaite* 1591 *ib*, *Deynesgate* 1417 *GrimsChamb*, *denysgate* 1522 *GrimsCB ii*, *Deansgayte* 1538 *ib* i, *-gate* 1568 *ib* i, 1578 *GrimsFC*, 1629 *GrimsMiscD et freq*, *Deanegate* 1670, 1683 *GrimsChamb*; the early forms in *Dane*– suggest that this is 'the Danes' street', *v*. **Danir**, **gata**. DEAN'S GATE TERRACE (lost), 1851 *Census*. DIAL SQUARE, – *square* 1842 White, – *Sq*. 1851 *Census*. DOCK ST. (lost), – *S*. c.1820, *N. Dock St*. c.1820, *South Dock Street* 1801, 1840, *West* – 1801, 1842 all *GrimsMap*, *New* –, *West Dock St*.,

1851 *Census*. DRUMMER LANE (lost), 1689, 1714 *GrimsCLeet*.
DUDLEY ST., 1851 *Census*. DUNCOMBE ST., 1869 *LindDep Plans*,
named from the family of Joseph *Duncombe* 1826 *GrimsCB xv*.

EASTGATE, 1851 *Census*, *Eastgt* (sic) 1842 White. EAST LANE
(lost), *la Estlane* 1411 LAAS vi, self-explanatory. EAST MARSH
LANE (lost), 1709 *GrimsCLeet*, *v.* East Marsh *supra*. EAST ST., –
street 1849 Hagar. EDWARD ST., – *street* 1842 White.

FINKLE ST. (lost), *Fynkelstrete* 1469 AD, 1480 *GrimsMiscD*,
Fynkyl– 1565 *GrimsCB i, fynkelstreate iuxta le bulringe* 1587
GrimsFC, Fynkel Streate 1595 *ib*; this is an obscure name which
has recently been discussed at length by Richard Coates "A breath
of fresh air through Finkle Street", *Nomina*, 18 (1996), 7–31. He
examines all the suggestions so far made and concludes that the
first el. is ME *fen(e)kel* 'fennel', but no certainty is possible; cf.
Finkle St., PN L **1**, 65–66 and *v.* Deansgate *supra*. FISH DOCK
ST., – *Rd.* 1851 *Census*. FISHER ROW (lost), *Fissherrawe* 1397,
Fisherrawe 1401, *Fisshr'* 1403 all *GrimsCt, Fyssherrawe* 1423,
1441 *GrimsChamb*, 'the fishermen's row', *v.* **fiscere, rǣw**.
FLEETGATE (lost), *Fletegate* 13 (p1269) *Bard*, 1492 *GrimsExtent*,
1521 *GrimsCB i, Flet–* Hy3 (1409) Gilb, *flete–* 1543 *GrimsExtent*,
fletgayt 1546 *GrimsChamb*, 'the street leading to the estuary,
creek' *v.* **flēot, gata**. FLESHEWER ROW (lost), *Flesshowerowe*
1393 *GrimsFC*, "lane called" *Flesshewerrawe* 1436 AD,
Flesshewar lane 1457 *TCC, Fleschewer layne* 1577 *GrimsFC*,
Flescher layn 1556 *GrimsCLeet*, 'the butchers' row, lane', from
ME **fleshhewer** 'a butcher', **rǣw, lane**. FLOTTERGATE, 1366
GrimsFC, 1411 LAAS vi, 1591 *GrimsCt*, 1622 *GrimsMiscD et
passim* to 1842 White, – *alias Ropery Lane* 1691 *Td'E*, – *als
Ropery Lane* 1691 *GrimsMiscD*, 1719 *Td'E, flotter–* 1556
GrimsChamb, 1580 *GrimsFC*, 1598 *GrimsMiscD*, 1664 *GrimsCB
ix, Flotiergat* 13 (Ed1) *Newh*, *–gate* 1401 *GrimsChamb*, 1419,
1422 *GrimsCt*, 1436 AD vi, *Flotyer–* c.1400, 1409 *GrimsChamb*,
1411 LAAS vi, *Flotergate* 1411 *GrimsCt*, 1518 *GrimsFC*, 1521
GrimsCB i, 1570 *GrimsChamb*, *–gaytt* 1525 *GrimsCB i, –gait*
1527 *GrimsChamb*, *flothergat'* 1525 *GrimsChamb*, 'the street of

the sailors', from a ME ***floter**, ***flotier** and **gata**; *Floter* is recorded as a surn. in Thuresson 85. For the alternative name *v.* Ropery St. *infra*; *v.* also Queen St. *infra*. The name has been reintroduced as that of a Mall on the plan of Freshney Place Shopping Centre. FLOWER ROW (lost), – *row* 1842 White, 1849 Hagar, – *Square* 1851 *Census*. FOTHERBY ST., 1851 *ib*, – *S.* 1801 *GrimsMap*, cf. *Fotherby's dole and spout* 1695 *GrimsChamb*, named from the family of John *Foterby* 1516 *GrimsCB i*, – *Fotherby* 1522 *ib*. FOUNDRY LANE (lost), 1851 *Census*. FRIAR LANE (lost), *Freyre lane* 1600 *TCC*, *Freres Lane* 1628, *Frier Laine* 1663, *Friers laine* 1671, *friers Laine* c.1700 all *GrimsCLeet*, *Fryar Lane* 1731 *Td'E*; there is no indication whether this is named from the Austin friars or the Greyfriars, cf. *Greyfriar Lane infra*.

GARDEN ST., 1807 *BRA 833*, 1851 *Census*, – *street* 1826, 1842 White, named from the family of William *Gardin* 1524 *GrimsCB i*, – *Garden* 1808 *ib xiv*. GARDENER'S LANE (lost), 1801 *GrimsMap*, named from the family of Ambrose *Gardiner* 1633 *GrimsCLeet*. GEORGE ST., 1801 *GrimsMap*, – (*being part of the present Turnpike Road*) 1804 *Td'E*, 1810 *LincsD*, 1851 *Census*. GREGORY ST., 1851 *ib*, from the surn. *Gregory*, cf. William *Gregory* 1842 White. GREYFRIAR LANE (lost), *Greyfrelane* (sic) 1417 *GrimsCt*, *Grayfrerelayne* 1518 *GrimsFC*, *venellam que ducit versus fratres minore* (sic) 1492 *GrimsExtent*, *venella que ducit Ad fratres minores* 1543 *ib*, named from the Grey Friars, *v. supra* and cf. *Friar Lane supra*. GRIME ST., 1801 *GrimsMap*, 1851 *Census*, cf. *Grimes Chappell yard* 1625, 1662, – *Chappel yarde* 1634, – *Chapple yard* 1690, *Grymes Chappel Yard* 1724, *Grimes Chappel* 1686 all *Terrier* and *Grime Green* 1792 *Yarb*; presumably named from the family of Walter *Gryme* 1400 *GrimsCt*. GRIMSBY LANE (lost), *Grimesbie laine* 1627 *GrimsCLeet*. GROPECUNT LANE (lost), *gropcontlayn* 1529 *GrimsCB i*, *Grapecuntte Layne* 1565 *GrimsCLeet*, *Grapecuntlane* 1566, 1573 *GrimsChamb*, *grape cunt laine* 1576 *ib*, *grapecunte layne* 1592 *GrimsFC*, *Grapecount laine* 1645 *GrimsCB viii*, *Grape-cunt Lane* 1685 *Td'E*, *grope Cunte layne* 1580 *GrimsFC*, *grope cunte* – 1581 *GrimsMiscD*, *Gropecunt*

Lane 1719, 1765, 1794 *Td'E*, *groping lane* 1625 *Terrier* and note
Crane Cunt Lane (sic) 1534 *GrimsCB i*, self–explanatory; it is a
common name for a Lovers Lane, cf. Grape Lane, PN YE 289,
which an 18th century antiquarian noted "tends not a little to
obscenity"; cf. *Sanctuary Lane infra*. GROSVENOR CRESCENT,
1851 *Census*. GROVE PLACE (lost), 1851 *ib*.

HAVELOCK ST. (lost), 1851 *ib*, *Havelocs St*. 1801 *GrimsMap*, cf.
Havelock Stone supra. HAVEN ST. (lost), 1801 *GrimsCB xiv*, 1801
GrimsMap, 1810 *Td'E et freq* to 1851 *Census*, self–explanatory.
HAVENSIDE ST. (lost), 1662 *Td'E*, 1695 *GrimsCB x*, 1804 *Td'E*,
the streete at the haven side Eliz *GrimsCt*, *Haven Side streete* 1666
GrimsCB ix, – *Streete* 1685 *Td'E*, – *Street* 1708 *ib*, 1799 *GrimsCB*
xiv, cf. *the hauen side* 1637 *ib viii*, *ye haven side* 1679
GrimsCLeet, *the* – 1690 *ib*, – *Havenside* 1736 *GrimsChamb*,
Haven Side 1789 *GrimsCB xiv*, self–explanatory. HAYCROFT ST.,
cf. *le Hay Croft* 1513 *GrimsCB i*, *hay crofte* 1528 *ib*, – *croft* 1547
GrimsCLeet, *haycroft* 1557, 1626 *ib*, *–crofte* 1587 *ib*, *Haycroft*
1634 *ib et freq*, *Heycroft* 1537 *AOMB 209*, *Heye crofte* 1540 *ib*
212, *Hacroft* p1600 *GrimsCLeet*, self–explanatory; it was the name
of an important field as is indicated by the wealth of reference and
became the name of a street. HIGH ST. (lost), *(the)* – 1696 *Td'E*,
1704, 1718 *GrimsCB x et freq* to 1851 *Census*, *the Highstreet als*
Saint Maries Street 1696 *Td'E*, *viam regiam* 1468, 1522 *GrimsCB*
i, 1548 *ib iii*, 1577 *GrimsFC*, *the kinges strete* 1480 *GrimsMiscD*,
– *Kinges Strette* 1512 *GrimsCB i*, – *kynges stret*, – *Kynges Hy Way*
1524 *ib*, – *comen hy way* 1515 *ib*, *viam altam* 1492 *GrimsExtent*,
alte vie 1543 *ib*, *altam viam* 1548 *GrimsCB iii*, 1692 *GrimsCLeet*,
alt' stret' 1586 *GrimsFC*, *the high streit* 1555 *GrimsCLeet*, *le hygh*
strete 1564 *GrimsFC*, 'the important, the principal street', *v.*
hēah, **strǣt**. It is once alternatively referred to as St Mary Lane,
cf. *Saint mary layne* 1591 *GrimsFC*. HOLME ST., 1851 *Census*.
HUMBER COURT (lost), 1851 *ib*, – *court* 1842 White. HUMBER
ST., 1851 *Census*.

IRISH GREEN (lost) 1851 *ib*; cf. *Contractors Row supra*.

KENT ST., 1851 *ib.* presumably named from an old Grimsby family, cf. Elizabeth *Kent* 1543 PRStJ, John *Kent* 1545 *GrimsCB iii* and *terr'* . . . *quondam Kentes grounde et nuper Kingstone grounde* 1586 *GrimsFC*; *Kingston(e)* is similarly an old Grimsby family, cf. Thomas *Kyngston* 1481 *GrimsCB i.* KING EDWARD ST., 1801 *GrimsMap*, – *North* 1851 *Census*, – *South* 1864 *Terrier.* KING ST. (lost), 1851 *Census.* KIRK LANE (lost), *kyrk lane* 1543 *GrimsExtent*, *Kyrke layne als Smythe layne* 1577 *GrimsFC*, *Kirke layne alite'* – 1591 *ib*, *Kirke laine alt' Smiths laine* 1633 *ib*; probably from the *Kirk* family, cf. Christopher *at Kyrk* (sic) *GrimsCB iii*, Thomas *Kyrck* 1565 *ib i* and cf. *Smith Lane infra.*

LACEBY RD, c.1832 *Yarb,* cf. *Lacebygate* 1457 *TCC*, the road to Laceby. LEVINGTON ST., 1851 *Census.* LITTLE COATES RD, *Cotesgate* 1457 *TCC*, *Coats gate* 1625, 1662, 1697, *Coates* – 1634, 1686 all *Terrier*, 'the road to Little Coates', *v.* **gata.** LITTLEFIELD LANE, *littlefield Lane* 1688 *GrimsCLeet*, *Little Feild Laine* 1705 *ib*, cf. Littlefield *supra.* LITTLE LANE (lost), *the luttyll layn'* 1555 *GrimsCLeet.* LOCK HILL, 1842 White, cf. *the Lock* 1799 *GrimsCB xiv*, *Intended Road to the Lock* 1801 *GrimsMap.* LOFT ST., *it was resolved that the Main Street in the Borough of Great Grimsby a* (sic) *foresaid leading from the East Bar to the Lock be henceforth and for ever called 'Loft Street' in honour of Major Gen'. Henry Loft M.P.* 1809 *GrimsCB xiv.* Dr Rod Ambler draws attention to the fact that, according to George Shaw, *Old Grimsby* 1897, this became Victoria St. in 1854 when the Queen visited the town to open the new dock, which became the Royal Dock. LONG CAUSEWAY (lost), 1826, 1842 White, 1840 *GrimsMap*, cf. *ye Causey* 1666 *GrimsCLeet*, *the Causeway* 1707 *ib*, *v.* **caucie.** LOVERS LANE (lost), 1840 *GrimsMap.* LOW ST. (lost), 1840 *ib.*

MANORHOUSE LANE (lost), – *lane* 1849 Hagar. MARKET STAITH ST. (lost), *a certain Street* . . . *called the East Marsh intended to be called* – 1801 *Td'E*, *a certain place* . . . *called or intended to be called* – 1811 *ib*, *Staith Street* 1800 *GrimsCB xiv*, for Staith, *v. The Staith supra.* MARKET ST., 1800 *ib*, 1851 *Census*, – *S.* 1801

GrimsMap. MARSH LANE (lost), *the marsh layne* 1649 *GrimsCB viii*, – *Marshe lanes* 1662 *GrimsCLeet*. MAUD ST. (lost), 1851 *Census*. MIDDLE LANE (lost), *le Middelane in Bryghou* 1392 *GrimsCt*. MILL ST. (lost), – *street* 1826, 1842 White. MOODY LANE, 1685, 1695 *GrimsChamb*, 1777 *GrimsCB xiii*, *Modie* – 1563 *TCC*, *the Mudye Laine* 1565 *GrimsCLeet*, *moodye layne* 1582 *ib*, *modie* – 1585 *GrimsChamb*, *moodie lane* 1630 *GrimsCLeet*, *le Moody laine* 1678 *Foster*, *Mudy* – 1684 *GrimsCLeet*, and cf. *Modie house* 1563 *TCC*, named from the family of Richard *Mody* 1525 *GrimsCB i*.

NACTON ST., 1851 *Census*. NELSON ST., – *St* 1851 *ib*. NEW ST., 1801, 1840 *GrimsMap*, 1851 *Census*. NORTH BRIDGE ST., *Bridge St. North* 1851 *Census*, cf. – *South* 1851 *ib*. NORTHGATE (later called Loft St. and now VICTORIA ST.), 1411 LAAS vi, 1419 *GrimsCt*, 1683 *MiscDep 161*, *viam regiam versus borial'* 1392 *GrimsFC*, *viam versus boria'* 1538 *GrimsCB i*, self-explanatory, *v*. **norð**, **gata**. NORTH LANE (lost), *la Northlane* 1411 LAAS vi, *the north layn* 1547 *GrimsCLeet*, – *northlayne* 1550 *ib*.

OLD BRIDGE TERRACE (lost), 1851 *Census*. ORWELL ST., – *St.* 1851 *ib*. OSBORNE ST., 1851 *ib*, – *row* 1826 White, named from the family of Ann *Osborn* 1723 PRStJ.

PARADISE COURT (lost), 1851 *Census*. – LANE (lost), 1840 *GrimsMap*, – ROW (lost), 1851 *Census*, cf. *Paradise* 1636 *GrimsCB viii*, *paradise* 1688 *GrimsCLeet*, *sewers yssuing into Paradise* 1639 *GrimsCB viii*, *Paradise Goate* 1687 *ib ix*, – *Goat* 1687 *GrimsChamb*, *paradice* – 1691 *ib*, – *drain* 1743 *GrimsCB xii*, *Paradise Drain* 1801 *ib xiv*; in towns *paradise* is sometimes a complimentary nickname, sometimes used ironically, but in early names can denote 'a pleasure garden'. No certainty is possible. PARK LANE (lost), *ye Park laine* 1694 *GrimsCLeet*, cf. *opposit' communem parcum* 1601 *GrimsFC*, the latter was in Deansgate. PASTURE ST., 1801 *GrimsMap*, – *street* 1826, 1842 White. PELHAM TERRACE, 1851 *Census*; no doubt named from the *Pelhams*, Earls of Yarborough, landowners in the borough. The name survives as Pelham Rd. PEPPERCORN WALK, – *lane* 1826, 1842 White, cf. *Pepper Corn Close* 1659, 1662, 1712, 1721 *GrimsCLeet, a close called Pepper Corne* 1696 *Td'E, a piece of Grounds called Pepper Corn* 1736 *GrimsCB xi, pepper Corne* (sic) 1697 *GrimsCLeet, Pepper Corne* 1725 *ib, Pepper Corn* 1842 *TA*, no doubt a reference to the rent of the close. PINFOLD LANE, cf. *pinfald* 1516 *GrimsChamb, the pynfalld* 1541 *ib, le pynfold* 1544 *GrimsCB ii, the pynfold* 1564, 1565 *ib iv, le pinfould* 1639 *GrimsBCB*, – *Pinfold* 1651 *GrimsCB viii et freq* to *Pinfold Hill* 1851 *Census, v.* **pyndfald**. POTTERY ROW (lost), – *row* 1842 White. PROSPECT TERRACE (lost), 1851 *Census*. PROVIDENCE PLACE (lost), – *Pla.* 1851 *ib*.

QUEEN ST., 1851 *ib*, – *or Flotter Gate* 1815 *Td'E*, cf. *Flottergate supra.*

RAGFOAL LANE (lost), 1736 *GrimsCB xi*, 1737 *GrimsChamb, Rag-foal* – c.1736 *GrimsLeases, Rag-hoal* – 1736 *Td'E*; the significance of *foal* here is not apparent, though the first el. is clearly the surn. *Ragg*, cf. Thomas *Ragge* 1575 *GrimsCB iv*, and cf. *Raggs close* 1645 *ib viii, David Raggs Close* 1673 *GrimsCLeet*. RAILWAY ST., – *St.* 1851 *Census*. RATTON ROW (lost), 1801 *GrimsMap*, – *rowe* 1636 *GrimsCB viii*, – *Rowe* 1637 *ib* and cf. *Raten hill* 1492 *GrimsExtent*; a common nickname of contempt in street–names, 'the rat–infested row', *v.* **ratoun** 'a rat', **ræw**. The comparative form means 'the rat–infested hill'. RED HILL ST. (lost), 1841 *GrimsMap*, cf. *Red hill* 1826. 1842 White. RILEY ST. (lost), – *St* 1851 *Census*, named from the family of William *Riley* 1805 PRStJ. EAST ROBINSON ST., *Robinson Street* 1851 *Census*. presumably from a long–established family in the borough, cf. Jacob *Robynson'* 1513 *GrimsBC* and *Robinsons Shopp* 1577 *GrimsFC, William Robinson howse* 1587 *GrimsCLeet*. RODGERS LANE (lost), – *lane* 1722 *ib*, named from the family of Christopher *Roger* 1587 PRStJ. ROPERY ST., –*laine* 1674, 1681, 1702 *GrimsCLeet*, – *Lane* 1688, 1707 *ib et passim* to 1824 *Td'E*, – *lane* 1697 *ib, Roperey Layne* 1701 *GrimsCLeet*, cf. *the Roperye* c.1560 *GrimsCLeet*, – *Ropery* 1803, 1834 *GrimsCB xiv, Capt Harris's*

Ropery 1832 *ib*, *Ropery* 1849 Hagar, self–explanatory and cf. *Flottergate supra*.

St James Terrace, 1851 *Census*; Dr Ambler points out that the name survives with a name stone in Bargate. St John's Lane (lost), *in vico nuncupat' modo Saynt John' hys lane* 1515 *GrimsCB i*, cf. *the Corner a for sanct Johnnys cherche stelle* [i.e. stile] 1529 *GrimsCB i*; this is the only reference to a church dedicated to St John, which is otherwise unknown. St Mary Gate, *Saintemariegate* 13 (p1269) *Bard*, *Sayntymary* – 1477 *GrimsCB i*, *Seintmary*– 1514 *ib*, *Saint maries gatte* 1560 *ib*, *St Mariesgate* 1611 *GrimsFC*, *Snt Maryes Gate* 1690 *GrimsCLeet*, *S. Marys gate* 1719 *Td'E*, *St Mary Street* 1722 *ib*, *Saint Mary's* – 1765 *GrimsCB xiii*, cf. *Sentmarikirklane* 1409 *GrimsChamb*, *Sayntmarykyrklane* 1499 *GrimsCB i*; it is normally called North and South St Mary Gate, *Northsayntmarygate* 1347 AD ii, *North saynt mari*– 1366 *GrimsFC*, – *saint mary* – c.1392 *ib*, *Northseintmarigate* 1399 *GrimsCt*, *Northseintmary*– 1401 *GrimsFC et freq*, cf. *Northseintmarilane* 1392 *GrimsCt*, *North Saint Marysgate or the High Street* 1697 *GrimsFC*; *Southseintmarigate* 1392 *GrimsCt*, 1394 *GrimsFC*, *South* – 1396 *ib*, –*saintmarigate* 1397 *GrimsCt*, –*seintmarygate* 1398 *GrimsFC*, – *sant marygate* 1457 *TCC*, *south saint marygate* 1492 *GrimsExtent*, *le Southseint marygate* 1507 *GrimsFC et freq*; today there are also East and West St Mary Gate, *E. St. Mary's Gate*, *W. S. Mary's Gate* 1801 *GrimsMap*, all named from the destroyed church of St Mary. Sanctuary Lane (lost), 1801 *GrimsMap*, 1851 *Census*, *Saintuarylayne* 1591 *GrimsFC*, *Sanckuarye layne* 1594 *GrimsMiscD*, *Sentuarielayne als Grapcuncte Lane* 1597 *GrimsFC*, cf. *the South Sanctuary* 1553–55 ECP and *Gropecunt Lane supra*. Gillett 79 comments, "The friars and nuns enjoyed the same rights of sanctuary as the parish churches. Indeed the popularity of the Austin friars in this connexion seems to have given Sanctuary Lane its name". Savile St. (lost), 1826 White. Scartho Rd, 1851 *Census*, cf. *Scarthougate* 1374 AD vi, *Scarthow gate* 1457 *TCC*, 'the road to Scartho', *v.* **gata**. School Lane (lost), *schole lane* 1639 *GrimsCB viii*, *Schoolhouse laine* 1676 *GrimsCLeet*; the reference must be to

the *Grammar School supra*. SCOT LANE (lost), *Scotelane* 1395
GrimsCt, presumably from the surn. *Scot*, though the earliest
reference to the family so far noted is Joseph *Scott* 1694 *GrimsCB*.
SCOTNEY LANE (lost), *Scotneylane* c.1400 *GrimsChamb*, *-lane*
1409 *ib*, *Scotnallane* (sic) 1492 *GrimsExtent*, presumably named
from the surn. *Scotney*. SHEEPFOLD ST., 1851 *Census*. SILVER
ST., 1722 *Letch*, 1752 *Foster*, 1799 *GrimsCB xiv et passim*; Mr
John Field draws attention to the fact that some Silver Streets led
to a supply of fresh water. SIX ACRES RD (lost), 1801, 1803
GrimsCB xiv, 1804 *Td'E*, cf. *the six acres* c.1600 *GrimsMap*
(*PRO*), 1636 *GrimsCB viii*, *Six Acres* 1670 *GrimsChamb et freq* to
1811–12 *GrimsCB xiv* and *Six acres Marsh* 1660 *ib ix*, – *Acres
Goat* 1685 *GrimsChamb* (*v.* **gotu** 'a sluice'), *the six acres dike*
1837 *Heneage*, self–explanatory. SMITH LANE (lost), 1766, 1777
GrimsCB xiii, *Smyth layne* 1536–38 *ib i*, *Smythe Lane als St Mary
Lane* 1568 *ib*, – *layne* 1584 *GrimsFC*, 1588 *GrimsCLeet*, *Smyth
laine* 1674, 1685 *GrimsCLeet*, *Smiths Lane* 1714 *Td'E*, *Smith's* –
1730 *ib*, no doubt named from the surn. *Smith*, cf. Gilbert *Smith*
1392 *GrimsCt*; *v.* also *Kirk Lane supra*. SMITHY LANE (lost),
Smithilane 1392 *GrimsCt*, cf. *domum vocat' le smythe* 1548
GrimsCB iii, *the smythy howse* 1560 *ib v*, *smythe house* 1585
GrimsChamb, *the Smiths forge* 1625 Heneage, self–explanatory,
v. **smiððe**. SOSTANGATE (lost), 1394 *GrimsChamb*, 1587, 1590
GrimsCLeet, *Sostang gate* 1705 *ib*, *Sowstange* – 1569 *GrimsCB iv*,
Sestan– 1402 *GrimsFC*, 1419 *GrimsCt*, 1519 *GrimsFC*, *Sastan*–
1405 *GrimsCt*, *Sastann*– 1596 *GrimsFC*, *Saystan*– 1528 *GrimsCB
i*; the forms here may be compared with those for *Sextongate*, PN
L 1, 98–99, though only a single spelling in *So*– was noted for the
latter. Perhaps the etymology is the same, 'Saxstān's road, street',
but it hardly seems likely that the same unrecorded OE pers.n.
would occur in the street–names of two places in the same county.
Dr Insley would prefer to interpret the Grimsby name as
containing ME *sextein*, *sextain*, *saxton* 'an officer of a church or
religious house who cares for the buildings, ornaments, vestments
etc., and who attends to burials, bell–ringing, etc., a sexton' <
MLat *secrestānus*, *segrestānus*, variants of *sacristanus*, *v.* MED,
s.v. *sextain*, Reaney s.n. *Sexten*, though the spellings in *So*–

present a difficulty. SOUTHGATE (lost), 1411 LAAS vi, 1424
GrimsChamb, 1450, 1460 *GrimsParlExp* and probably to be
identified with *viam regiam versus austrum* 1366 *GrimsFC*,
venellam uersus austr' 1516 *GrimsCB i*, self–explanatory, *v.* **sūð**,
gata. SOUTH ST. (lost), – *S.* 1801 *GrimsMap*, – *St.* 1851 *Census*.
SPITAL LANE (lost), *hospitall' lane* 1515 *GrimsCB i*, *le
Spittlehouse lane* 1638 *ib viii*, referring to the hospital of St Mary
Magdalene and St Leger *infra*. SPRING ST. (lost), *Lower* – 1801
GrimsMap, 1851 *Census*, *Upper Spring S.* 1801 *GrimsMap*, *Upper
Spring Street* 1851 *Census*, *Spring S. Ter* 1851 *ib*, cf. *Spring
garden* 1842 White. STRAND ST., 1851 *Census*. SWAN LANE
(lost), 1682 *Td'E*, *Swaynlane* 1394 *GrimsChamb*, *Swainlane* 1401
ib, *Swayne layne* 1582 *ib*, *Swanne lain* 1531 *GrimsCB i*, – *Lane*
1570, 1573 *GrimsChamb*, – *lane* 1576 *ib*, – *layne* 1598
GrimsMiscD, *Swan layn* 1546 *GrimsChamb*, –*lane* 1565, 1692 *ib*,
1719 *Td'E*, *Swane Lane* c.1560 *GrimsCLeet*, – *layne* 1585
GrimsChamb; a similar variation of forms between the earlier
Swayn–, etc. and *Swan–* is found in *Swain Bridge supra* so perhaps
the first el. here is **sveinn** 'a young man, a servant'.

THESIGER ST., 1851 *Census*. TOMLINE ST., 1851 *ib*, no doubt
from the *Tomline* family which, as Mrs Bettie Watkinson points
out, owned land here. TORONTO PLACE (lost), 1851 *ib*. TOWN
HALL ST., – *St.* 1851 *ib*. TOWN ST. (lost), 1709 *Td'E*, 1732
GrimsCB xi, *the townes streete* 1660 *Td'E*, *the Townes Street* 1729
ib. TRELL LANE (lost), 1699 *GrimsCLeet*, – *laine* 1671, 1674,
1683 *ib*. TRIANGLE (lost), 1851 *Census*. TURNPIKE RD, (*the*) –
1794 *GrimsCB xiv et passim* to 1820 *GrimsMap*, *the Turnpike*
1788 *GrimsCB xiv et passim* to 1812 *ib*, *Turnpike* 1840 *GrimsMap*,
Louth Turnpike Road 1840 *EnclA*, and note *it is unanimously
agreed that the Turnpike Road intended to be made from Great
Grimsby Haven from a place called Upper Sands Ends to Wold
Newton Church and Irby–Mill Field shall go over Seamour white
Bridge* . . . 1765 *GrimsCB xiii*.

UNION PLACE (lost), 1851 *Census*. UPPER STAITH (lost), *upper* –
1869 *LindDep Plans*, cf. *The Staith supra*; it ran from the Old
Dock.

VICTORIA ST., 1872 *Padley*, – *St.* 1851 *Census*, – *North*, – *Street
West* 1851 *ib*; it was apparently earlier *Northgate*, then Loft St.

WATTAMS LANE (lost), – *lane* 1705 *GrimsCLeet*, cf. – *house*
1701 *ib*, from the surn. *Wattam*, cf. William *Wattam* 1654 PRStJ.
WEELSBY RD, *Welsebe lane* c.1600 *GrimsMap (PRO)*, *Weelseby
layne end* c.1634 *Terrier*, the road to Weelsby. WELHOLME RD,
1851 *Census*. WELLOWGATE, 1397 *GrimsCt*, 1460 *GrimsParlExp*,
1511 *GrimsFC*, 1522 *GrimsCB i*, 1535 VE iv *et passim*, –*gat* 1513
GrimsCB ii, – *Street* 1701 *Td'E*, – *Lane* 1705 *GrimsCLeet*,
Welhougat 1344 *GrimsFC*, –*gate* 1344 *ib*, 1361 AD vi, 1392
GrimsChamb, 1395 *GrimsCt*, *Welhow*– 1362 AD vi, 1403
GrimsCt, 1543 *GrimsExtent*, – *gate* 1625 Heneage, *Welhowegate*
1452 *GrimsCB i*, 1500 *GrimsFC*, *Wellowe gayte* 1564 *GrimsCB iv*,
–*gaite* 1569 *ib i*, – *gate* 1582 *GrimsCLeet*, 1638 *GrimsMiscD*,
Wellow gate 1670 *GrimsCLeet*, – *Gate* 1712 *GrimsCB xii et
passim* to 1851 *Census*, *Wellogayt* 1540 *GrimsCB iii*, –*gate* 1595
GrimsFC, *Wellagate* c.1600 *GrimsMap (PRO)*, 'the road to
Wellow *supra*' *v.* **gata**. WELHOWSTOKELANE (lost), 1471
GrimsCB i, cf. *Wellowestokes* 1394 *GrimsChamb*, *wellow stocke*
1576 *ib*, – *stock* 1570, 1573 *ib*, the meaning of *stoke*, etc. here is
uncertain. WELLOW MILL LANE (lost), *Wellow mill layne* c.1634
Terrier, – *Mill Lane* 1692 *GrimsCLeet*, 1762, 1788 *Terrier*,
self–explanatory. WESTGATE (lost), *Westgate* 13 AD ii, 13 AD vi,
self–explanatory, *v.* **west**, **gata**. WESTLANDS AVENUE, cf.
Westland Corner 1851 *Census*. WEST MARSH LANE (lost), 1712
GrimsCLeet, 1797 *GrimsCB xiv*, 1851 *Census*, *west marsh laine*
1672 *GrimsCLeet*, *West Marsh* – 1679 *GrimsChamb*, – *lane* 1699
GrimsCLeet, cf. West Marsh *supra*. WEST ST., – *S.* 1801
GrimsMap. WHITE HALL YARD (lost), 1851 *Census*. WHITGIFT
WAY, – *St.* 1851 *ib*, named from the surn. *Whitgift*, cf. Henry
Whyttgyft 1539 *GrimsBCB*. WOOD ST., – *St.* 1851 *Census*.
WORSLEY ST., 1851 *ib*; as Dr Rod Ambler points out this must

have Yarborough connections, for the title of the eldest son is Lord *Worsley*.

YARBOROUGH DRIVE, cf. *Yarbro' terrace* 1826, 1842 White, *Yarborough* – 1849 Hagar, cf. *Yarborough Top* 1851 *Census* named from the Earls of *Yarborough*, landowners in the borough.

CHURCHES, HOSPITALS & OTHER RELIGIOUS HOUSES

Note: The names in this section are those alluding to the dedication of a church, hospital, &c. The names of chantries and friaries have already been included among the Major Names *supra*.

ST ANDREW (lost), "the king's hermitage of St. Andrew" 1342 Pat, *Ecclesiam sci Andree* 1492 *GrimsExtent*, *Eccl'iam s'c'i Andree* 1491 *Surv*, situated a little to the north of St Leonard's Priory. It was a chapel formerly served by a hermit, *v*. Gillett 1 and 76.

ST JAMES, *ecclesiam Sancti Jacobi* 1155–58 (1334) Ch, 1226–28 Fees, *ecclesia S. Jacobi* 1209 LAHW, *ecclesie Sancti Jacobi* 1226 Welles, *ecclesia* – 1251 (m13) NCot, 1291 Tax, *Grimesby Sancti Iacoby* 1254 ValNor, *ecclesiam Sancti Jac'* 1275 RH, *ecclesie S. Jacobi* 1307 Austin, – *Sancti Jacobi* 1344 *GrimsCB i*, 1420 *GrimsCt*, – (*in Denesgate*) 1441 *GrimsChamb*, 1477, 1500 *GrimsCB i*, 1516 *ib ii*, *ecclesia sancti Iacobi* 1381 Peace *et passim* to 1543 *GrimsExtent*, *Saynt james kirke* 1481 *GrimsCB i*, *Sant Jamys church* (sic) 1524 *ib*, *Saynt James* 1565 *GrimsCLeet*, *templam Scte Jacobi* 1557–78 *GrimsFC*, *St James Churche* 1582, e17 *GrimsCLeet*, – *Church* 1658 HollesM *et passim*, for details *v*. Gillett 82–84. The 1481 form in *kirke* is worthy of note.

ST LEONARD'S PRIORY (lost), *conventum de Grinnesby* (sic) 1239–40 RRG, "the church of St. Leonard without" *Grimmesby* 1258 Ch, *Sancti Leonardi extra Grimesby* 1297 RSu, "prioress & nuns of St. Leonard's" 1313 Pat, *priorissa sancti leonardi* 1405

GrimsCt, "prioress and convent of" *Grymmesby* 1406 Pat, *domus sancti Leonardi iuxta Grymesby* 1401 RRep, *capella* – 1409 ib, *priorissa Sancti leonardi de Grymesby* 1416 *GrimsCt, the pwre* [i.e. poor] *hows of nownys of Grymysby* 1474–80 HMCRep, *priorisse monial' sci leonardi iuxta Grymesby* 1490 *GrimsCB i, the monialium Sancti leonardi* 1515 *ib, domum . . . S'ti leonardi de Grymesbie* 1540 *AOMB 212, moniales Sci leonardi* 1543 *GrimsExtent*; it was situated where Grimsby College is and for details *v.* Gillett 75–76.

St Mary (lost), *ecclesia beate Marie* c.1240 IB, – *Beate Marie* 1291 Tax, 1428 FA, "church of St. Mary" 1241, 1253, 1262, 1277, 1305, 1356 Pat, *ecclesiam sancte Marie* 1244–45 RRG, – *Beate Mar'* 1275 RH, *B. Marie* 1263, 1270 RRGr, *Grimesby S. Marie* 1279 ib, *ecclesie sanct Marie* 1424 *GrimsCt, Ecclesia b'te marie* 1492 *GrimsExtent, ecclesie beate marie* 1493, 1500 *GrimsCB i, Grymysby Marie* 1526 Sub, *Saynt Marysse* 1491 HMCRep, *Seint Mary Churche* 1510 *GrimsCB i, Seyntt Marie Kyrke* 1537 *GrimsCLeet, sanct mare churche* 1547 *ib, Sant Mar. churche* 1579 *Terrier, ecclesie parochis beate marie* 1586 *AddReg i, the parsonage of S' marie* 1588 *GrimsCLeet*; the 1537 form in *Kyrke* is worthy of note. The exact date of the demolition of St Mary is unknown, but the two parishes of St Mary and St James were consolidated in 1586, *v. AddReg i*, f. 71. The former gave its name to St Mary Gate *supra* and its Church Yard was still being referred to in the 19th century, *v. Old Church Yard supra*.

St Mary Magdalene and St Leger Hospital (lost), *leprosurum Sancte Marie Magdalene* 1291 RSu, *lepresorum hospit' sancte mar' magd' extra Grimesby* 1330 *BReg iii*, "the hospital of St. Mary Magdalene and St. Leger" 1315 Pat, "the hospital of St. Mary Magdalene" 1335 ib, *ste mare magdalane* 1370 *GrimsCt, Hospitalis beate Marie Magdalene extra barras ville de Grymesby* 1469, 1476 *GrimsCB i, hospital beate marie magdal' extra barr' de Grymesby* 1495 *ib, le Spitell* 1394 *GrimsCt, del Spitell* 1396 *ib* (p), *Hospitall'* 1403 *ib, Hospit' marie magdalene* 1441 *GrimsChamb*, *(the) Spyttle howse* 1469 *GrimsCB*

i, *–howse* 1476, 1495 *ib*, *– house* 1568 *GrimsCB iv*, *Spitilhous*
1512–13 *GrimsBCB*, *Spittilhouse* 1514–15 *ib*, *ye Spytylhows* 1519
GrimsCB ii, *the Spetylhouse* 1521 *ib*, *one Hospitall or Spyttell*
hows 1542 *ib iii*, *the Spittle howse* 1577 *Terrier*, *hospitall or*
spyttyll howse of Mary Magdaline 1585 *GrimsLeases*, *the Spitle*
house 1630 AASR xl, *Spittlehouse* 1634 *GrimsCLeet*, *–howse*
1646, 1648 *GrimsCG viii*, *v*. **spitel** 'a hospital'; cf. *Spital Lane*
supra. It was situated "on the south side of the town and on the
west side of Bargate", Gillett 80.

WELLOW ABBEY (lost), *locum ubi sita est abbatia, qui dicitur*
Welhou 1155–58 (1334) Ch, "church of Wellow" Hy2 (1460) Pat,
abbatem & conuentum de Grimesbi 1193 Dane; the abbey is very
frequently referred to as "of Wellow" less so "of Grimsby"; for
early spellings of the former, *v*. Wellow *supra*. The Augustinian
abbey was dedicated to St Olaf and St Augustine and for details,
v. Gillett particularly 69–75.

INNS, PUBLIC HOUSES & HOTELS

THE ANCHOR (lost), *the Sign of the Anchor heretofore the Sign of*
the Ship 1731 *T'dE*. BLACK SWAN (lost), 1842 White, 1849
Hagar; it was in Flottergate. BLUE BELL (lost), 1842 White, 1849
Hagar; it was in Loft St. BRITANNIA (lost), *– Public* (sic) 1851
Census. THE BULL (lost), *vnum tav' le bull* 1545 *GrimsCB iii;* this
is the earliest named tavern so far noted in the borough. THE BULL
AND SUN (lost), *a Public House in the East Marsh called –* 1809
ib xiv. CARRIERS' ARMS (lost), 1842 White. CROWN AND ANCHOR
(lost), 1842 ib, 1849 Hagar; it was in Silver St. DUKE OF
WELLINGTON, *Duke of Well Inn* (sic) 1851 *Census*. DUKE OF
YORK (lost), 1842 White, 1849 Hagar; it was in Lower Burgess
St. FLEECE (lost), 1842 White, 1849 Hagar; it was in Loft St.
FOUNTAIN INN, *Fountain* 1842 White, 1849 Hagar. THE GRANBY
INN, *Granby Inn* 1795 *GrimsCB xiv*, 1815 *Dixon*, 1831 *GrimsCB*
xiv, 1843 *Nelthorpe*, *– Hotel* 1852 *Census*; public meetings were
held at the Granby in the late 18th century, *v*. also *Turret Hall*

supra. GRANTS ARMS (lost), 1851 *Census*. GREYHOUND (lost), 1842 White, 1849 Hagar; it was in Baxtergate. HAVELOCK ARMS (lost), 1851 *Census*. HONEST LAWYER (lost), 1851 *ib*; Dr Ambler points out that this name has been reused for a modern public house in Ladysmith Rd. HOPE AND ANCHOR, 1842 White, 1849 Hagar. HUMBER HOTEL, 1842 White, 1849 Hagar, 1851 *Census*. JOLLY SAILORS' (lost), 1842 White, – *Sailors* 1849 Hagar. KENT ARMS, 1851 *Census*. OLD KING'S HEAD, 1851 *ib*, *King's Head* 1842 White, 1849 Hagar. LEEDS ARMS (lost), 1842 White, *Leeds'* – 1849 Hagar. LONDON TAVERN (lost), 1842 White, 1849 Hagar. LORD NELSON (lost), 1849 *ib*; it was in Loft St. MARINERS' TAVERN (lost), 1842 White, 1849 Hagar; it was in Loft St. MASON'S ARMS (lost), 1851 *Census*; it was in Silver St. QUEEN'S HEAD, *The Queen's Head Public Ho* 1798 *Hill*, *The Queens Head Inn* 1804 *Td'E*, *Queen's Head* 1815 *Dixon*, 1842 White, 1849 Hagar, 1851 *Census*. RED LION (lost), 1842 White, 1849 Hagar; it was in Burgess St. ROSE AND CROWN, 1842 White, 1849 Hagar. ROYAL HOTEL (lost), 1851 *Census*. ROYAL OAK (lost), 1849 Hagar. SARACEN'S HEAD (lost), 1851 *Census*. SHIP HOTEL, *Ship* 1842 White, 1849 Hagar. STAR AND GARTER (lost), 1842 White, 1849 Hagar; it was in Bull Ring Lane. STEAM MILL (lost), 1842 White. STEAM PACKET TAVERN (lost), 1842 White, *Steam Packet* 1849 Hagar; it was in Loft St. THE SWAN (lost), *The Swan Ale House* 1798 *Hill*. TEMPERANCE HOTEL (lost), 1842 White; it was at Lock Hill. WHEATSHEAF, *Wheat Sheaf* 1842 White, 1849 Hagar; it has been relocated to more modern buildings. WHITE HART, 1842 White, 1849 Hagar. YARBOROUGH HOTEL, 1838 *Nelthorpe*, 1851 *Census*, – *Arms* 1842 White, 1849 Hagar; like the Wheatsheaf, this has been relocated to more modern buildings.

FIELD-NAMES AND LOST MINOR NAMES

Forms dated 1239, 1312, 1330, 1389, 1406 are Cl, 1258 Ch; 1272, 1293 *Ass*; 1276 RH; 1284 *HarlCh*; 1297 *GrimsSR*; 13 (13) *Alv*, 13, 1374, 1469 AD; 1322, 1369 *FF*; 1335, 1374, 1436, 1469 Pat; 1372, 1390 Misc; 1373, 1387, 1395 Peace; 1375, 1464,

1467, 1468, 1475 Fine; 1450 *GrimsParlExp*; 1451, 1612
HMCRep; 1480, 1622, 1640, 1670 *GrimsMiscD*; 1491 *Surv*;
1492, 1535 *GrimsExtent*; 1503 Ipm; 1509, 1634, 1639 *GrimsBCB*;
1535–46 *MinAcct*; 1537 *AOMB 209*; 1540 *AOMB 212*; 1552 *MM*;
1579, 1601, 1625, 1634, c.1634, 1662, 1671, 1686, 1690, 1697,
1706, 1718, 1724, 1762, 1788 *Terrier*; c.1600 *GrimsMap* (*PRO*);
1612 *Shaw*; 1615 *MiscDep 161*; 1625 Heneage; 1641 LNQ i; 1658
HollesM; 1678 *Foster*; c.1736 *GrimsLeases*; 1768, 1808, 1837
Heneage; 1792, c.1832 *Yarb*; 1798 *Hill*; c.1820 *GrimsMap*; 1825
LincsD; 1831 *Monson*; 1840 *EnclA*; 1842 *TA*; 1851 *Census*. Forms
with a date followed by +, e.g. 1405+, are *GrimsCt*, those
followed by –, e.g. 1470–, are *GrimsChamb*, those followed by *,
e.g. 1569*, are *GrimsCB*, those followed by x, e.g. 1571x, are
GrimsFC, those followed by =, e.g. 1677=, are *GrimsCLeet* and
those followed by >, e.g. 1615>, are *Td'E*.

(a) Abby Cl 1788 *Heneage*, – head–land 1762, – Headland (*abbay
headland* 1601, *Abby* – 1724, *v.* **hēafod–land** and cf. *the abbey land* 1579,
The Abbey – 1634, *Abby* – 1690), Abbey Leys 1792 (*v.* **lea** (OE **lēah**)
'meadow, pasture' in the pl.; all named from Wellow Abbey *supra*); Bogs
Flg 1792; Bowis's Cl 1788 *Heneage* (named from the family of Richard
Bowis 1777 PRStJ); Brat Green, – Wong 1792 (*v.* **brot** 'a small piece of
land', **grēne**², **vangr** 'a garden, an in–field', as elsewhere in the borough);
Broughton Orchard 1842 (1663=, 1720=, 1722=, named from the family
of Thomas *Broughton nuper de Louth* 1676>, though *Broughton* is an old
family name in Grimsby, cf. Thomas *Broghton* 1470–); But bank 1842 (*the
Butt bank* 1736>, *Butt banks* c.1736, cf. *le buttes* 1405+, *the* – 1546=,
1565=, 1582=, 1590=, probably referring to the archery butts, *v.* **butt**);
Butcher closes 1814+ (*Butchers Closes* 1678=, cf. *Butcher Lane supra*);
Edward Butterwick's Gardens 1788+; Calf Gate 1815* (this is comparable
with *shep–gate* and must be from *calf–gate* denoting pasturage or right of
pasturage for a calf); the Carr 1815* (*v.* **kjarr** 'a bog, a marsh', as
elsewhere in the borough); Chamberlains Ley 1800*, – leys, – Lands 1800>
(*v.* **lea** (OE **lēah**), **land**, belonging to the borough *chamberlains*); Castor
Hole 1792> (the significance is not apparent, though the reference must be
to Caistor or to a family name derived from it); a close called Chapel 1762
(it belonged to *Nuns Fm supra*); Chantry Cl 1765* (*the Chauntre close*
1565=, *chanterie* – 1569*, *ye Chantry* – 1667=), Chantry Field–Lands

1800*, – Lands 1800 > (1735*, *Chauntrelandes* 1547, *Chaunterye landes* 1642*, *the lands belonging to the Chauntery of Grimsby* 1697 >), Chantry Pingle 1802* (*v.* **pingel** 'a small enclosure', as elsewhere in the borough and cf. *Chauntriedayle* 1457 (*v.* **deill** 'a share of land')), *the Chauntrie ground* 1557 =, – *groundes* (*modo pertinen' gramatic' Schole*) 1586x, 1597x; the explanation is given in the 1697 > form, cf. *The Chantry supra*); Clay Pits 1792 > (*Clay pitts* 1670 =, cf. *Clay Pitt Close* 1692 =, *Claypitt* – 1705 =, *Clay Pit* – 1723 =); Coalhouse Yard 1766* ((*le*) *Colehouse–yard* 1685-, 1692, 1695-, – *coale house yard* 1687-, cf. *le Coale yard* 1682- and *unum domum vocat'a Coole House* 1566*); the common 1799*, Grimsby Common 1806*, the Commons 1840 (*the comons* 1537 =, *the Comon* 1660 =, cf. *the commown felld* 1555 =, – *comenfeldes* 1588 =); Cook's Green 1764 >, Cooks – 1794 > (1692 >, 1710 >, *Cookes Greene* 1685 >, *Cooks green* 1719 >, named from the family of Robert *Cowk* 1547 =, Paul *Cooke* 1621 *Inv*); Cow Cl 1792 >, c.1820, 1840 (*Cowe close* 1540); Cradle Bridge Wong 1792 > (*v.* **vangr**); Cross Drain 1799*; Cross Mires 1792 >; Deadman Flg 1792 (cf. *Dedemansheuedland* 1374 HMCRep, –*maneshedeland* 1457, self–explanatory, *v.* **dede–mann, hēafod–land**); the desmesne flg 1792 > (cf. *the demeyn landes* 1524*); Dolphin c.1820 (appears to be the name of a marker in the channel from the sea); Dove Coat Cl 1798, – Cot Cl 1842 (*dovecotclose* 1528x, *Doue coate Close* 1672 =, *duffcoat* – 1685 =, *dufcoate close* 1693 =, *Dovecoate Close* 1720 =, *Dufcoat Cloas* 1746 =, self–explanatory); Duckhole 1792 >; East–end Closes 1811*, East end Closes 1825, 1832*, – End Closes 1835*; (the) East Field 1762, 1788, 1792 >, 1840 ("the east field" 1374 HMCRep, *the east felde* 1579, – *feild* 1601, – *East feild* 1662, – *Feild* 1686, 1697, *East Field* 1724, *Grimsby East Feild* 1731 > (*v.* **ēast, feld**; one of the open fields of the borough); the eight acres wong 1792 > (*v.* **vangr**); Epsom Cl 1788 *Heneage*; the fallow field 1787*, – Fallow Field 1814*, 1816* (*le fallow feild* 1634, *the falow* – 1735 =, self–explanatory); Wet and fat pasture 1777* (*Fatt pasture* c.1581 +, *fatte* – c.1600, *Fatt*– 1612, *fat* – 1645*, 1687-, *fatt* – 1670-, 1689 =, *Fatt* – 1727*, *Fat pasture commonly called Twelveman's Goose gates* 1710 >, self–explanatory and *v.* Wet and fat pasture in f.ns. (a) *infra* and *Goosegates supra*); the five and twenty lands flg 1792 > (a consolidated holding of twenty–five selions, *v.* **land**); Fox Cl 1798, c.1820, 1842; Fox Tail 1798 (Mr John Field draws attention to the use of *foxtail* as the name of a plant, one of various species of grass with soft brush–like spikes of flowers, especially *Aopecurus spp*, at least one of which is a serious pest on arable land); the Fryars' Cl 1792 > (*the Close next the Friers* 1672 =, cf. *a* *place . . . called the Fryers Lands* 1724>, *Fower leys called . . . the Fryers leys* c.1600 *Dep*, *v.* **lea** (OE **lēah**) in the pl.; named from the *Grey Friars supra*); Gallows Gutter 1792> (1720=, 1723=, - *Guttor* 1746=, *v.* **goter** 'a gutter'); Gallows Hill 1788*, 1805* (self-explanatory); Glebe Wong 1792> (*v.* **vangr**); Gold Garths 1792> (*Goldgarthe* 1491, 1543, *vno crofto vocat gold garthe* 1492, *goldyn garthis* (sic) 1527*, *Gould Garthes* 1627=, - *Garths* 1723=, *Gollgarth* Eliz+, *Goulegarthes* 1628=, - *Garthes* 1633=, 1673=, 1682=, -*garths* 1653=, - *Garths* 1673*, *Goulgarthes* 1639*, 1662=, -*gars* (sic) 1696=, *the Gowlgarthes* 1656*, *Gowlgarths* 1698=, *le Goole garthes* 1684=, *Goldgarrs* 1688=, - *gare* 1697=, - *garthe* 1707=, - *garths* 1720=, probably 'the enclosures where gold flowers grow', *v.* **golde, garðr**; the first el. appears to have been later confused with **goule** 'a ditch, a stream, a channel'); Grimsby Field 1831, 1851 (*campo de Grymesby* 1374, 1426, *campis de* - 1465*, *y^e felde* c.1600, *Grimsbye Feild* 1665=, self-explanatory); the Grip(s) 1792 (from ME **grip(e)** 'a ditch, a drain'); Gutter wong 1792 (*v.* **goter, vangr**); the furlong being headland & fellow 1792 (*v.* **hēafod-land** 'a strip of land on which the plough is turned'; *fellow* is no doubt used in the sense 'a counterpart, a match', *v.* NED s.v. 4b; cf. *the headland and his fellow* PN L **2**, 12); Hell Parlour furlong 1791 (no doubt a derogatory nickname); High-cross mires wong 1792; the High Field 1792 (*the high felldes* 1547=, *in alto campo* 1582=, self-explanatory); Humphrey Walk 1792 (named from the family of John *Humphry* 1754 *GrimsLeases* and **walk** 'a stretch of land used for pasturing sheep', common in L); Ings's (sic) 1797* (*la Inges* 1425+, cf. *the inges dike* e17=, *v.* **eng** 'meadow, pasture', as elsewhere in the borough); Ings Meadow 1788 *Heneage*, 1797* (cf. preceding); Kings Close Corner, - Wong 1792 (cf. *Kings leas* 1642*, *v.* **vangr, lea** (OE **lēah**) in the pl.); the Knowles 1792 (*v.* **cnoll**); Langleys wong 1792 (named from a long-established Grimsby family, cf. Thomas *langley* 1570 *Inv*, Maria *Langley* 1639* and **vangr**); Leak Hill 1792; Little Cl 1798, 1842 (*little Close* a1600=, *the Little Closes* 1719>); Long Furlong 1792; Long Ings 1792 (1706, 1732*, cf. Ings's *supra*); Long Marfur, Marfers 1792 (*v.* **marfur** 'a boundary furrow'); the Long Marsh 1812*; Thos Lusby's Marsh 1754* (*Lusby* is a common Grimsby name); Markham Hill 1805* (*Markham* is a well-established local surn., cf. William *Markham* 1441-); Marsh Cross Ditch 1799*; the Mere Gate 1792 (cf. *the mere* 1579, *v.* **(ge)mǣre** 'a boundary, land on a boundary', **gata** 'a road, a way'); Mile Stone Wong 1792 (*v.* **vangr**); the North End 1792; (the) North Field 1792, 1800*, c.1832, 1840; North Ings 1792 *v.* **eng**); Nuns Acre Wong 1792 (*v.* **vangr**), Nuns Cl 1762, Nun's -

1788 (*nonnes close* Eliz+, *the Nunnes close* 1625, 1634, 1662, – *Nunns Close* 1672=, 1686, 1706, 1724, *Nuns* – 1718, *Nunns fould* 1634= (v. **fald** 'a fold'), *y^e nonnes groundes* 1579, *the nunes headland* 1579, *nonns* – 1601, *the Nunnes* – 1634, 1662, *the Nuns Headland* 1697, – *headland* 1724, *Nuns head land* 1762 (v. **hēafod–land**), *Nunnsmyln'* 1397+ (v. **myln**), *the Nunns yard* 1707=, all named from the nuns of St. Leonard's Priory *supra; v.* also Nuns Corner *supra*); Panny Bottom (sic) 1792; Panton furlong 1792 (cf. *Panton marsh* 1677=, named from the family of Richard *Paunton* 1557 *Inv*); Paul Green furlong 1792 (named from an old Grimsby family, cf. William *de Paule de Grymesby* 1374x); Peacock Dale, – Green, – Wong 1792 (cf. *Pecoke furlonge* 1540, named from the family of Peter *Paicocke* 1563*); the Penny platts 1765–6*, Penny Plats 1794*, 1797*, 1812*, c.1820, c.1832, – Plots 1840 (*Penyplat* 1425+, *Penneplattes* 1523–, *le penyplattes* 1525–, *(the) penny plattes* 1537= *et freq* to 1585–, *penny playtts* 1546–, – *playttes* 1547=, –*plates* c.1600, *peny plattes* 1601*, *pennie plats* 1634, *Penney Platts* 1670=, *penny plats* 1676–, *Penny Platts* 1689–, *v.* **plat**[2] 'a plot, a small piece of ground'; *penny* presumably refers to the rent); Pinder Mere 1792 (*v.* (ge)**mǣre**), The Pindars Grass 1815* (cf. *Pinder Marfer* c.1634, – *Marfar* 1706, *v.* **marfur**; named from the borough *pinder*); Pingle(s) 1797* (*the pyngyll* 1555=, *Pingle* 1657x, *pingle* 1720=, *little Pingle* 1657x, 1677*, *y^e little pingle* 1697=, *v.* **pingel** 'a small enclosure'; there are several f.ns. called *Pingle* in the borough); Piper Well 1792; Pitham 1765–6*, 1777*, – Nooking 1792 (*Pytham nooke* 1690=, *Pittam Nooke* 1691=, *Pitham nooke* c.1700=), Great –, Little Pitham Cl 1798, Pitholm c.1820, Pitholmes 1840, Pitholme 1842 (*pittham* (sic) 1425 (m16)*, *Pyttom* 1436, 1441–, –*dyke* 1457, *Pitholme* 1472*, 1478=, 1612, *Pyte–* 1478–, *Pytt–* 1500=, *Pyt–* 1514*, *pit* – 1515–, *pit–* 1527–, *Pitholmes* c.1600, *pyttham* 1540*, *pyttam* 1546–, 1570–, *Pitham* 1556–, 1614x, 1645* *et passim* to 1719>, *Pittam* 1576–, 1639*, 1678=, *Pittham* 1670=, cf. *pittam dike* 1712=; the name is derived from from **pytt** 'a pit, a natural hollow' and **holmr** 'raised ground in marsh', 'river–meadow'; forms in –*ham* etc. for –*holme* are common in north L. The significance of this name is difficult to determine. It is shown on both the c.1600 and c.1820 maps as a small island of land between Little Field and Haycroft); Priest Green 1792 (1706, self–explanatory, *v.* **grēne**[2] 'a grassy spot'); Pudding Poke Nook, – furlong 1792, – Marsh 1812* (*pudding Poak nooke* 1706, a fanciful name for soft, sticky land); S. Rails Cross 1752*; Rainbow Wong 1792 (presumably an in–field (*v.* **vangr**) "ploughed concentrically with a curved boundary" Field 179); Rush Wong 1792 (cf. *Rush Close*); Rye Hill 1792; Sand Hills 1788*, c.1820, East –, West Sand hills 1788 *Heneage*, Sandhills 1792 (*Sandhylls* 1403+, *Sandehills* 1540, *Sand hylls* 1546-, *-hylles* 1566-, *-hilles* 1562-, 1573-, 1582-, *Sande hills* 1576-, *Sand Hill* 1707=, *Sandall* c.1600, self-explanatory, *v.* **sand**, **hyll**; it was situated to the east of Fresh Ings and Salt Ings and is described by Oliver 30 as 600 feet in length by 400 feet broad); Upper Sands Ends 1765* (cf. *futtway to the Sands* 1724=); Scartho Clife Corner 1792, - Corner Furland (sic) 1792, - Furlong (*furland* is a variant of *furlong* in north L), Scarthoe Meer 1762, 1788, Scartho Mere 1792 (*Scarthow mere* 1457, *Scarthoe meere* 1625, 1634, 1662, - *Maire* 1677*, - *Meere* 1686, 1697, *Scartho Meer* 1718, - *Mear* 1724, *Scarthow Mear bank* 1706, 'the boundary with Scartho' (an adjacent parish), *v.* (**ge**)**mǣre**), Scartho Spring Rundle 1792 (*v.* **rynel** 'a runnel, a small stream'); Seven Acres c.1820 (1707=, (*the*) *7 Acres* 1676=, 1679=, *Seaven acres* 1685=, - *Acres* 1724=); Shearman Holme 1798 (*Shermanes Holme* 1684=, named from the family of William *Sherman* 1349+ and **holmr**); Shepherd's House 1762, Shepherds - 1788, Shepherds House Furlong 1792 (named from the family of Robert *Shipperd* 1655 PRStJ); Short Ings 1792 (1732*, *the short ings* 1682=, cf. Ings's *supra*); the short leys 1792 (*v.* **lea** (OE *lēah*) 'meadow, pasture' in the pl.); Mrs Somerscales Farm 1751* (*Somerscailes nooke* 1690=, *Somerscale's Farm* 1732, Ann *Somerscales, widow* is named in the 1751* document and for an earlier member of the same family, cf. Daniel *Somerskales* 1611x); the South End 1792; South Field 1792, 1832, 1840, the South or Weelsby side - 1792, South or South East - 1800> (*the south feld* 1579, self-explanatory); Spital Hill 1792, Spittal Hill 1842 White, Spittle Green 1792 (*Spitill grene* 1540, *Spittle greene* 1703=, cf. *Spytelcroft* 1475 (*v.* **croft**), *Spytelgarth* 1475, *yᵉ spetyll garthes* 1483*, *Spittelhows garth* 1511-12+ (*v.* **garðr** 'an enclosure'), *Spytelhedeland* 1457 (*v.* **hēafod–land**), *Spytelland* 1457, *yᵉ Spittlehouse lands* 1670, 1674>, *Spittle land* 1670-, 1682-, 1695-, 1731 (*v.* **land**), *Spittle Closes* 1670=, - *Close* 1677*, 1681= *et freq* to 1720= (*v.* **clos(e)**) (*v.* **spitel**, **grēne**², all named from the hospital of St. Mary Magdalene and St. Leger *supra*); Standmarsh 1792; Swains Cl 1820* (probably from the surn. *Swain*); Swine garth wong 1792 (*v.* **garðr**, **vangr**); Syke flg 1792 (*v.* **sík** 'a small stream, a ditch, a trench'); Tanners Cl 1798 (1698>, 1719>, probably named from the family of Nicholas *Tanner* 1566 PRStJ); the Tethering Grounds 1823* (it was in the Little Field); Thornhil 1792, - Hill, Thorne - 1823*, (*Thorne hill* p1600=, 17=, self-explanatory); Thorn Tree Marsh 1813*; Three Acres Dale 1792 (*v.* **deill**); Three Corner furlong 1792; the Toll Carr 1817* (*v.* **kjarr**); the Town Well 1789*, Town or Common Well 1794*, 1818* (*coēm fontem* 1573-, *aqua stagna siue fonte* 1583x, *le coēm fontem* 1626=, *Common well* c.1700=, 1705=, *-well* 1720=, cf. *Old Well* 1819*); Tunnel Wong 1792 (*v.* **vangr**, the reference perhaps being to *Wellow Tunnill* in f.ns. (b) *infra*); Tup Flg c.1820; Tupham Flg 1788*, 1794*, Tupholme – 1792, 1840 (*Topeholme* 1540, *tuppam dyk* c.1550=, *Tupholme Dike* 1634=, 1670=, 1712=, 1724=, – *ditch* 1681=, *Tuppum Dike* 1673=, – *dike* 1683=, cf. *Tupholme foreland* 1697=; this is probably identical in origin with Tupholme LSR and means 'the raised ground in marsh where tups are found' *v.* **tup** 'a ram, a tup', **holmr**, with **dík**); Freehold land called the Waste 1808, 1837 (cf. *yᵉ Queens Wast* 1710>); Weelsby Hedge 1792 (the boundary with the adjacent parish of Weelsby); West Cl c.1820 (1687x, 1712=, 1724=; it adjoined Bargates Fm); the West Fld 1762, 1788 *Heneage* (*North west feld, sowth West feld* 1457, *the west Fild* 1560=, – *feild* 1601, 1634, – *Feild* 1686, – *West feild* 1690, self–explanatory); West Mere 1792 (*v.* (**ge**)**mǣre** 'a boundary, land forming a boundary'); West pasture 1754*; the Wet pastures 1766, Wet and fat pasture 1777*, – Pasture 1787*, 1798*, Wet and Fat (sic) 1797*, 1801*, 1811*, 1814 (*wete pasture* c.1581+, *Wett Pasture* c.1600, 1625, *wett pasture* 1670–, 1679–, c.1700=, 1701, *Wett* – 1699=, *wet* – 1645*, *Wetpasture* 1692=, *Wett and fatt pasture* p1600=, – *& Fatt pasture* 1674=, 1677=, – *and fatt pasture* 1681=, 1707=, 1720=, *Wett and Fatt pasture* 1688=, – *& fatt pasture* 1712= (*v.* also Wet and fat pasture *supra* under F; self–explanatory); Wild Goose Flg 1792; Woofers Flg, Woo furrows Wong 1792 (*Wlfo* 1425+, *Wolfowhyll* 1457, *pasture voc' Wolfo* 1468–, *a marshe* . . . *callid Wulfoo* 1471*, *woolfo* c.1581+, *Wolfoes als wolfo(e)* 1612, *Littell Wollfo* c.1600, *litle wolfoe* 1617*, *a Marsh called Woulfo* 1615 (probably 'the spur of land' or 'the mound where wolves are found', *v.* **wulf**, **hōh**, **haugr**. The area is now built up and the topography cannot be seen in detail); Yarborough Green Dale 1792 (named from the Earls of *Yarborough*, prominent land–owners in the borough).

(b) *Addams Close* 1690= (named from the family of William *Addames* 1580 PRStJ); *Akerheued* 1352 (*v. Seeacrehede infra*; note the use of *acrehead* as an appellative in 2 *acrehedes* 1457); *La Almeson hous* 1335 (a house built in the King's highway in which to entertain poor persons coming to the town, from ME *almes(se)–hous*; note also *le almonshouse* (sic) 1516–); *Anderson's house* 1712>, *Andersons House* 1728>, 1730>, – *Workhouse* 1732> (named from the family of Elizabeth *Anderson* 1701>); *ashe close* 1577x; *ayrisdale* 13 (13) (from the ME surn. *Ayr*, cf. Henry *Ayr*, coroner 13 AD vi (*v.* Reaney s.n. *Ayer* (1) and **deill** 'a share of land'); *Baily Close* 1537* (perhaps to be identified with *the bayliffe close* e17=, from ME

bail(l)i, baillif); *the baily croft* 1480 (cf. prec.); *domus . . . voc' a
Barkhowse* 1535–46 (from ME **bark–hous** 'a tannery'); *Bolyngtonland* 1457
(Robert *Bolyngton* is named in the document); *Boothes close*, *– house* 1640
(named from the family of Philip *Booth* 1553 PRStJ); *atte Bothe* 1419, 1423
(p) ('the temporary shelter, shed, etc.', *v.* **bōth**); *Boy Close* 1736*, *Boyland*
1615>, 1673> *et passim* to 1697> (cf. *Boy Lane supra*); *Bradlay feld*
1457, *bradley feld syd* 1579, *Bradley fields side* 1625, *– feildes side* 1634,
– fields side 1662, *– Feild Side* 1686, *– feild Side* 1690, 1697 (referring to
the neighbouring parish of Bradley); *Bradley house* 1666= (named from the
family of Robert *Bradley* 1578 PRStJ); *Brase Close* 1622 (named from the
family of John *Brasse* in the same document); *the brick garth* 1698=,
Brickyard 1705=, *the Brickyarde* 1723> (the interchange of *garth* and *yard*
is noteworthy); *Bristows Close* 1691= (named from the family of Thomas
Bristow 1681 *Inv*); *ter vocat brus land* 1532x (named from the family of
William *Brusse* 1492); *Bull Bank* 1737–; *Caldesyke* 1457 (*v.* **cald, sīk** 'a
ditch, a trench'); *Candelarhedeland* 1457 (from ME **candeler** 'a
candle–maker' or the derived surn. and **hēafod–land**); *Canonenge*, *–land*,
–hedeland 1457 (*v.* **canoun, eng** 'meadow, pasture' and for *Canon*, *v.*
Canonbig supra); *capon furlong* 1601, *Capon furres* 1625, *– furs* c.1634,
Cappon furres 1662, *Capon Furs* 1697, *Cappam Furres* 1634, *– Furrs* 1686,
Cappam–furrs 1690 (*v.* **furlang**, of which *furres* is a common pl. form; the
first el. is probably the surn. *Capon*, for which *v.* Reaney s.n.); *Caterall
thinge* 1576, *Catterall thinge* 1582x (from the surn *Caterall*, cf. Robert
Caterall 1510*, and **þing** 'property, possessions', as elsewhere in the
borough); *Cavething* 1492 (cf. *Caue Close* 1678; from the common Grimsby
surn. *Cave*, cf. Alexander *de Caue* 1297, John *de Caue* 1349x, Robert *Cave*
1590=, Philip *Cave* 1681 PRStJ, and **þing**); *le cheker* 1565*, *– checker*
1569*, 1582– (*v.* **cheker** 'a chequer', which denoted the variegated
appearance of the field); *the Church close* 1677=, *church –* 1696=, *(the)
Church Close* 1705=, 1707=, *ye Church Cloase* 1709=; *y^e Citicke bancke*
1645* (the reading is uncertain); *clayton is putt* 1565*, *Mrs Claytons Green*
1691>, *Claytons –* 1719>, *terras Georgii Clayton* 1691>, *Mrs Claytons
Long Close* 1697> (from an old–established Grimsby family, cf. John
Clayton 1581 *GrimsQR*, with **pytt, grēne²** and **clos(e)**); *Cockhall garth*
1582x; *colby thyng* 1546–, *colbie –* 1559–, 1562–, *– thinge* 1565–, 1576–
(from the surn. *Colby*, cf. Elizabeth *Colby* 1492, and **þing**); *colston pytt*
1546–, 1565*, *coulston pytte* c.1560=, *le Couston pitt* (sic) 1627=, *Coulson
Pit* 1685–, *Coulston's pitt (house)* 1712>, *Coulstons Pitt (house)* 1728>,
Coulsons Pitt House 1730>, *on the said Wast ground a Tenement formerly*

stood which was called Coulsons 1732> (from a long–established Grimsby family, cf. John *Colson'* 1392+, *J. Colson* 1450, Alexander *colston'* 1547*, and **pytt**); *Constable Shoppe* 1570*; *the Covent closess* (sic) c.1581+ (from ME **covent** 'a convent' and **clos(e)**; NED s.v. *convent* points out that the latinized spelling *convent* was introduced c.1550 and by c.1650 superseded the ME form; cf. Covent Garden PN Mx 167); *Coxsey Close* 1663=, *Coxsy* – 1691=, *Cobsey* – 1676=, 1685-, 1691= *et passim* to 1731>, – *close* 1677=, *Copsey Close* 1678= (named from the surn. *Cobsey*, cf. *Cobsey Lane supra*); *Craine house end* 1670= (named from the family of Thomas *Craine* 1576 PRStJ); *cros Lea* 1706; *Crossemare* 1457 (presumably a boundary marked by a cross, *v.* **cros**, **(ge)mære** 'a boundary, land on or marking a boundary'); *Croxby Mede* 1503 (named from the surn. *Croxby*, cf. Thomas *de Croxby* 1368+, and **mæd** 'a meadow'); *Cuthardesdale* 1457 (from the a ME surn. *Cuthhard* and **deill** 'a share or portion of land'); *le dunghill* 1569* (there are numerous reference to *dunghills* in the Borough records, *v.* Gillett 2, 4, 115); *del Dyke* 1327, 1339, 1366x, *Dyke* 1402+, 1403+, *Dike* 1332 all (p) (*v.* **dík**); *Empringhams land* 1642* (named from the family of Peter *Empryngham* 1436 AD, Richard *Emperingham* 1577x); *del Fal* 1276, 1284, 1312 all (p) (obscure); *le fierbeacons* 1585- (self–explanatory and cf. Beacon Hill, PN L **4**, 114–15); *Fishborne Closes* 1689- (presumably named from the surn. *Fishborne*, but none had been noted in the source searched); *Fleetwoods land* 1693x, *–lands* 1699> (named from the family of Thomas *Fleetewood* 1615>); *the forland ingges* 1579 (*forland* is no doubt for *forlang*, cf. *lez Fourlongis* 1540); *foulthomes close* (sic), *Foulthomes* – 1642> (obscure); *frostland* 1402+, *Frost-* 1436 AD (presumably from the surn. *Frost*, but none has been noted in the sources searched); *Fyrsfurlanges* 1457 (*v.* **fyrs** 'furze', **furlang**); *Garratts ground* 1637= (probably from the surn. *Garratt*); *le Garthes* 1537, *the grange and farm called the Garths* 1625 (*v.* **garðr**); *Gibsons garth* 1625 (named from the family of John *Gibson* 1591 *Inv* and **garðr**); *Graynesbyland* 1457 (John *Granesby* is named in the document); *Gresynges* 1465- (probably 'the grass meadows, pastures', *v.* **gærs**, **eng**); *Grymsbye close* 1640, *Grimsbye Close* 1665=, *Grimsby* – 1670=; *Grymesbygare* 1457 (*v.* **geiri** 'a triangular plot of land'); *grymesbie headland* 1579, *the headland of Grymsbye* 1601, *Grimesbie headland* 1625, 1634, *Grimsby* – 1662, 1690, – *head Land* 1706 (*v.* **hēafod–land** 'the head of a strip of land used for turning the plough'); *Grymsby Orchyard* 1714>, *le orchard* 1683-, *the Orchard* 1731>; *Grymesbysyke* 1457 (*v.* **sík** 'a ditch, a trench'); *Grymesdale* 1457 (probably from the family of Walter *Gryme* 1400+ and **deill** 'a share of

land'); *Guevares howses* 1678, 1685 (from the *Guevere* family, John
Guavary 1593 PRStJ; the houses were in Moody Lane and cf. *Robt Kitchine
& M' Guevara howses are chosen Baley howses for this year followinge*
1649*; *messuagio vocato Halshamplace* 1395x (named from the family of
Peter *de Alsham de Grimsby* 1358x and **place** 'a plot of ground, a
residence'); *Harpum care* (sic) p1600= (named from the surn. *Harpham*, cf.
Ann *Harpam* 1618 PRStJ, and **kjarr**); *harsies close* c.1600 (the first el. is
presumably a surn. derived from the OE pers.n. *Heresige*); *a close of John
Hatcliffes* 1625, *Hatcliffes close* 1634, 1668, 1690 (self-explanatory);
Heldecroft 1492 (perhaps 'the croft on the slope', *v.* **helde**, **croft**); *Henneage
Close* 1699 (the *Heneage* family were landowners in Grimsby and were
long-established there, cf. John *Henege* 1521*); *Hill Close* 1664=, 1720=,
1724= (probably from the surn. *Hill*, cf. *Widdow Hill* 1666= and *otthe Hill*
1427+ (p)); *the hirn'* 1450 (p) (*v.* **hyrne** 'a corner of land, etc.');
Hokkescrofte 1537, *Hocks Croft* 1625 (the first el. is perhaps a side-form of
the surn. *Hook* with early shortening, the second being **croft**); *home Closes*
1720= (self-explanatory); *hor closes* (sic) c.1600 (obscure); *Howfildes* 1457
(probably from **haugr** 'a mound' and **feld**); *humberstone thinge* 1566-,
Humberstone – 1574-, – Thinge 1576- (from the surn. *Humberstone*, cf.
John *Humberston* 1552 PRStJ and **þing**); *Hylfurlanges* 1457 (*v.* **hyll**,
furlang); *Jug close* 1540 (perhaps named from the shape of the field);
kageler thyng 1546-, *kakley – 1559-, kaklay – 1562-, Kakley thinge* 1566-,
1569-, 1570- (the first el. is perhaps a byname based on ME *cakeler*
'chatterer', with **þing** 'possession, property', as suggested by Dr Insley);
molendino de Kaldehal' quod pertinet ad manerium de Grimesby 1239
(perhaps 'the cold nook of land', *v.* **cald**, **halh**); *Kalkerthorp' iuxta magnam
Grymesby, Calker-, Carkel-* 1293 (*v.* **þorp** 'a dependent outlying farmstead
or hamlet'; the first el. is obscure); *Kircross Furlanges* 1457 (the first part
of this name is probably 'the church cross', *v.* **kirkja**, **cros**); *le Kyllett wood,
le Kyllette woodes* 1566* (obscure); *Lang gairs* 1659= (*v.* **lang**, **geiri** 'a
triangular plot of land'); *litle Coates sike* 1634, *Little Coates* 1686, *little
Coats Sike* 1690 (from the adjacent parish of Little Coates with **sík**); *lytill
croft* 1481* (self-explanatory); *Loyds Close* 1712= (cf. *M' Lloyd* 1692=);
long Close 1670-, 1676-, 1687-, 1693=, 1697>, *y^e – 1690=, (the) Long
Close* 1691>, 1725= *et passim* to c.1736, *The long Close (which heretofore
had belonged to The Chantry)* 1691*, *Ms Susanna Claytons Long Close*
1731> (it was in *Newbigging*); *unum croft' voc' lyas close* 1521* (perhaps
from ME *lias* 'a bluish limestone rock, lias' with **clos(e)**); *Mathewland* 1457
(no doubt from the surn. *Mathew* and **land**); *le milnecroft* 1392+, *– myln*

croft 1492 (self-explanatory); *Morleys Close* 1720=, *Morley* - 1722=, *Morleys Marsh* 1694-, 1695 (from the Morley family, cf. *M^rs; Morley* (sic) 1692=); *Mustelowe thynge* 1576, *Mustlow thing* 1731 > (no trace has been found of the *Mustlow* family; *v.* also þing); *Mydby* 1404+ (p) (the form is late, but this may be compared with Midby, PN L 2,19 for which it was suggested that it may be a partial anglicization of Scand. **miðr í bȳ** literally 'middle in the village', comparable to *Northiby infra*); *Newarks Close* 1696=, *Newarkes Pingle* 1707= (named from the *Newark* family, cf. William *Newark* 1692=, with **clos(e)** and **pingel**); *New Brigg or Clow* 1703*, *y^e New Bridge Haven* 1710 > (for *clow*, *v.* PN L, **4** xv, where it is pointed out that the meaning is 'a dam for water', 'a sluice or floodgate', *v.* NED s.v. *clow* sb. 1a); *Newe close* 1540; *the new Goate* 1709 > (*v.* **gotu** used in L of 'a sluice', as Mr Arthur Owen has pointed out); *all ye tementes* (sic) *in yis town called new purches* 1484* (self-explanatory); *Northiby* 1492 (p) (literally 'north in the village' from Scand. **norð í bȳ**, cf. *Mydby supra*); *Ogles Yard* 1727 > (named from the *Ogle* family, long-established in the borough, cf. Philip *Ogle* 1393+); *le oister pittes* 1585 (from ME *oistre* 'an oyster' and **pytt**); "a garden called" *Osyergarth* 1469 ('the enclosure where osier willows grow', from ME *osier* and **garðr**); *Oxe close* 1540; *The Parsonage close* 1634, - *Close* 1686, 1690; *Petches Close* 1691- (named from the family of Thomas *Peche* 1517*); *peddemilme* 1396+, *Pedmulln'* 1397+, *-mylne* 1404+, 1405= (the mill is named after the family of *Galf' Pedd* 1371+); *peueryll house* 1507* (from the surn. *Peverel*, cf. William *peuerell* 1511*); *pickridge Close* 1662* (the reading is doubtful); *the Pittles* 1625 (apparently from ME **pightel** 'a small enclosure, a croft', but the nasalized form **pingel** is normally found in L); *le pittes extra brighogait'* 1524* (*v.* **pytt**); *Potters yard* 1694*, *ye potters yard* 1705=, *Potters Yard* 1707=, 1709 >, *potters yard* 1720= (probably self-explanatory, but note that the surn. *Potter* is found in the borough, cf. Robert *Potter* 1691 PRStJ); *Procters Close* 1676= (*Mr Procter* is mentioned in the same document); *Pykerdales* 1425+ (*v.* **deill** in the pl.; the first el. is ME *pīker(e)*, *picker* 'a thief' used as a byname or surn.); *Pyland, -hedeland* 1457 (from the surn. *Pye*, on which *v.* Gillett Index, with **land** and **hēafod-land**); *Ringes Leas* 1677 (from the surn. *Ring*, cf. William *Ring* named later in the same document, and **lea** (OE **lēah**) 'meadow, pasture' in the pl.); *super Rodes* 1457 (presumably from OE **rōd** 'a rood of land' in the pl.); *placea terr' vast vocat Ros pog iuxta symwhit bryg* 1546-, *ter' vast' voc' Rose Poge* 1556-, *plac' terr' voc' Roes pogge* 1562-, *placea terr' vocat Rose pogge* 1566-, 1570-, *plac' terr' voc' Rose Pog* 1581x and cf. *Pogrounde* 1452 Gillett (named from *Rosa Pogge* 1403+, *Rose Poge* 1465-, - *pogge* 1468-, the family having been noted as early as John *Pog'* 1390-); *Russling Close* 1720=; *le Ryndell* 1457 (*v.* **rynel** 'a runnel, a small stream'); *Ryngstake thyng* 1515* (no doubt from the surn. *Ringstake* and **þing**, but no member of the family has been noted in the sources searched); *Saltcotes* 1500-, 1515-, -*cottes* 1527-, cf. *le saltcootes hyllis* 1528- (*v.* **salt, cot** 'a hut, a shed', for use in salt-making; it was in the East Marsh); *le Salt marche* (sic) 1520*, *the salt marshes* 1645* (self-explanatory); *Sandholme* c.1550= (*v.* **sand, holmr**); *Sandou* 1335, *Sandehowe* 1372, 1375 Orig, 1375, *Sand-* 1373 IpmR, 1477*, 1537, -*how* 1625, *Sandow* 1692-, 1695-, 1700=, *Sandy* 1681-, 1687-, 1690=, 1702=, 1721=, *Sandye* 1697=, *Sanday* 1670-, 1679-, 1707=, 1720=, 1722=, *Sandey* 1722=, cf. - *nooke* 1694= ('the sand mound, hill' *v.* **sand, haugr**; Watson 8 states "a mound (Abbey Hill) with a spring or well at the foot was called 'Well-hoe' and not far away a sand hill received the descriptive name 'Sand-hoe.'"); *le Sandput* 1393- (*v.* **sand, pytt**); *Seeacrehede, -enge, -hedeland, Seland* 1457, *See close* 1565, - *Close* 1576-, *Sees close* 1569-, 1573- (named from the *del See* family, on which *v.* Gillett Index; *v.* also **eng, hēafod-land, land** and **clos(e)**; *acre-head* is not found in dictionaries, but must represent a ME ***aker-hede** denoting a headland in the (common) field, cf. *Akerheued* in f.ns. (b) *supra*); *the shepe closse* 1607*, (*the*) *Sheepe Close* 1660=, 1670-, 1679*, 1689=, 1720*, 1724*, *Sheep* - 1682-, 1693=, 1697=, 1705=, 1711=, 1722= (self-explanatory); *Sheep house* 1706, 1718; *les Sheldecoft* (sic) 1491, *lee* - (sic) 1492, *Sheylld-* 1543, *Scheld'* - 1546-, *a Close called Sheldeclose* 1510*, *Shiele close* 1565-, *Sheld* - 1573-, *Shielde* - 1576-, *shilde-* 1582-, *Scheldes* - 1585-, *unum claus' vocat' Sheildes* - 1590= (the first el. is uncertain, but could be **sceld** 'a shield, protection', used in p.ns. of 'a shelter', **sceldu** 'a shallow place', or the ME surn. *Sheld*, with **croft** which appears to have been replaced in the 16th century by **clos(e)**. It was situated next to St. Mary's church); *sheryff crofte* 1559-, *Shiriff Close* 1577x, *Sheriff close* 1580x (*v.* **croft** and **clos(e)** named from the *Sheriff* family, cf. Robert *Sheryff* 1417-, 1477*); *Shyllgarthe* 1543 (the first el. is obscure; *v.* **garðr**); *Shoppe Close* 1689= (cf. *le Cornershop'* 1417-); *Silver buton Close* 1722= (obscure); *Simson's Close* 1700-14=, *Sympsons shop* 1650>, 1709*, 1712>, *Simpsons* - 1730>, - *Shop* 1732> (named from the family of William *Symson* 1545*); *aquares vocat sinkers* 1576x, *sinckers* 1588x, *the Sinks*, y^e *Sink* 1692=, y^f *Sinks* 1693=, 1712=, *Synks* 1698=, *the Sinkes* 1707=, (*the*) *Sincks* 1713=, 1722= (from dial. *sink* and *sinker*, both recorded in NED of a conduit, drain, sewer and a cesspool or drain respectively. The two were clearly used interchangeably as references from *GrimsCLeet* suggest, cf. the appellative use in *synkes Ryndylls or Sewers* 1555 and *any synkers and Rundelle* 1565); *Six Acres Close commonly called Alderman Swangates* 1702 >, *Six acres Closes called Alderman's Swangates* 1710 > (cf. *Aldermens Swangate* 1716 and *v. Swangates* in f.ns. (b) *infra*); *Slefordgrounde* 1441- (presumably named from the surn. *Sleford* though none has been noted in the sources searched); *Snaythland* 1424- (presumably from the surn. *Snayth* and **land**); *M. Somerfoules Close* c.1700 (*M*ʳ. *Somerfoule* is named in the same document); *Somertemyng* 1394-, *-ynges* 1403+, *Sumertymyng* 1513-, *- iuxta portum maris* 1515- ('the meadow(s), pasture(s) only used in summer-time', from ME *somer-tyme* and **eng**, a name unique in this survey); *le Spowte* 1569* (*v.* **spoute** 'a spout, a gutter'; it is described as being *ad finem borial' pastur'*); *Spring garthe* c.1506=, *the sprynge garth* 1565=, *-garthe* 1585x, *(the) springarthe* 1587=, 1587x, *Springarth* 1591x (perhaps 'the enclosure by the copse' rather than 'by the spring', *v.* **spring, garðr**); *M*ʳ. *Spurrs Shop* 1719 > (from a member of the family of Helen *Spur* 1601 PRStJ); *Stallings* 1540; *Mydel-, North-, Sowthstaynmare* 1457, *Mydle -, northe -, South Stannemers* 1540 ('the stony boundary, land on or forming a boundary', *v.* **steinn, (ge)mǽre**; this may be the same as Standmarsh in f.ns. (a) *supra*); *starcroft* 1645* (perhaps from **star** 'sedge' and **croft**); *the slooks* (sic) 1707=, *the stocks* 1720= (the two refs. are to the same place); *a place now called by the name of the Stone Stairs* 1709 > (they were used for taking water out of the Haven for brewing); *the Stuble Feilde* 1671=, *le Stuble feild* 1684=, *Stubble -* 1707= (self-explanatory); *Swangates* 1692- (cf. *Six Acres Close commonly called Alderman Swangates supra*. The compound *swan-gate* has only been noted in the survey in Grimsby, but it was presumably formed on the analogy of the common L **shep-gate** and therefore denotes a pasture, pasturage for a swan, in each instance so far noted in the pl., cf. *Goosegates supra*); *Swanland* 1692-; *(le) Sykehouses* 1566* *v.* **sík** 'a small stream, a ditch', **hūs** in the pl.); *takelhouse Close* 1665=, *(le) great Tackle house Close* 1687x, 1687 >, *the Great tackle house Close* 1719 >, *Great Takell Close* 1696= (named from a long-standing Grimsby family, cf. John *Takyll'* 1397+); *Talbet house* 1684= (named from the family of William *Talbotte* 1570 *Inv*); *Molend' de Templar* 1492 (self-explanatory); *Tharrold Close* 1662 (from an important Grimsby family, cf. Robert *Thorhald'* 1509); *Therlyngland* 1401+ (the reading is uncertain); *Thimelbie close* 1568* (from the surn. *Thimbleby* cf. Richard *Thymolby* 1520*); *litill thorndall* 1527- (*v.* **þorn, deill** 'a share, a portion of land'); *Thorne Close* 1615; *Mrs Todds Pingle* 1662*, *Todds*

Close 1692–, 1707=, 1711= (from the surn. *Todd*, cf. Nicholas *Todd* 1607 PRStJ, with **pingel** and **clos(e)**)); *le Tollehilles* 1464, *Lez* – 1468, 1475, *tolehyll* 1500–, *Tolehil(l)s* 1513–, 1518*, *toll hyll* 1546–, *le tolhilles* 1559–, *Tulehilles* 1480, *Crofto vocat' Tulehyll* 1491, *–hill* 1492, *tulehyll'* 1543, *Tulehilles* 1570–, *– hilles* 1572–, *–hils* 1576–, *Tulie hilles* 1582–, *tulihilles* 1585–, *Tully Hills* 1670– *et passim* to 1719> (Dr Insley suggests that this is a compound of the ODan pers.n. *Tōli* and **hyll** in the pl., the place being descibed as *monte molendin' ventritic'* 1566–. He comments that there has no doubt been association of the first el. with the common noun *toll* as a result of popular etymology, and points out that the *–u–* spellings reflect the raising of ME [o:] > [u:] in the first stage of the Great Vowel Shift); *the Towne bridge* 1641; *the Town Close* 1737–; *the towne mill* 1639*; *Tramerscroft* 1393, *Tramberkerr* (sic) 1402+ (*v.* **kjarr**; Dr Insley suggests that *Tramer–*, *Tramber–* is 'the pool frequented by cranes', *v.* **trani, mere**[1]); *Turfhowdayle*, *– hyll* 1457 ('the turf mound', *v.* **turf, haugr**, with **deill** and **hyll**); *Tweed Close* 1695– (named from the *Tweed* family, cf. Edward *Tweede* 1559 PRStJ); *le vine garthe* 1577 (self–explanatory, *v.* **garðr**; it is described as *a walled garden*); *Walthamland* 1457 (presumably from Waltham, a nearby parish, or a derived surn. and **land**); *Wathe, Watheland* 1457 (*v.* **vað** 'a ford' with **land**); *foss voc' a met water dik* (sic) (*a met* is obcure; *v.* **wæter, dík**); *le Wayour* 1392x, *– Wayer* 1393–, *lee wayer* 1492 (*v.* **weyour** 'a pond'); *Wele* 1390–, 1394+, 1395, 1402+, 1406 all (p), *Weele* 1393+ (p) (it is uncertain whether this is a topographical surn. of local origin); *Welesbymere* 1457 ('the boundary with Weelsby', *v.* (**ge)mære** and cf. Weelsby Hedge in f.ns. (a) *supra*); *Wellecroftgarth* 1390 (*v.* **wella, croft** with **garðr**); *Wellow bancke* 1588=, *y^e Wellow bancke close* 1654>, *Wellow Tunnill* 1736*, 1736>, *Willow Tunnell* (sic) c.1736 (named from Wellow *supra*); *West Carre banck* c.1581+ (*v.* **west, kjarr**); *y^e house and close called Westerbyes* 1647*, *the House & Close called* – 1664* (named from the surn. *Westerby*, cf. Thomas *Westyby* 1423+, Mathew *Westerby* 1638x); *westgayrthe* (sic) 1508* (*v.* **west, garðr**); *terram . . . nuper appellat Whiteheade Landes* 1576x, *Whiteheade thinge* 1582x (named from the surn. *Whitehead*, cf. John *Whithede* 1518*, with **land** and **þing** 'property, possessions'); *Whyteland, –hedelandes* 1457 (no doubt from the surn. *White* with **land** and **hēafod–land**); *Atte Wode* 1327, 1339, 1369, *del* – 1392+, *atte Wod'* 1332, *– Wod* 1364x, 1369+, 1374+, 1382+, *attewod* 1344x all (p) (self–explanatory); *y^e Wrastling Close* 1699= (presumably where wrestling took place); *Mr wrights howse* 1673>, *Whrights howses* (sic) 1678>, *a Cottage or Tenement . . . which was hertofore Called Mr Wrights*

Houses 1726 > (named from a long-established family in the borough, cf. John *Wryghte* 1450); *le Wyllowes* 1559–; *Wymarke Croft* (sic) 1543 (no doubt from the surn. *Wymark*, though none has been noted in the sources searched); *Wyndle Crofte* 1492 (named from the surn. *Windle*, cf. Robert *Wyndyll* 1539, and **croft**); *Wynehowe* 1436 AD (Dr Insley suggests that this is perhaps a compound of the OE pers.n. *Wine* and **haugr**, though the form is late); *Yffyffynge house* (sic) 1583x (probably a surn., but the form is obscure).

Healing

HEALING

> *Hechelinge* 1086 DB
> *Heghelinge* 1086 DB, *–inga* c.1115 LS
> *Hegelinge* 1086 DB, 1166 RBE (p), 1180 P (p), 1235 Dugd vi,
>   *–ing'* Hy2 LN (p), 1208 Cur (p), 1218 Ass (p), *Heigeling*
>   Hy2 (e14) Selby, *Hegling'* 1201 FF, c.1240 IB, *–inge* 1212
>   Fees, *–yng'* 113 (e14) Selby
> *Heiling'* eHy2, Hy2 (e13) *Ncot*, 1199 Memo (p), 1202 Ass (p),
>   1208 P (p), 1208 FF (p), 1209 P (p), 1221 Welles, Hy3
>   (e14) Selby, *–inga* 1166, 1167 P (p), *–inge* 1193, 1194 ib
>   (p), 1196 ChancR (p), 1197 P (p), *Heilling'* 1219 Ass (p)
> *Heyling'* 1242–43 Fees, 1252 Cl, 1269 RRGr, 1281 QW, 1316
>   FA, 1344 Fine, 1354 Orig, *–inge* 1563 *BT*, *–ingge* 1282
>   Ass, 1318 Selby, *–ingg* 1303 FA, *–yng* 1291 Tax, 1311
>   Ipm, 1327, 1332 *SR*, 1340 Ipm, 1354 Cl, 1354 Fine, 1360,
>   1380, 1404 Pat, *Heyeling'* Hy3 (e14) Selby
> *Heylinges* 1254 ValNor, 1285 RSu, 1353 Ipm
> *Hailinges* 1180 P (p)
> *Helling'* 1191 P (p), Hy3 (e14) Selby
> *Helinge* 1195 P (p), 1554 PrState, 1555, 1558 InstBen, 1576
>   LER, 1585 SC, *–ing'* 1198 P (p), Hy3 (e14), 1284 Selby,
>   *–ing* 1365 AD ii, 1526 Sub, 1553 Pat, a1567 LNQ v, 1576
>   Saxton, 1610 Speed, *–yng* 1346 FA, 1353, 1359 Ipm, 1366
>   AD ii, 1369 Misc, 1369 Pat, 1373, 1375, 1385 Peace, 1395

Ch *et passim* to 1634–42 Holles, *–ynge* 1385 Cl, 1556 LNQ
xiv
Helinges 1212 Cur (p), *–ynges* 1427 Cl
Hecliga (sic) Hy2 Dane (p)
Heheling 1212 Fees
Heigling 1221 Guis
Healyng 1566 *BT*, *–ing* 1590, 1596, 1601, 1668 *ib et passim*,
–inge 1664 *Terrier*

'The followers, the people of Hægel', *v.* **–ingas**, the first el.
being the unrecorded OE pers.n. **Hægel*, found also in the
identical Hayling (Ha). OE **Hægel* belongs to the Germanic root
contained in OE, OSax *haga* 'an enclosure', cf. also OE
hagusteald 'a bachelor, a warrior, the landless member of a
following' and the OSax pers.n. *Hagelin*, *Heilin*. Healing is in
origin a group–name denoting a body of people bound by kinship
or lordship, *Hægel* being the name of the leader. Healing became
a p.n. when the *Hægelingas* settled in what is today Healing. It is
the only such p.n. formation found in the North Riding of Lindsey,
though such group–names form the first el. of Immingham,
Killingholme, Stallingborough and the lost *Lopingham*, in the same
area, PN L **2**, 163, 193, 268 and 149.

AYLESBY RD, 1853 *EnclA*. EAST FIELD (lost), 1824 O, 1853
EnclA, *the east fealde* 1601, *East fielde* 1613, *the East field* 1638,
1679, *– feild* 1664, *– feeld* 1668, *– feald* 1690 all *Terrier*, *– Field*
1748 *Dixon*, 1822 *Terrier*, *v.* **ēast**, **feld**; one of the open fields of
the village. FIELD HO, cf. *campo de Heyeling'* Hy3 (e14) Selby,
– Heglyng' 113 (e14) ib, *campis de Helyng'* 1421 *AD*,
Healingefeilde c.1590 *Terrier, Healing Field* 1828 Bry, *v.* **feld**,
commemorating the great field of the village. GREAT COATES RD,
Great Coates and Grimsby Road 1853 *EnclA*. HALL. HEALING
BECK (local), *Heghlingbek* Hy3 (1301) Ch, *Helingbeck'* 1263 (e14)
Selby, Hy3 (e14) ib, Ed1 (e14) ib, *the becks* 1613 *Terrier, v.*
bekkr 'a stream'. HEALING COVERT. HEALING ROOKERY.
HEALING WELLS, *Healing Well* 1824 O, *Healing Wells Close* 1839
TA (Riby), cf. *Litlewelberg'*, *Sutewelleberg'* Hy3 (e14) Selby, *v.*

lȳtel, **wella**, **berg** 'a hill', *Sute-* is from **sūð** 'south'. HEALING
WELLS FM is *The Folly* 1828 Bry. MANOR HO, *Maner* – 1907 *TA*
(Altered Apportionment). THE MEADOWS, *the Meadow* 1679
Terrier. MILL HILL (lost), 1824 O. MOAT, 1824 ib. NORMANS
DENE, cf. *little Norman* (sic) 1613 *Terrier*, obscure. OLDFLEET
DRAIN, for forms, *v.* the same name in Great Coates *supra* and
Oldfleet Drain PN L **2**, 269. PASTURE PLANTATION (lost, approx.
TA 223 121), 1828 Bry. THE RECTORY, *the parsonage* 1601, –
Parsonage 1638, – *howse* 1613, *–house* 1678, *– parsonage house*
1690, 1698, 1706, *The Parsonage House* 1724, *One thatched
dwelling house* 1822 all *Terrier*, cf. the Parsonage headland in
f.ns. (a) *infra*. STALLINGBOROUGH RD, 1853 *EnclA*. TOOT HILL
(lost), 1824 O, *– hill* 1679 *Terrier*, *v.* **tōt–hyll** 'a look–out hill'.
WELLS RD, *Healing Wells Road* 1853 *EnclA*. WEST FIELD (lost),
1824 O, *the weast fealde* 1601, *– West fielde* 1613, *– west feald*
1634, *– field* 1638 *et freq* in *Terrier* to *the West Field* 1822 *ib*,
1853 *EnclA*; one of the great fields of the village *v.* **west, feld**.

FIELD-NAMES

Forms dated 1235 are Dugd vi, ii; 113 (14), Ed1 (14), Hy3 (14)
are Selby; 1327, 1332 *SR*; 1365, 1366 AD ii; 1385 Peace; c.1590,
1601, 1623, 1634, 1638, 1664, 1668, 1679, 1690, 1698, 1706,
1724, 1822 *Terrier*; 1748 *Dixon*; 1792, 1851, 1871, 1872, 1874,
1876, 1877, 1910 documents transcribed by Mr P.J. Steel of
Immingham; 1813 *MiscDon 397*; 1839 *TA*; 1853 *EnclA*; 1907 *TA*
(Altered Apportionment).

(a) Adams Cl 1792, 1871, 1874, 1877, Adams' – 1876 (from the surn.
Adams); Arden Wd 1907; Aylesby Cl 1792, 1871, 1877 (named from
Aylesby, a neighbouring parish); the Beck Lane or Shepherds Lane 1853 (cf.
Healing Beck supra); Bellrise 1792; Brick Pasture 1853, – Cl 1871 (cf.
Brick–Hill Close 1748); Briggs Cls 1861 (from the surn. *Briggs*, cf. John
Briggs 1781 *BT*); Caister rd 1822 (*Caster way* 1613, *Caister gate*, *Caister
high way* 1724, 'the road to Caistor', *v.* **gata**); 1st. –, 2nd. Caistor Rd Plot
1871 (*v.* **plot**); the – 1822, Church Cl 1872 (*yᵉ church close* 1613, *Church*

– 1724, cf. *ad ecclesiam* 1327, 1332 both (p), *v.* **cirice, clos(e)** and cf. Kirk Cl *infra*); Church Rd 1853; Coates Cl 1792, – Hedge 1822 (*great cotts hedge* 1601, *Great Coates* – 1668, *Cotes* – 1613, *Coates* 1634, 1679, *Coats* – 1664, 1706, *Cotes-hedge* 1638, *Coats hedg* 1690, *Cotes hedge* 1698, – *hedg* 1724, the boundary with the neighbouring parish of Great Coates); Corn Cl 1853; Cow Cl 1792 *et passim* to 1910; Eight Acres 1910; Foal Cl 1910; Furze Cl 1792, the – 1853, Low – 1851 (*ye firr close* 1690, *ye Firr* – 1698, *ye firrs* – 1706, *ye firr* – 1724, *Furze Close or Wood Close* 1748, *v.* **fyrs** 'furze'); Gallinbers 1853, Gallimber Hill 1910 (*Galghenberg'* Hy3 (14), *high* –, *low Gallinburg* 1690, *high Gallin burs* 1698, *ye high* –, *Low Gallinburs* 1706, *ye high Gallinburs*, *Low Gallinburg* 1724, *Gallinders* (sic) 1748, 'gallows hill', *v.* **galgi, –en^2, berg**); Gorse Covert 1871 (*v.* **gorst, cover(t)**); the – 1853, Green Carr 1874, 1877 (*grenker* Hy3 (14)), *Healing Green Carr* c.1590, *green–Cars* 1638, *the Green Carr* 1748, *grene carre hedge* 1601, *greencarr* – 1613, *Green carr* – 1664, *green carr* – 1668, *Green Carr* – 1679, 1690, *ye green Car* 1698, *green Car* – 1706 (*v.* **grēne^2, kjarr** 'a bog, a marsh', as elsewhere in the parish); Healing Clough 1813 (*v.* **clōh**); Healing Cover (cf. Gorse Covert *supra*); Home Allotment 1871, 1876, the – 1871, Home Cl 1876, 1877, – Fd 1851, – Plat 1851 (*v.* **plat** 'a plot of ground'); the Hop Yd 1753; Horse Cl 1792; Great Intack 1851, Intake 1871, Intack 1872, 1876 (*v.* **inntak**); Kelk Cl 1792, 1851 (– *close* 1690, 1698, 1706, – *Close* 1724, from the surn. *Kelk*); Kirk Cl 1872, Kirk's – 1874 (*the kirke close* 1601, – *kirk–close* 1638, *kirke close* 1664, 1668, 1690, *kirk* – 1679, 1698, cf. *at Kirk de Helyng* 1385 (p), *Kirk green* 1706 (*v.* **kirkja, clos(e)**; it appears that there was both a Kirk Cl and a Church Cl in Healing, cf. the Church Cl *supra*); Loft's Slawns 1851 (from the surn. *Loft*, cf. William *Loft* 1839 and *v.* The Slawn *infra*); Long Cl 1871 (1748); the long furlong 1822 (*the Long forlong* 1601, – *long furlong* 1679, *y^e* – 1690, 1698, 1706); Lords Cl 1851, 1874, 1877; Mareham 1822 (1707, 1724, *marame* 1601, *maram* 1613, 1664, *mayram* 1634, *Maram* 1668, *Marham* 1679, 1690), Mareham Green 1822 (*maram green(n)e* 1601, – *greene* 1613, *Marum–green* 1638, *maram Greene* 1664, *Marame green* 1668, *Marham Green* 1679, 1698, – *green* 1690, *Mareham grene* 1706, – *Green* 1724, probably 'the boundary water–meadow' from (**ge)mǣre** and **holmr** with **grēne** 'a grassy spot', cf. Marams Drain in the f.ns. (a) of Barrow upon Humber, PN L **2**, 22); Far Marsh 1853; Million's Cl 1851, Millions – 1871, 1874, 1876 (perhaps to be identified with *Milling Close* 1748, *v.* **mylen** 'a mill'); Old Cow Cl 1851; (1st) Old Fd 1910; the Old Green 1822, the Town Green 1853 (*v.* **grēne** 'a (village) green'); Old Inclosure 1839; Old Pasture

Lane 1853; Open field land 1839; Palliter Cl 1871; the Parsonage headland 1822 (*the parsonage headland* 1613, *a headland of the Parsonage* 1679, *a parsonage headland* 1724, *v.* **hēafod–land** and The Rectory *supra*); Pasture Occupation Rd 1853; High –, Low Railway Pce 1871, (Low) Railway Cl 1876, 1877; The Rectory Orchard etc. 1907 (cf. The Rectory *supra*); Rush Pasture 1792, 1851, 1871 (cf. *Rush Carr* 1697, 1706, *– carr* 1690, *– Car* 1698, *v.* **risc**, **kjarr**, replaced in later forms by **pasture**); Sedge Pasture 1851, 1871 (*v.* **secg**); The Slawn 1822, – Slawns 1853, (Top) Slawns 1871 (*the slawne* 1613, 1664, (*the*) *Slane* 1638, 1668, *yᵉ Slawn* 1690, 1698, 1724, *the Slaun* 1698, *yᵉ slaun* 1706, 1724, *High–Slawn* 1748, perhaps referring to *slane* 'a turf-cutting spade' (*v.* NED s.v.), used in some topographical sense); Poor Sowers 1792, The – 1853, 1877, Sours 1876, The Meadow –, 1st Meadow –, 2nd Meadow – 1871, Bottom – 1872, – Sowers 1874 ('land with acid soil', *v.* **sūr**); Stack Green 1874 (*Starkergate* Hy3 (14) (*v.* **gata**), *starke care greene* 1601, *Starcar-green* 1638, *Starkar Greene* 1664, *Starker green* 1668, *– greene* 1679, *Stackers green* 1698, *Stacker –* 1706, 1724, *Stark Car* 1724, *v.* **kjarr** with **grēne** 'a grassy spot'; the first el. is ME **star(e)**, **starre** (from ON **storr** 'bent-grass') 'any of several sedges or reed grasses, sometimes used as thatch, marram grass (Ammophila arundinacca) or sand sedge (Carex axinana), or the greater fox sedge (Carex vulpina)', *v.* MED); Stallingborough hedge 1822 (*stalingbrowghe hedge* 1601, *Stallingborough –* 1613, 1679, *Stallingurgh –* 1638, *Stalingborough –* 1668, *Stallingbrough –* 1690, *Stallinbrough hedg* 1698, *Stallinburgh Hedge* 1706, *– hedge* 1724, cf. *Stallingburgh field* 1638, *Stallingbrough feild* 1664, referring to Stallingborough, an adjacent parish); Short Stocks 1874; Sweet Briar Hill 1910; Talbot's Well 1822 (*talbot well* 1601, 1664, *Tabot-well* (sic) 1638, *Talbott Well* 1668, *Talbuts well* 1698, *Talbots –* 1706, 1724, *Talbuts Well* 1690, from the surn. *Talbot*); Thorn Tree Plat 1851, – Platt 1872, 1874 (*v.* **plat**); Toft Carr 1822, 1871 (*v.* **toft**, **kjarr**); Town Side Rd 1853 (cf. *Towne gate* 1613, *v.* **gata**); Wellbourn 1876, Wellbound Cl 1910 (probably cf. *Welburn lane* 1690, *Wellbourn –* 1698, *Wellburn –* 1706, *well bourn–lane* 1724; Wells Gate 1853 (cf. *terram Mathæi ad fontem* 113 (14), *v.* **wella**); the West Fd (Drain) 1853; Wood cl 1874, 1877 (*yᵉ wood close* 1690, 1698, 1706, and cf. *yᵉ wood* 1724, *v.* **wudu**, cf. Furze Cl *supra*).

(b) *Aldeuat* Hy3 (14) ('the old ford'. *v.* **ald**, **vað**); *Apparaters Close* 1698, *Apparater –* 1706 ('the apparitor's close', land assigned to an officer of the ecclesiastical court or a similar functionary); *Aubestik'* Hy3 (14) ('Aubi's rod, pole', *v.* **sticca**, the pole in question being no doubt one used to mark a boundary; the first el. is the AScand pers.n. *Aubi*, a short form of

Auðbjorn, etc., for which *v.* SPNLY 37); *Bair Dale* 1748 (*v.* **bere, deill**); *calueker* Hy3 (14) (*v.* **calf, kjarr**); *the carre* 1613, – *Care* 1634, – *Carr* 1638, – *car* 1664, – *Carrs* 1668 (*v.* **kjarr**); *Cottiger close* 1724 ('land allotted to one or more of the cottagers'); *crucem de Heling'* Hy3 (14) ('(at) Healing Cross'); *Crumdikgate* Hy3 (14) ('the road to *Crumdike* (the crooked dike)', from **crumb, dík** with **gata**); *y*^e *fallow feild* 1698, 1706; *y*^e *far close* 1698; *Fulriskes* Hy3 (14) ('the foul rushes', *v.* **fúl, risc**, in a partially Scandinavianised form); *Glaghemberg* Hy3 (14) (obscure); *one lea buting on y*^e *grip* 1690 (*v.* **grype** 'a ditch, a drain' and cf. the use of *grip* in *a grip* 1724); *Hagh "of" Heling* 1365, – "of" *Heylynge* 1366 both (p) (*v.* **haga** 'an enclosure'); *y*^e *hall field* 1679 (*v.* **hall**); *Holmare* Hy3 (14) ('the hollow boundary' or 'the boundary in the hollow', *v.* **hol, (ge)mære**); *howl greene* 1679, – *green* 1690 (*v.* **grēne²** 'a grassy spot') *y* *long Furrow* 1668; *Merkelgrene, Merkles, Merkeles* Hy3 (14) ('the boundary green', 'the boundary pasture land', *v.* **mercels** 'a (boundary) mark', **grēne, lǽs**); *Methelberg'* Hy3 (14) ('the middle hill', *v.* **meðal, berg**, a Scand compound); *gayram willelmi Molendarii* Hy3 (14) ('the gore of William the Miller', *v.* **geiri**); *Milnegate* Hy3 (14) (*v.* **myln, gata**); *Newecroft* 1235 (*v.* **nīwe, croft**); *Normagar'* (sic) Hy3 (14) (the first el. is perhaps a corrupt form of the ME pers.n. *Norman*); *Paghland'* 113 (14) (obscure); *the parsonage grownd* 1601, – *ground* 1613, 1679, 1690, *the Parsonage grounds* 1638, – *personage Ground* 1664, *y*^e *Parsonage ground* 1706, *y*^e *Parsonage landes*, – *meadow* 1613, *the Parsonage–land* 1638, – *parsonage land* 1664, *y*^e *Parsonage land* 1668, *y* *parsonage land* 1706 (cf. *The Parsonage headland* in (a) *supra* and *The Rectory supra*); *Rauenker* Hy3 (14) ('the ravens' carr', *v.* **hrafn, kjarr**); *Redemare* Hy3 (14) ('the reedy boundary land', *v.* **hrēod, (ge)mære**); *viam de Riby* Hy3 (14) ('the road to Riby'), *Riby hedg* 1690 (*v.* **hecg**, referring to Riby, a neighbouring parish); *Rowe mare* 1601 ('the rough boundary land', *v.* **rūh, (ge)mære**); *Rubertmar'* Hy3 (14) (*v.* **(ge)mære**; the first el. is perhaps a corrupt form of the pers.n. *Hubert*); *super Scot* Hy3 (14) (i.e. a misreading of *Stoc*, with *c* for *t* and *vice versa*; probably *v.* **stocc** 'a tree–trunk, a stump' used as a boundary marker); *Stocsozcheuedland* (sic) Hy3 (14) (*v.* **hēafod–land**; *Stocsozc–* is obscure); *Sinker grene* (sic) 1634, *Swyn–carr–green* 1638 (*v.* **grēne²**), *Swine carr* 1601, *Swincarr* 1613, *Swine Carr* 1664, *Swin Carr* 1679, 1690, 1724, – *Car* 1698, 1706 (*v.* **swīn, svín, kjarr**); *Staynemare* Hy3 (14) ('the stony boundary (land)', *v.* **steinn, (ge)mære**); *the townes end* 1613; *turfecarr* 1601, *Turfcar* 1613, *turf–car* 1638, *turf carr* 1668, *Turf –* 1664, *Turff Carr* 1679, *Turf –* 1690, *turf Car* 1698, – *car* 1706, *Turfe Close* 1748 (*v.* **turf**, kjarr); *the Vine Yards* 1748; *Wardell's Farm* 1748 (from the family of Nicholas *Wardall* 1642 LPR); *Wilson Close* 1748 (from the surn. *Wilson*, cf. Thomas *Wilson* 1642 LPR); Withcarr (*end*) 1613 (*v.* **víðir, wīðig** 'a withy, a willow', **kjarr**); *Yghelkerholm* Hy3 (14) (from **ighil** 'a leech', **kjarr** with **holmr**).

Holton le Clay

HOLTON LE CLAY

Holtun 1086 DB, *-tone* (2x) ib, *-ton* 1565, 1641 *BT*, (*- in le Clay*) 1633 *BT*, 1634 *Terrier*, 1667, 1669, 1672 *BT*, 1698 *MiD*, 1724 *Haigh*, (*- in le Claie*) 1635 *BT*, (*- le Clay*) 1671 *Terrier*, 1686 *BT*, 1690 *Terrier et passim*

Houtona c.1115 LS, *-ton* (') 1200 P (p), 1201 Cur, 1212 Fees, 1240 RRG, 1242–43 Fees, 1263 FF, 1275, 1276 RH, 1287 Cl, 1290 RSu, 1291 Tax, 1297 *AD*, 1298 Ass, 1303 FA *et passim* to 1602 *Terrier*, (*- "by" Grimesby*) 1291 Ipm, (*- iuxta Humberstan*) 1295 *Ass*, (*- "by" Humberstayn*) 1297 AD, (*- juxta Grimysby*) 1303 FA, (*- "by" Wathe*) 1396 AD, (*- iuxta Greate Grimsbie*) 1590 *BT*, (*- le Clay*) 1720 *ib*, *Howtona* Hy3 (1409) Gilb, 1406, 1408, 1415 Cl, 1431 FA, 1478 Cl, 1496–98 *MinAcct*, 1535 VE iv *et passim* to 1576 LER, *-tonne* 1610 *BT*, (*- juxta Tetteney*) 1503 Ipm, (*- next tetnay*) 1584 *Foster*, (*- Iuxta great grimsbe*) 1588 *BT*, (*- iuxta Tetteney*) 1588 *ib*, (*- in Le clae*) 1604 *ib*, (*- iuxta grimsbie*) 1607 *ib*

Hotton' 1166 P, *-tuna* 1167 ib

Hutun Hy2 Dane (p)

Hocton' 1202 Ass, *Houcton* (*- "near" Grimesby*) 1276 Cl

Hauton' 1254 ValNor, *Hawton al Holton in le Clay* 1723 SDL

Houghton (*- "by" Grymesby*) 1352 Ipm, 1475–77 *MinAcct*, 1519 DV i, 1523–24 *MinAcct*, 1526 Sub, 1546–47, 1609 *MinAcct*, 1616 *BT*, 1779 *EnclA* (Tetney), *Howghton* 1496–98 *MinAcct*, *Howgeton* 1534 LP vii

Howlton 1563 *BT*, 1576 Saxton, 1610 Speed, 1653 *ParlSurv*,
1697, 1703 *Terrier*, (*– in le Claie*) 1615 Admin, *Houlton*
1610, 1619, 1623 *BT*, (*– nexte to great Grimsby*) 1614 *ib*,
(*– in the Clay*) 1626 *ib*, (*– in Clay*), 1649 WillsPCC, (*– le
Clay*) 1652 *Rad*, 1682 *Haigh*, (*– in le Clay*) 1668 *ib*, 1678
BT, 1682 *Haigh*, 1692 *BT*, 1719 *Haigh*

'The farmstead, village, estate on a hill–spur', *v*. **hōh**, **tūn**,
identical with Holton le Moor PN L **3**, 31 and Holton cum
Beckering LSR. It is described as being near Great Grimsby,
Humberston, Tetney and Waithe, and today is distinguished as –
le Clay, situated as it is on the clay.

BEACONHILL FM. CHURCH LANE, *the Church lane* 1652 *Rad*,
1822 *Terrier*, cf. *ad Ecclesiam de Houton* 13 AD vi. FURZE
PLATTS, cf. *the Furrs*, *– Fursies*, *– Furseis* 1609 *DuLaMB*,
Houlton furrs 1652 *Rad*, *the furzeside* 1733 *Nelthorpe*, *v*. **fyrs**
'furze', **plat**² 'a small piece of land', as commonly in north L.
HOLTON CROSS COVER (lost), 1824 O, cf. *at Crosse de eadem*
[i.e. *Houton*'] (p) 1385 Peace, *v*. **cros**, and Holton Cross in
Waltham, PN L **4**, 184. HOLTON GRANGE, "grange in" *Howton*
1535–37 LDRH, *Howton' graunge* 1535–46, 1543–45 *MinAcct*,
Howton –, Firma unius grangiæ 1537–38 Dugd iv, *Howton grange*
1544 LP xix, *Grange F*. 1828 Bry; the references here are to more
than one **grange** and in the 16th century they belonged to
Humberston Priory, Hagnaby Abbey and St Katherine's Hospital,
Lincoln. HOLTON LODGE is *Holton F*. (sic) 1824 O. MILL LANE,
cf. *in ripam molendini* Hy3 (1409) Gilb, *Mill Dam Close* 1840 *TA*;
the lane leads to Waithe Mill *infra*. MOTOR HALT was on the now
disused railway line. NORTH END FM, cf. *le Holme ex parte
boriali de Howton'* 1496–98, *– ex parte borial' de Houghton'*
1523–24, *– ex parte Boriali de Hougheton'* 1546–47, *– ex parte
boreal' de Houghton'* 1609 all *MinAcct*. NORTH FIELD FM.
PARSONAGE BARN (lost, approx TA 294 027), *Pars. B*. 1828 Bry.
SOUTHFIELD (local), cf. *Southfield Hedge* 1773 *Nelthorpe*.
TETNEY LANE, *Tetneygate* 1733 *ib*, *v*. **gata**. VICARAGE, *the
vicaridge house* 1602, *– vicarage house* 1634, 1638, *vicarige –*

1671, *the Vicaridge* 1690, *there is neither Vicarage House Garden or Orchard* 1822 all *Terrier*. WAITHE MILL, 1840 *TA*; it is *Water Mill* 1765 *Plan*; the now disused mill is actually in Holton parish, but for additional forms, *v.* Waithe Mill, PN L **4**, 179. THE WELLINGTON (lost, approx TA 286 025), 1828 Bry.

FIELD-NAMES

Principal forms in (a) are 1840 *TA*; forms dated m12 are *AD*; Hy2 Dane; n.d. AD; eHy3 (1409), Hy3 (1409) Gilb, Hy3 *HarlCh*; 1332 *SR*; 1421–23, 1451–53, 1475–77, 1496–98, 1523–24, 1546–47, 1609[1] *MinAcct*; 1431 FA; 1457 *TCC*, 1609[2] *DuLaMB 119*; 1652 *Rad*; 1668, 1682, 1690, 1703, 1719, 1724, 1817, 1870 *Haigh*; 1675 *Em*; 1686 LNQ xviii; 1733 *Nelthorpe*; 1822 *Terrier*.

(a) Mr Beatniffe's Farm 1822 (named from the *Beatniffe* family, cf. John *Beatniffe* 1697 *Terrier*, Richard *Beatniffe* 1822); Beck Cl (*v.* **bekkr**); Bull Garth (*v.* **garðr**); Burnt House Garth (*v.* **garðr**); Corner Cl; Cow Cl; the East Fd 1822 (*in orientali campo* eHy3 (1409), *in campo orientali de Howtona* Hy3 (1409), *the Easte feild* 1609[2], – *Eastfield* 1733, 'the east field', *v.* **ēast, feld**, one of the great fields of the parish, cf. *in occidentali campo* in (b) *infra*); Ferraby Cl; Gallows Lane Cl (cf. *galtre* m12, *galtremar* eHy3 (1409), *Galtremere* 1457 (*v.* **(ge)mære**), *–hyll* 1457, *South Gautrey Hill* 1609[2], *Gawtry hill* 1733, and cf. *Galtregrene* 1457, *v.* **galga, galgi** 'gallows', **trēow**, with **hyll** and **grēne**[2]); Holt Cl (*v.* **holt**); Hotel yard and Garden; House Homestead and Long Garth (*v.* **garðr**); Keelby Cl; Lidgard's Cl (from the surn. *Lidgard*, cf. Joseph *Lidgard* 1708 BT); Old Garth (*v.* **garðr**); Old Orchard; Paddock; Parsonage Cl; Pepper Corn House and Garden (probably alluding to the payment of a nominal or pepper–corn rent); Pinder's Garth (named from the *Pinder* family, cf. William *Pinder* 1652 *Rad*, with **garðr**); Pingle (*v.* **pingel**); Sixteen Acres; Tenney Garth (from the surn. *Tenney* and **garðr**); Twelve Acres, Two Acres; Waterhouse Cl; water-mill 1817 (*water myll* 1609[2]); Winley Garth (*v.* **garðr**).

(b) *Arthura Peice* (sic) 1733 (*v.* **pece**); *Athelberd holm* eHy3 (1409) (from the ContGerm pers.n. *Adalbert* with **holmr**); *Barlynges land* 1457 (named from the surn. *Barlings*, cf. Thomas *Barlynges* named in the same document, with **land**); *beane lands, – furlonge* 1609[2] (*v.* **bēan, land, furlang**); *Benest* (sic) Hy3 (1409); (*Short*) *Blemans* 1733; *Blodesmare* 1457 (from the ME surn. *Blode* and (ge)mǣre 'a boundary, land on or forming a boundary'); *Bothemare* (sic) 1421–23, *Brothmare* 1451–53, *Brothem'* 1475–77, *Brodmersshe* 1523–24, 1546–47, *Brodmarshe* 1609[1] (all refer to the same piece of land; the first el. is uncertain, the second is **mersc**); *Boymare* 1457 (the first el. is ME *boy* but in what sense is uncertain; the second is (ge)mǣre); *Bran lands* 1733; *Brigdale* 1421–23, *Briggedaile* 1451–53, *Briggedale* 1496–98, *Brygdale* 1523–24, 1546–47, *Brigesdale* 1609[1] (*v.* brycg, Scandinavianised, deill); *Butlarhede* 1457 (from the surn. *Butler* and hēafod 'a headland in the common field'; John *Botelar* is named in the document); *Butt green* 1733 (*v.* butt[2] 'an archery butt', grēne[2] 'a grassy place'); *Cartys hill* 1609[2], *Curtashill* (*green*) 1733 (named from the *Curtesse* family, cf. John *Curtesse* 1632 *Inv*, and hyll with grēne[2]); *Cathowe* 1421–23, 1451–53, 1475–77, *Chathowe* 1523–24, 1546–47 (*v.* cat(t), haugr 'a mound, a hill', denoting a hill frequented by the wild cat); *Cattsay* 1733; atte *Celer* 1332 (p); at *Chapel de Houton* eHy3 (1409), 1431 (p) (cf. *Chapelhedeland* 1457, *v.* chapel(e), hēafod–land); *Coldwat'gate* 1451–53 (*v.* cald, wæter with geat or gata); *Crasshills* (*Dyke*) 1733; *Crofts Meer* 1733 (*v.* croft, (ge)mǣre); *Crow Green* 1733 (from crāwe or the surn. *Crow* and grēne[2]); *Dawhedelandis* 1457 (probably from the surn. *Daw* and hēafod–land); *dokdall* 1421–23, *dokedale* 1451–53, *Dokdale* 1475–77, 1496–98, *Dokedale* 1523–24 (*v.* docce 'a dock', deill 'an allotment, a share of the common field'); *dykdale*, 1421–23, 1451–53, *Dykedale, Dikedale* 1496–98, 1523–24, 1609[1], *Dickedale* 1523–24, *Dikedale* (*iuxta Grymesdale*) 1546–47, 1609[1], *Duckedale* (sic), *Dikedole* 1475–77 (*v.* dík, deill); *dounlandaile* 1451–53, *doulandale* (sic) 1475–77, *Dounlandale* 1496–98, *Dounelandale* 1523–24, *Dounellandale* 1546–47, *Downelandale* 1609[1] (apparently from dūn 'a hill' with land and deill); *Dunghill Whong* 1733 (*v.* vangr); *Engedyke* 1457 (*v.* eng, dík); *Estarbyes hill* 1609[2] (from the surn. *Esterby*, cf. Leonard *Esterbie* 1592 *BT*); le *Estland'* 1421–23, – *Estlaunce* 1451–53, *Estlaunce* 1475–77, *Estalaune* 1496–98, *Estlande* 1546–47, *Eastland* 1609[1] (*v.* ēast, land; –*launce* forms perhaps represent land in the pl.); in *campo de Houton'* 1421–23, in *Campo de* – 1451–53, in *campis de Howton* 1457, in *campo de Howton'* 1496–98, in *Campis de Houghton'* 1523–24, 1546–47, in *campis de* – 1609[1], cf. *Feldedyke, Feldwyll* (sic) 1457 (*v.* feld, with dík and wella); le *fenne* 1451–53, les *fences* (sic) 1475–77, le *Fenne* 1496–98, 1523–24, 1546–1547, 1609[1] (*v.* fenn); *Fulmar* Hy3 (1409); *Furr Hills* 1733 (*v.* fyrs, hyll); *Furwell* n.d. (*v.* wella); *Fyshers hill* 1609[2] (presumably from the surn. *Fisher* and hyll); *Gards furlong* 1609[2]; le *Gares*

1457, *Gares* 1733 (*v.* **geiri** 'a triangular piece of ground'); *Goose green Hill* 1733 (*v.* **gōs, grēne**[2], as freq in the parish, with **hyll**); *Garseholme* 1457, *Grasnam* 1733 (perhaps 'the water–meadow where grass grows', *v.* **gærsen, holmr**, the latter frequently has reflexes in *–ham, –am* in north L); *atte Grene* 1332 (p), *Green Close* (*End*) 1733 (*v.* **grēne**[2], here no doubt the village green); *Grendere* 1451–53, *Gronder* 1475–77, *Grenedere* 1496–98, *Grynder* 1523–24, *Gryder* (sic) 1546–47, *Greenederry* 1609[1] (obscure); *Gretehedeland* 1457 (*v.* **hēafod–land**; the first el. may be **grēat** 'big'); *Groinesdale, Gronnedeles deile* 1421–23, *Grynnesdale* 1451–53, 1496–98, *Grynesdale* 1475–77, *Grymesdale* 1523–24, 1546–47 (the forms of the first el. are confused, as freq in *MinAcct*, but Dr Insley suggests it may be a ME nickname from *groin* (OFr *groin, groigne* 'snout') applicable to a person with a large nose; the second el. is **deill** 'a share of land'); *Hallemor* eHy3 (1409), *Halmar'* 1421–23, 1475–77, *Hallemarre, –more* 1451–53, *Hallemere* 1496–98, *Halmere* 1523–24, *hall meare* 1609[2], *Hallmore* 1609[1] (from **hall** with an uncertain second el.); *Halylees* 1457 (apparently from **hālig** 'holy' and **lea** (OE **lēah**) 'meadow, pasture' in the pl.); *Harry leys* 1733 (from the surn. *Harry* with **lea** (OE **lēah**) 'meadow, pasture' in the pl.); *del Hawe* 1421–23, *Hawe* 1451–53, 1609[1], *le Hawe* 1475–77, 1496–98, *le Haugh'* 1523–24, *Haughe* 1546–47 (*v.* **haga** 'an enclosure'); *Hell'* 1421–23, *le Hill'* 1451–53, 1609[1], *le hill'* 1475–77, 1496–98, 1546–47, *le hyll'* 1523–24 (*v.* **hyll**); *le Hieghes* 1421–23, *le Heighes* 1451–53, 1496–98, *les Heighes* 1475–77, *Highes* 1546–47 (*v.* **hēah**[2] 'a high place, a height' in the pl.); *Hole* eHy3 (1409), 1457, *the hole* 1609[2], *the Hole, Hole Furlong* 1733 (*v.* **hol**[1] 'a hole, a hollow'); *le Holme* 1421–23, 1451–53, 1496–98, 1523–24, 1609[1] (*v.* **holmr** 'higher ground in marsh'); *Holton dike, – Hill* 1686; *two Dales called . . . Houlton Dales* 1675 (*v.* **deill** 'a share of land'); *Holton lane End* 1733; *Hotemare* 1421–23, *Hetemarre* 1451–53 (obscure); *houed landale* 1421–23 (*v.* **hēafod–land** 'the head of a strip of land left for turning the plough', with **deill**, with the replacement of **hēafod** by the cognate ON **hǫfuð**); *Housedykes* 1733 (*v.* **hūs, dík**); *Humberston Gate* 1733 ('the road to Humberston', *v.* **gata**); *the Inngs, the Inngs dale, Inggs gate* 1609[2], *the Ings* 1652, 1733 (*v.* **eng** 'meadow, pasture' in the pl.); *Kechynland* 1457 (from the surn. *Kitchen* and **land**; William *Kechyn* is named in the document); *Kynsoneland* 1457 (from the surn. *Kynson* and **land**; Robert *Kynson* is named in the document); *Lady Lands* 1733 (probably selions dedicated to Our Lady, *v.* **land**); *Langmer'* 1421–23, *langmare* 1451–53, *longmare* 1523–24, *longemare* 1546–47, *Longnare* (sic) 1609[1], *Longmeare* 1609[2] (*v.* **lang, (ge)mǣre** 'a boundary', as elsewhere in this parish); *Lareland* 1457 (perhaps from **leirr** 'clay' and **land** 'a selion', as freq in the parish); *Littelblamild* Hy3 (1409) (*blamild* probably means 'the dark soil', *v*. **blár, mylde**, prefixed by **lȳtel, lítill**); *Langelandes* 1457, *longlands*, *Longlands dyke* 1609[2], *Longlands* 1733 (*v*. **lang, land**); *lord scropelandes* 1457 ('Lord Scrope's lands'); *Maidenchairs Furlong* 1733 (*v*. **furlang**; *Maidenchairs* is obscure); *in pratis de Houton'* 1421–23, 1451–53, *in prat' de Houghton'* 1496–98, 1546–47, 1609[1], *in prato de Houghton'* 1523–24 ('in the meadow(s) of Holton'); *Mydylgate* 1457 (*v*. **middel, gata** 'a road', freq in the parish); *in ripam molendini* Hy3 (1409) ('the bank of the mill [stream]'), *le mylnedore* 1421–23, *Milnemere alias Milndore* 1451–53, *Milnmore* – 1496–98, 1523–24, *Milmore al' Milnedoure* 1475–77, *Milnemore al' dict' le Mylnedore* 1546–47, *Milncrowe* (sic) 1609[1] (*v*. **myln, mōr**, with **dōr** 'an entrance gate or door' in the alternative forms, presumably referring to water–mill in (a) *supra*, cf. also Mill Lane *supra*); *le Northfenne* 1421–23, *North'fenne* 1451–53, 1496–98, *Northfennes* 1475–77, *Northefenne* 1546–47, *Northfenne* 1523–24, 1609[1] (*v*. **norð, fenn**, cf. *Westfenne infra*); *Nuns Close* 1652 (named from the nuns of Grimsby); *Old Well Hill* 1733; *Petham* 1733 (*–ham* is a common reflex of **holmr** in north L; the first el. is perhaps **pēte** 'peat'); *all that . . . Close or* (sic) *pasture . . . comonly called . . . Pickard* 1668, *all y[t] other Close of pasture . . . commonly called* – 1682, *all that other Close of pasture . . . comonly called Pichard* (sic) 1690, – *comonly called . . . Pickard* 1703, – *comonly called . . . Pickard* 1719 (named from the *Pickard* family, cf. *Rychard Pyckard* 1577 *Inv*); *Raker hyll* 1457; *Rannmore Hill* 1733; *Riddesdale* 1451–53, 1496–98, *Ridesdale* 1475–77, *Redale* (sic) 1523–24, 1546–47, *Reddesdale* 1609[1] (the first el. is uncertain); *Rokarres* 1457, *Long Rowdker hill, Rowkers* 1609[2], *long* –, *short Rookas Hill, Rookas Side* 1733 (perhaps from **rūh** 'rough', **kjarr**, with **hyll** and **sīde** 'a hill–side'), *Rose Whong* 1733 (*v*. **vangr**); *Routhmar* eHy3 (1409) (probably 'the red boundary land', *v*. **rauðr, (ge)mǣre**); *Rush greene* 1609[2] (*v*. **risc, grēne**[2]); *Saltergate* 1457 ('the salters' road', *v*. **saltere, gata**); *Sandecotes* 1421–23, 1475–77, 1496–98, 1523–24, *Sandcotes* 1451–53, *Sandcot'* 1546–47, *Samotes* (sic) 1609[1] (*v*. **sand, cot**); *Sandome* 1457, *Sandeholme* 1421–23, *Sandholme* 1451–53 (*v*. **sand, holmr**); *Sandy gate*, – *grene* 1609[2] (*v*. **sandig, gata** with **grēne**[2]); *Scalumsyke hyll* 1457 (*Scalum*– is obscure); *Starkere* 1457 (from ME **star(e)**, **starre** and **kjarr**, cf. Stack Green in Healing f.ns. (a) *supra*); *Sheep Hill* 1733 (self–explanatory); *Slawstead furlong* 1733 (*v*. **furlang**; *Slawstead* may be from **slāh** 'a sloe' with **stede**); *Smalemar* eHy3 (1409) (perhaps 'the narrow marsh', *v*. **smæl, marr**[1]); *South Gares Nooke* 1733 (*v*. **sūð, geiri** in the pl., with **nōk** and cf.

le Gares supra); *Southlange* 1421–23, *Southlande* 1421–23, 1451–53, 1523–24, *Southland'* 1475–77, 1609[1], *South'lande* 1496–98, 1546–47 (from **sūð** 'south', **land**, with **lang**[2] 'a long piece of land' in the earliest form); *Sowthalhedelandes*, *Sowthall landes*, *Sowthalwange* 1457 ('the south hall', *v*. **sūð, hall**, with **hēafod–land**, **land** and **vangr** 'a garden, an in–field'); *Standale* 1451–53, 1475–77, 1496–98, 1546–47, 1609[1], *Stan'dale* 1523–24 (*v*. **stān, dalr** 'a valley'); *Stanname* 1609[2]; *Starcass Hill* 1733 (obscure); *the streete*, *Holton streete* 1609[2], *Street Hedge* 1733 (*v*. **strǣt, hecg**); *Suthlongfurowes* eHy3 (1409) (*v*. **lang, furh** 'a furrow' in the pl., prefixed by **sūð**); *Swinstisyke* 1451–53, *Swyncksty syke* (sic) 1609[2] ('pig–sty sike, i.e. streamside meadow', *v*. **swīn, stigu, sík**); *les Sykes* 1421–23, – *Sikes* 1451–53, 1475–77, 1496–98, *le Sykes* 1523–24, *les Sykes* 1609[1], *the syke* 1609[2] (*v*. **sík**); *Tetney Gate* 1733 ('the road to Tetney' (an adjacent parish), *v*. **gata**); *Thachowe* (sic) 1496–98 (*v*. **þak** 'thatch', **haugr** 'a mound'); *Thiefhole* 1733 ('the hollow frequented by thieves', *v*. **þēof, hol**[1]); *Thirnewellsic* eHy3 (1409) (*v*. **þyrne** 'a thorn–bush', **wella**, with **sík**); *Tuafletes* Hy2, Hy3, *twafletes* Hy3, *Twaflatte(s)*, *Towadeflates* (sic) 1421–23, *Twaflattes* 1451–53, 1475–77, *Tawflates* 1496–96, *Twy flates* 1523–24, *Twyfflattes* 1546–47, *Toweflate* 1609[1] 'the two streams', *v*. **twā, flēot**, cf. the same name in Tetney parish, s.n. Twafleet in f.ns. (a) *infra*); *Wathehallandes* 1457 (lands belonging to *Wathall*, PN L **4**, 179); *Wath lane end* 1609[2], *Waythe Gate* 1733 ('the lane, the road to Waithe', *v*. **gata**); *Wellow Thing* 1668, 1682, 1690, 1703, 1724, – *thing* 1719 (the second el. is **þing** 'property, premises', no doubt belonging to Wellow Abbey in Great Grimsby); *Westenges* Hy2, Hy3 (*v*. **west, eng**); *Westfenne* 1421–23, 1451–53, *West fenne* 1496–98, 1523–24, *Westefenne* 1546–47 (*v*. **west, fenn**); *in occidentali campo* eHy3 (1409), – *campo de Houton* Hy3 (1409), – *Camp' occid'* 1457, *Holton West feild* 1609[2], *the Westfield* 1733 (*v*. **west, feld**, one of the great fields of the parish, cf. the East Fd in (a) *supra*); *Westosgotacre* Hy3 (1409) (from the ME pers.n. *Ōsgot*, an anglicized form of ON *Ásgautr*, ODan *Āsgut*, with **æcer**, prefixed with **west**); *Witherhawe* 1457 (*v*. **víðir** 'a willow', **haga** 'an enclosure'); *Wrae* 1457 (*v*. **vrá** 'a nook, a corner of land'); *Wyndinds* (sic) 1609[2] (no doubt for *Wyndings*, for which *v*. PN L **2**, 173, s.n. *wynedyngs*); *Wynn Green* 1733 (from the surn. *Wynn*, cf. George *Win* 1621 BT, with **grēne**[2]); *Wynnowbryghyll* 1457 (*Wynnow–* is obscure); *Ynglemare* 1457.

Humberston

HUMBERSTON

Humbrestone 1086 DB, 1440, 1444 Visit, 1526 Sub, *–ston*
1226 ClR, 1530 Wills iii, *Humberston* 1242–43 Fees, 1294
Ass, 1310 Cl, 1312 Pat, 1322 Pap, 1331 Ipm, 1331 Cl, 1346
FA, 1368 Pat, 1375 Peace, 1402, 1428 FA, 1450 Pap, 1451
Cl *et passim*, *–stone* 1309 Pap, 1421 Fine, 1431 FA, 1446
Fine, 1557 Pat *et passim* to 1638 *MiscDon 238*
Humbrestan Hy2 Dane, Hy2 (1461) Pat, 1223 Cur, 1226 FineR,
Humberstan Hy2 Dane (p), 1202 Ass (p), 1212 Fees, 1235
IB, 1238 RRG, 1266 Cl, 1273 Ipm, 1275, 1276 RH, 1291
Tax, 1292 Ipm, 1303 FA *et passim* to 1450 Cl, *–stane* 1323
Pat, 1353 Ipm, 1355 *Cor*, 1372 Misc *et passim* to 1458 Pat
Humberstein c.1115 LS, 1180 P (p), 1203, 1208 FF, 1209 P
(p), 1219 Ass (p), p1220 WellesLA, 1231 Welles, 1240
RRG, – *steyn* p1220 WellesLA, 1241 RRG, 1254 ValNor,
1258 Pat, 1278 Fine, 1289 RSu, 1291 Tax, 1295 *Ass*, 1428
FA, *Humbrestein* 1191 P (p), 1202 Ass (p)
Humbrestam (*–m* = *–in*) 1155–58 (1334) Ch, *Humbrestain*
1164–81 (l13) YCh v, *–stayn* 1267 Cl, 1310 *FF*, *–stayne*
1440 Visit
Humberstayn 1235 IB, 1242–43 Fees, 1244 Cl, 1247 Lib, 1258
Cl, 1262 RRGr, 1266 Misc, 1272 *Ass*, 1274 RRGr, 1282
Pat, 1291 Tax, 1295 RSu, 1296 *Ass*, 1298 Pat *et passim* to
1423 Pap, *–stayne* 1319, 1331 Pat, 1373 Peace, 1375 *FF*,
Humberscam (*–scam* = *–stain*) 1203, 1204 P both (p),
–stain 1224 FF, 1226 Welles, 1245 FineR, 1230 *HarlCh*,
1233 RA ii, 1293 RSu, 1296 *AD*
Humerstain' 1228 Cur, *–stein'* 1230 ib
Homeston (sic) 1552 *HumbD*, *Homerston* 1576 Saxton, 1607
Camden, 1610 Speed, *Humerston* 1608 *LRMB 256*

'The stone by the R. Humber', *v*. **stān**, forms in *–stein*, *–stain*
are from the cognate ON **steinn** 'a stone'. Of the stone itself,

Holles in 1634 reports, "here upon ye Shoare lyes a great Boundry blew Stone just at ye place where Humber looseth himselfe in ye German Ocean". Kirkby 18 states, "The boulder clay of the ridge contains stones of all sizes . . . The larger of these 'erratics' have been used as boundary marks . . . One or two serve as mounting blocks for horsemen . . . The largest of these 'erratics', measuring 4 feet x 3 feet x 2 and a half feet, lies buried in the field known as First Newcroft, on Kirby Fm".

According to Kirkby 19, "In the 1930's the Post Office authorities, to avoid confusion with Humberstone, Leicestershire, changed the official spelling to Humberston. At the present time [1953] the sufixes –on and –one are both used".

BANK PLANTATION (lost, on coast at approx TA 336 049), *the Bank Plant*, 1828 Bry. BEESTON FM was created from lands belonging to Grange Farm "at the instance of Lord Carrington" in 1910, *v*. Kirkby 177. BUCK BECK, *bucbek'* 1298 *Holywell*, *buckbeck* 1724 *Terrier (Scartho)*, self–explanatory, *v*. **bucc** 'a buck, a male–deer', **bekkr**. CHERRY GARTH, *le Chirigarth* 1298 *Holywell*, *the Cherry garth* 1678, 1687 *HumbD*, *Cherry Garth* 1705 *ib*, 'the enclosure where cherry–trees grow', *v*. **chiri**, **garðr**. CHURCH LANE, *the Church way* 1573 *Terrier*, *Kyerke Way* (sic) 1577–80 *ib*, *Church Lain* 1707 *Marshall*. The interchange of OE **cirice** and ON **kirkja** is noteworthy. FIR PLANTATION (lost, approx TA 303 042), 1828 Bry. GRAMMAR SCHOOL (lost), 1828 Bry. HUMBERSTON BECK (local), 1702 *Haigh*, *Humberstonbeck* 1609 *MinAcct*, *Humberson becke* 1686 *Terrier*, *Humberstone becke* 1706 *Foster*, *v*. **bekkr**; this is apparently an alternative name for Tetney Beck *infra*, and formed in part the boundary between Humberston and Tetney. HUMBERSTON FITTIES, *les Fitties* 1599 *HumbD*, *Sea banckes comonly called the Fyttyes* 1612 *Foster*, *the Fittyes* 1616, 1617 *ib*, *Fittizs* 1707 *Marshall*, *Humberston Fittys* 1775 *Yarb*, – *Fitties* 1828 Bry, for a detailed discussion, *v*. The Fitties PN L **4**, 116–17, where 16th century spellings are given. HUMBERSTON GRANGE, 1824 O, *Botany Bay or Grange Fm* 1828 Bry, the alternative name in 1828 is a nickname of remoteness, for the Grange is on the boundary of the parish. Grange here appears to be a late use of **grange**, common in L for 'a homestead, a farm–house, esp. one standing by itself remote from others', *v.* EDD s.v. 2. The form *ye No:* [i.e. *North*] *Grange* 1686 *Terrier* has been noted, but there is no indication of its site. KIRBY FM (local), named from the family of William *Kirby* 1745 Kirkby. MANOR FM is *Abbey Farm* 1704 *HumbD*, 1708 Kirkby and is *Hall F.* 1828 Bry, cf. *the Abby* 1653 *HumbD*. PEAK'S LANE, *Peack Lain* 1707 *Marshall*, cf. Peaks Fm in Weelsby *infra*. PIPE LANE, cf. *a place called badpypes* 1686 *Terrier*, *Badd pipes* 1706 *Foster*, *padpipes* (sic) 1705 *HumbD*, presumably from **pīpe** 'a pipe, a conduit'. SOUTH SEA LANE, *Sea Lane* 1828 Bry. TETNEY RD, 1707 *Marshall*, – *Gaite* 1573 *Terrier*, *v.* **gata**, leading to Tetney. THE VICARAGE, *ye vicarage house* 1577–80 *Terrier*, cf. *the Vicaridge Garth* 1703 *ib*, *v.* **garðr** 'an enclosure'. THE WALKS (lost, approx TA 303 043), 1828 Bry, *v.* **walk**, denoting land used for the pasture of animals, especially sheep, common in L. WENDOVER LANE (local), named from Viscount *Wendover*, son of Lord Carrington, *v.* Kirkby 100 and 175.

FIELD-NAMES

Undated forms in (a) are 1935 Kirkby. Forms dated 1289, 1298, 1298 are *Holywell*; 1327, 1332 *SR*; 1375[1] Peace; 1375[2] *FF*; 1523–24 *MinAcct*; 1537–38 Dugd iv; 1573, 1577–80, 1686, 1703 *Terrier*; 1567, 1579, 1587, 1612, 1615, 1618, 1624, 1630, 1660, 1667, 1669, 1686, 1692, 1705, 1706 *Foster*; 1584, 1638 *MiscDon 238;* 1608 *LRMB 256*; 1678 *FLMisc*; 1707 *Marshall*; 1728 *Td'E*, 1805 Kirkby. Forms with a date followed by *, e.g. 1501*, are *HumbD*.

(a) Abbey Green (1707, cf. *ye abbay close* 1686, *abby lands* 1573, named from Humberston Abbey and cf. *Scite . . . formerly being the Monastery of Humberston* 1612); Anthony Bank (cf. *Ant(h)ony farme* 1580, presumably from the surn. *Anthony*); Ash Garth (– *garthe* 1704*, cf. *the Ash Close* 1678*, 1687*, 1705*); The Auds; Back Cl; Bailey Hill (named from the *Bailey* family, cf. Francis *Baylie* 1660); Baldings Walk (probably named

from the surn. *Balding* and **walk** 'a sheep walk' as elsewhere in this parish);
Barn End Cl; The Bogs; Braywater (1705*, perhaps from ON **breiðr** 'broad'
and **wæter**); Bristlewells; Chestnut Holt (*v.* **holt** 'a wood, a thicket'); Gt –,
Lt Clover (sic); Cottagers' Cl; Cow Cl; Crow Holt or Monks' Walk (*v.* **holt,
walk**); Far Walk (*v.* **walk**); Gaudsgarth (*gaudsgathe* (sic) 1608, *v.* **garðr** 'an
enclosure', as elsewhere in the parish; Dr Insley suggests that the first el.
may be a surn. derived from ME *gaud* 'a trick, fraud'); Goose Paddles (*v.*
gōs; *paddle* 'a wading place' is found only rarely in f.ns., cf. Cow Paddle
PN L **1**, 22); Goxhill Cl (from the surn. *Goxhill*, cf. Lawrence *Goxhill* 1747
Kirkby); Halfway Cl; Hall Cl (cf. *le halle garthe* 1552*, *v.* **garðr**); Hill Cl;
Home Seed Plat 1805; Honey Holes (perhaps alluding to sticky soil); Horse
Cl, – Fd; Horse Marsh Cl; House Plat (*v.* **plat**[2] 'a small piece of land', as
elsewhere in the parish); Humberstone Cl (for the *Humberstone* family, *v.*
Kirkby 175); Kirman Garth (from the surn. *Kerman*, cf. Richard *Kermond*
1746 *BT*, – *Kerman* 1760 *ib.*); Madame Betty (sic); Marsh Cl; Milking Hill
1805, 1953 (*milkinghill* 1686, *Milking hill dike* 1706); Mucky Plat (*v.* **plat**[2]);
Newcroft (1573, – *crofte* 1608, – *Croft* 1704*, *the New Croft Close or Long
Close* 1705, *Newcroft Close or long Close* 1734*, self–explanatory); North
Ings (*north Inges* 1587, *North* – 1608, *le* – 1628*, *the North Ings* 1630,
North Inggs 1705*, *v.* **norð, eng** 'meadow, pasture', as elsewhere in this
parish); North Leas ((*the*) – 1692*, 1705*, 1734*, *northelease* 1608, *le
North* – 1638, *the North leaze* 1646*, – *leas* 1678*, – *leazes* 1707*, *v.* **norð,
læs** 'pasture, meadowland'); Parkers Sea Plat (from the surn. *Parker*, cf.
David *Parker* 1770 *BT*, and **plat**[2]); Peake Plat (cf. Peak's Lane *supra* and *v.*
plat[2]); Plantation Walk (*v.* **walk**); Resting Hill 1805, 1953; Rood Dales
(probably 'quarter–acre allotments', *v.* **rōd, deill**, as suggested by Mr Field);
Far –, Middle –, Second Rundles 1603, The Rundles 1953 (*Rundells* 1573,
Rundalls 1628*, 1634*, *the Rundles* 1705*, cf. *Rundillbanks*, *–furregate*
1573, *the rundall banke* 1686, *v.* **rynel** 'a runnel, a small stream'); Salt Cl
(cf. *Salt Dales* 1705*, *v.* **deill** 'a share, a portion of land', as elsewhere in
the parish); Scotch Firs; Sea Plat (cf. Parkers Sea Plat *supra*); Home Seed
Plat 1805 (*v.* **plat**[2]); Seed Marsh Cl, Gt Seeds; Smallams (*the* – 1686, cf.
Smallame Gaits 1573, *Smallomes gate* 1706, *v.* **smæl, holmr**; *–am*, *–om* are
frequent reflexes of **holmr** 'raised land in marsh, etc.' in north L); Sod
Walls (Mr Field suggests this probably means 'land hedged with turf
banks'); South Ings (1704*, *Southinge, Sowth–* 1608, *le South Inges* 1628*,
the – 1634*, *the south–Inge* 1630, *ye So: ings* 1686, *South Inggs* 1705*, *the
south Ings* 1706, *v.* **sūð, eng**); South Marsh (1692*, 1705*, – *mershe* 1608,
le South Marsh 1628*, *the South Marshe* 1634*, 1692*, self–explanatory,

v. **sūð, mersc**); South Plat (*v.* **plat**^{2}); Spit Box (sic); Swath Walk (*v.* **swæð** 'a track', later 'a strip of grassland', **walk**); Tetney Field (from the neighbouring parish of Tetney); Thrunsco Plat (cf. *Thyernescobrig'* 1298, *Throuske Becke* (sic) 1573, *Thrunscowe Inges* 1608 (*v.* **brycg, bekkr** and **eng**), from Thrunscoe in Cleethorpes parish and **plat**^{2}); Washdyke Walk (*v.* **wæsce** 'a place for washing (sheep)', **dík**); Well Garth (*v.* **wella, garðr**, and cf. *Well Syke close* 1678*, 1687*, − *Close* 1705*); Wendover Paddock (cf. Wendover Lane *supra*); Willson Plat, Willsons Sea Plat (from the surn. *Wilson*, cf. Thomas *Wilson* 1638 *BT*, with **plat**^{2} and **sæ**).

  (b) *les akerheuedes* 1298 (*v.* **æcer, hēafod** 'a headland in the common field' as elsewhere in the parish; note the appellative use of this compound in *vno akerheued* 1298 and *One other peice of meadow called an acrehead* 1573; the word is common in the 1573 *Terrier*); *Aires's Bank* 1728 (from the surn. *Aires* with **banke**); *Wm Allisons Mead* 1707 (*v.* **mæd**; in a number of examples in this parish *Mead* is qualified by a personal name); *Aloupittes* 1298 (*v.* **pytt**; the first el. is probably the AN bird-name *aloue* 'a lark'); *Bakehouse Close* 1704*; *le baland* 1298 (*v.* **land**); *Bamikermare* 1573 (*v.* **kjarr, (ge)mære**; *Bami-* is obscure); *Banckmare, Banck Mare Wonge* 1573, *a green called banck mare* 1686 (*v.* **banke, (ge)mære** 'a boundary, land on or forming a boundary' as elsewhere in the parish, with **vangr** 'a garden, an in-field', and perhaps cf. Bank Plantation in f.ns. (a) *supra*); *Ralph Bassnip Mead* 1707 (*v.* **mæd** and cf. *Wm Allisons Mead supra*); *baxter dale* 1686 (from the surn. *Baxter* and **deill**); *Bell-Gaite, -gate* 1573 (presumably from the surn. *Bell*, though this has not been noted before Martin *Bell* 1666 *BT*, with **gata** 'a way, a road', 'land by a road', as elsewhere in the parish); *berefurlanges* 1298 ('the barley furlongs', *v.* **bere, furlang**); *berg* 1298 ('the hill, the mound', *v.* **berg**); *Bilburnes Lands* 1573 (the *heires of Bilburne* were occupiers in 1573); *(the) Bottom Close* 1678*, 1687*, 1706*, *the bottom Close* 1705* (self-explanatory); *bounehoumare, − marehill'* 1298 ('the hill, the mound where beans grow', *v.* **baun, haugr**, a Scand. compound, with **(ge)mære** and **hyll**); *Bradinge* 1585*, 1587, *Brady* (sic) 1707 (*v.* **brād, eng**); *braytengpittes* 1298 (cf. *terram Henr' brayt* 1298, *v.* **eng, pytt**); *broxwelles* 1298 (probably from **brocc** 'a badger' and **wella**); *Brummet farme* 1686 (named from the *Brummet* family, cf. William *Bromett* 1688 *BT*); *Brusssells hill* 1707* (perhaps to be identified with Bristlewells in f.ns. (a) *supra*); *burghou* 1298 (*v.* **burh** 'a fortified place, etc.', **haugr** 'a mound', but the significance here is unknown); *Land called a Butt* 1573 (*v.* **butte** 'a strip of land abutting on a boundary'); *the Butts* 1573 (probably a reference to shooting butts, *v.* **butt**^{2}); *Candlesby thyng* 1548 (from the surn. *Candlesby* and **þing** 'property, possessions' as elsewhere in the parish); *Castello* 1327, *Castell'* 1332 both (p) (this is unlikely to be a

local topographical surn.); *Charleslande* 1523–24 (from the surn. *Charles* with
land); *Sac*[h] *Chessman Mead* 1707 (*v.* **mǣd** and cf. *W*[m] *Allisons Mead supra*);
Cock Garth 1706 (*v.* **cocc**[2], **garð**; perhaps a cock–fighting enclosure); *a
parcell of Land called a common Greene* 1573 (cf. *Atte Grene* 1327, 1375[1]
both (p), *v.* **grēne**[2]); *Conne Greene, Congrenegate, Congrenehole* 1573 (*v.*
coninger); *Corne Fields* 1705* (*v.* **feld**); *Corn heads* 1686 (*v.* **corn, hēafod**);
the Cow marsh 1706; *Crosse gate* 1706 (*v.* **cros, gata**); *Cudgell greene* 1707*;
meadows called a Daile 1573 (*v.* **deill** 'a share, a portion of land' as elsewhere
in the parish); *Thomas Dannatts Cottages* 1667, *Danats Farme* 1705; *Dilcocke
thing* 1660[1], 1660[2], – *thinge* 1670* (named from the *Dilcock* family, cf.
William *Dilcocke* 1562 *Inv*, and **þing**); *Dixons Cottage* 1705 (named from the
Dixon family, cf. William *Dicson* 1538 *Inv*); *Ralph Dodson Mead* 1707 (*v.*
mǣd, and cf. *W*[m] *Allison's Mead supra*); *Docken Grave* 1573; *Donnesham
Dike* 1573 (the reading of the first part of the name is uncertain); *Dowdswell's
house* 1667, *W*[m] *Dowdswell Mead* 1707 (named from the *Dowdswell* family;
Thomas *Dowswell* is named in the 1667 document; *v.* **mǣd** and cf. *W*[m]
Allison's Mead supra); *Drawewater dyke* 1573; *in orientali campo de
Humberstayn* 1289, *in oriental' campo* 1298, *in Campo orient'* 1573, *in orient'
Campo de Humeston* (sic) 1628*, *in orien' Campo de Humerstone* 1638, *le
Eastfield, le Est field, este feeld* 1608, *the Easte feilde* 1630, *East Field* 1704*,
the East feild 1706 (*v.* **ēast, feld**, one of the great fields of the parish, cf. *in
borialibus campis, the south feilde, y*[e] *West feild infra*); *y*[e] *East forlong* 1686
(*v.* **ēast, furlang**); *faldenges, Faldhenges* 1298 (*v.* **falod** 'a fold', **eng**); *Farr
becks* 1707 (*v.* **bekkr**; *farr Ings* 1705 (*v.* **eng**); *in campis de Humberstan*
1298, *Humberstone Field* 1728, cf. *y*[e] *fyelde syde* 1577–80 (*v.* **feld**); *lez Firres*
1573 (*v.* **fyrs** 'furze'); *footbal close* 1704*; *Christ Fridington Mead* (sic) 1707
(*v.* **mǣd** and for the *Fridlington* family, *v.* Kirkby 177; cf. also *W*[m] *Allison's
Mead supra*); *Furrewell Greene, the long Furwells* 1573, *forwels green* 1686;
Garods Garth 1734* (from the surn. *Garrod* and **garðr**); *Garwonge,
garwange* 1608, *Garwong* 1706* (*v.* **geiri** 'a triangular piece of land', **vangr**
'a garden, an in–field' as elsewhere in the parish); *Gleselandes* 1298 (*v.* **land**;
the first el. is obscure); *N*[o] –, *S*[o] *Goat* 1707 (*v.* **gotu** 'a sluice'; they were near
the sea); *Gye Close, Gye Farm* 1704* (no doubt from a surn.); *Halton Close*
1573, 1705*, – *Lands* 1573; *Hausk(e)mare* 1573 (*v.* (**ge**)**mǣre**; the first el. is
obscure); *Holton dike, – hill* 1686 (*v.* **dík, hyll**), *Howlton feild* 1608, *Howton
Field Mare* 1573 (*v.* (**ge**)**mǣre**) (referring to the neighbouring parish of Holton
le Clay); *Higden landes* 1584 (from the surn. *Higden* with **land**); *crofto . . .
vocat Hodgebell* (sic) 1646*; *Holmehill* 1573 (*v.* **holmr** 'raised land in marsh,
etc.', **hyll**); *Hounds mare* 1573 (*v.* (**ge**)**mǣre**); *Hubbarmare* (sic) 1573,
hubar–, hawber – 1578*, *Hubbart –* 1686 (presumably from the pers.n. or

derived surn. *Hubert* and **(ge)mǣre** 'a boundary, land on a boundary'); *Hundon mear* 1686 (*Hundon* is probably a surn. here with **(ge)mǣre**); *the Ing(e)s* 1573, *ings of Humberston* 1686, cf. *Inges meade* 1608, *ings and dale* 1686, *Ings dyke* 1686 (*v.* **eng** 'meadow, pasture', with **mǣd**, **deill**, and **dík**); *Jekell lande* 1552* (named from the family of Johm *Jekyll* 1585* and **land**); *Kellgate* 1646* (probably from the surn. *Kell*, cf. Martin *Kell* 1665 Kirkby and **gata** 'a road, land by a road'; the surn. *Kell* is a short form the ON pers.n. *Ketill*, which is recorded in Humberston in Henry *Ketill'* 1332 *SR*); *kidger grene* 1585*, 1587 (presumably from the surn. *Kidger* with **grēne²** 'a green, a grassy place'); *Lamb Close* 1704*; *Lea Close* 1704* (*v.* **lea** (OE **lēah**) 'meadow, pasture'); *litle close* 1608; *Litle far* (sic) 1667; *yᵉ marfrey* 1686 (*v.* **marfur** 'a boundary furrow'; *marfrey* is a variant form of the more common *marfer*); *le marked gate* 1298 (perhaps 'the road to the market', *v.* **market**, **gata**); *Mar tofte wong* 1578* (*v.* **toft** 'a messuage, a curtilage', **vangr**; *Mar* is uncertain); *le Mere* 1298 (*v.* **(ge)mǣre**); *mikelmare, –hill* 1298, *a green called Mickmare* 1686, 1706 ('the great, big boundary (land)', *v.* **míkill**, **(ge)mǣre**); *Midle furlong, yᵉ midle forlong* 1686 (*v.* **furlang**); *yᵉ Mile Green* (sic) 1686 (probably 'the mill green', *v.* **myln**, **grēne²**), *the milne close* 1573, *Mill Close* 1704*, *the Olde Milne Gate* 1573 (*v.* **gata** or **geat**); *Milster green* 1686; *the Moate Syde* 1704*; *Mossey Greene* 1573, *mossaie gate* 1578*, *– grene* 1578*, 1707* ('the mossy grassy place' *v.* **grēne²**); *Myre Firres* 1573, *Mire firrs* 1686 (*v.* **mýrr**, **fyrs** 'furze'); *le mires* 1298 (*v.* **mýrr**); *Neuland' de Humberstayne* 1375¹, 1375² both (p), *newe lande* 1608, cf. *Newland dale* 1686 (*v.* **nīwe**, **land** with **deill**); *the new close*, 1646*, *New –* 1669, *the New Close* 1706; *Edward Noble Mead* 1707 (*v.* **mǣd** and cf. *Wᵐ Allison's Mead supra*); *a dike called the noone layers dike* 1706 (*v.* **dík**; Mr Field suggests that this may allude to a place favoured by cattle resting at midday); *north becke* 1585*, *– Becke* 1587 (*v.* **bekkr** and cf. *Sᵒ Bek infra*); *the North End* 1573, 1705* (*v.* **norð**, **ende¹** and cf. *the South End infra*); *in boriali campo de Humberstan* 1296, *in borialibus campis* 1298 (*v.* **norð**, **feld** and cf. *in orientali campo de Humberstayne supra*, *the south feilde, yᵉ West feild infra*; Mr Field points out that North Fields seem to have been merged with one of the others (or to have been renamed) since there is no record of it after 1298); *No: forlong* 1686 (*v.* **norð**, **furlang**); *(the) North Marsh* 1573, 1634*, 1692*, 1707*, 1734*, *north marshe* 1585*, *north –* 1587, *le North mershe* 1608, *in borial' Marisco* 1628*, *in Boriale Marisco de Humberstone* 1638 (*v.* **norð**, **mersc** and cf. *yᵉ Southmarsh infra*); *le Noutegate* 1298 ('the cattle road', *v.* **naut**, **gata**, a Scand. compound); *the Oak Tree farme* 1667, *Oake Tree Farm* 1704*, *Oake tree house* 1678*, *the house . . . commonlly knowne by the name of the Oake-tree* 1678, *Oake tree Farme* 1705*); *Oak Wood* 1707; *un' selio vocat'*

Osberne 1298 ('a selion called Osbern'; *Osbern* as a pers.n. goes back either to AScand *Ōsbeorn* < *Ásbjorn* or to Norman *Osbern*, which can be derived from OSax *Ōsbeorn* or from AScand *Ōsbeorn*, as noted by Dr Insley; Mr Field points out that the naming of a selion in this way is noteworthy); *owt land* 1686, *(the) outlands* 1705*, 1706 (*v*. **ūt, land**); *Palcett Greene* 1646*; *Pallmere Close, Pallmer Headland* 1573 (*v*. **hēafod–land**), *Pallmer Wange* 1573 (*v*. **vangr**), *one Messsuage or tenement Called palmer landis* 1618, *Palmer Landes* 1624 (*v*. **land**; all named from the *Palmer* family, cf. John *Palmer* 1603 *BT*); *Pange garthe* 1670* (*v*. **garðr**); *patchett close* 1608 (*Griffin Patchet* was the tenant in 1608); *Pedekocholme* 1298 (perhaps from the ME surn. *Pedecok* and **holmr**, though Dr Insley prefers to see *Pedekoc* as being from AN *pé –, pie de coc*, a translation of ME *cokkesfot* 'columbine'); *Jnᵒ Porthous Mead* 1707 (*v*. **mǣd** and cf. *Wᵐ Allison's Mead supra*); *porte bedds* 1686; *(the) Queens Lands* 1573, *yᵉ queenes grounde* 1577–80; *Wᵐ Robinson Mead* 1707 (*v*. **mǣd** and cf. *Wᵐ Allison's Mead supra*); *Routhaumare* 1298 ('the red mound', *v*. **rauðr, haugr** (a Scand. compound), with **(ge)mǣre**); *Rows mare* 1573, *Rows New Close* 1707 (from the family of Robert *Rowse* and **(ge)mǣre**); *Sage Close* 1705; *Sandey Gate* 1646* (*v*. **sandig, gata**); *the sea bankes* 1578*, *yᵉ Sea bank* 1686 (self-explanatory); *seares close* 1608 (presumably from the surn. *Seare*); *Shifts close* 1686 (probably alluding to *shifts* in crop rotation, as discussed s.n. *a shift Acre* in the f.ns. of South Ferriby PN L **2**, 116 and cf. Shift cls in Immingham f.ns. (a) ib, 169); *Skeldremare (Gate)* 1573; *un selion' apud Skyre* 1298 (Dr Insley suggests that this is 'a selion at the rocky outcrop', from ME *skar(re), skir(re)* 'a rocky cliff, a crag, a jagged outcropping' of Norse origin, cf. ON *sker* 'a skerry', *v*. MED, s.v. *scarre* n. (2)); *Smith close* 1583 (this was a toft occupied by *the heires of Smith* 1573); *Sᵒ Bek* 1707 (*v*. **sūð, bekkr** and cf. *northe becke supra*); *the South End* 1573 (cf. *the North End supra*); *the south feilde* 1630; *the south Marshe* 1573, *Sowth marshe* 1608, *yᵉ South marsh* 1686, *the South marsh* 1706, cf. *the South Marsh Close* 1728 (cf. *the North Marsh supra*); *Stone hole* 1706; *Tagg–Greene* 1573, *Tags Close* 1734* (probably from **tagga** 'a young sheep' with **grēne²** 'a grassy place' and **clos(e)**); *Tethering grounds* 1573, *tetheringe grounde* 1579, 1585*, *Tetheringe ground* 1628* (self-explanatory; this was in the West Field); *Thistilbarghe* 1573 (*v*. **þistel, beorg** 'a hill'); *Thorndayles* 1298 (*v*. **þorn, deill**); *Thorney Firrs, – Greene, – Leaze* 1573 (*v*. **þornig, fyrs** and **lǣs**); *Town Fields* 1707*; *Wᵐ Tweed Mead* 1707 (*v*. **mǣd**); *Johm Usells Med* (sic) (*v*. **mǣd** and for this and the preceding, cf. *Wᵐ Allison's Mead supra*); *Waltham streete* 1686 (*v*. **strǣt**), *Wattom Gate, wattam Gaite* 1573, *Waltham gate* 1578* (*v*. **gata**, no doubt the same as the preceding name), *Wattam Feild marre* 1373 (*v*. **feld, (ge)mǣre**) (all with reference to the adjoining parish of Waltham); *Waterson Farme*, *Watersons Garth*, 1705, *Waterton Farme*, *- Garth* 1734* (from the surn. *Waterson*, *Waterton* with **ferme** and **garðr**); *Webster farme* 1667 (from the *Webster* family, cf. Mary *Webster* 1646 *Foster*); *a Messuage or tenement knowne and Called by the name of Welles* 1615 (named from the family of *Lord Welles* 1686 *Foster*); *weste close* 1608; *in occidentali campo* 1298, *in Campo occident'* 1573, *in occident' Campo de Humberstone* 1628, *le westfield*, *weste feeld*1608, *the west feild* 1634*, *le westfeilde* 1656*, *West feild* 1705*, 1707* (*v.* **west**, **feld**, one of the great fields of the parish, cf. *in orientali campo de Humberstayn*, *the south feilde supra*); *West furlong* 1573, *ye weste forlong* 1686 (*v.* **west**, **furlang**); *westsikequarter* 1608 (*v.* **west**, **sík** 'a ditch, a trench' with **quarter**, for which cf. Chapel Field Quarter in Goxhill, PN L 2, 121–22); *Whauberdale*, *Whawber daile* 1578* (the first el. is probably a surn.; the second is **deill**); (*the*) *whip close* 1646, 1669, *the Whipp close* 1706; *Alan Whiting Cowgarth* 1686* (*v.* **cū**, **garðr**); *Mollendinum ventriticum* 1537–38, 1564*, *nouum molendinum ventriticum* 1552*, *Wyndemyll* 1567, *- Millne* 1686*, *Wind Millen* 1586, *- Mill* 1692, *–miln* 1706* (self-explanatory).

Irby upon Humber

IRBY UPON HUMBER

Iribi (2x) 1086 DB
Irebi 1086 DB, c.1115 LS, 1166, 1167 P both (p), 1202 Ass, –*by* 1242–43 Fees, 1254 ValNor, 1257 FF, 1276 RH, 1304 Ipm, *et passim* to 1502 ib, *Yrebi* 1181, 1182 P both (p), 1185 Templar, 112 RA ix, 1200 P, 1201 Ass (p), 1204 Cur, 1210 P (p), –*by* 1237 Cl, 1261 FF, 1265 RRGr
Hirebi 1157–63 Dane, 1212 Fees, *Hyreby* 1210–12 RBE, 1242–43 Fees, 1338 Pat
Irreby c.1240 RA iv, 1282 Ipm, 1291 Tax, 1306 RA iv, 1316, 1346 FA, 1375 Peace, 1428 FA
Irbi 1275 RH, *Irby* 1303 FA, 1306 RA iv, 1306, 1317 Misc, 1327 SR, (*- "by" Layseby*) 1328 Banco, 1329 Pat, (*- iuxta Leysseby*) 1332 FF, 1346 FA, 1375, 1381, 1395 Peace, 1402 FA *et freq*, (*- super Humbre*) 1401–2 FA, (*- next Gret*

Grymesby) 1527 Wills ii, *Irby alias Ireby alias Erby be Swallow* (sic) 1741 *PT, Irbie* 1576 LER, 1724 *Terrier*
Hirby Hy2 (1409) Gilb, 1383 Peace, *Hyrby* 1267–73 RA ix
Yresbi 1222 Welles
Urby 1303, 1428 FA
Eirby 1504 Cl, 1504 Pat
Erebye 1576 Saxton, 1610 Speed, *–by* 1577 Harrison
Erby 1589 (1658) HollesM, 1625, 1634, 1638 *Terrier, –bie*
1613 *Td'E*
Earbie 1623 *Td'E, Eareby* 1638 *Terrier*

'The farmstead, village of the Irishmen', *v. Íri* (*Íra* gen.pl.),
bȳ. The reference is probably to an isolated settlement of
Norwegian Vikings from Ireland, or perhaps to Irishmen who
accompanied the Vikings to England. Irby is *upon Humber* in
contrast to Irby *in the Marsh*, LSR. It is also distinguished above
as near Laceby and Great Grimsby.

BARTON STREET, cf. *the streete close* 1625, *yᵉ street(–)close* 1634,
1638, (*the*) *Street Close* 1718, 1724, 1781, 1822, 1838 all *Terrier*,
1800, 1833 *Yarb* and *Street Close alias Deadmans grave* 1679, *the
street close –* 1686 both *Terrier*; this is the name of a presumed
pre-Roman trackway along the eastern edge of the Wolds leading
to Barton upon Humber. CHURCH LANE (local), cf. *Church and
Church Yard* 1837 *TA*. GLEBE COTTAGE, cf. *the Glebe Land* 1822
Terrier. IRBY DALES, *the dales* 1612, 1638, 1662, 1690, *yᵉ Dales*
1671, 1674, *the –* 1697, 1706, 1724, 1762, *Irby Dales* 1748 all
Terrier, v. **dalr** 'a valley' in the pl. IRBY DALES WOOD, *– Dale
Wood* 1824 O, *The Dales Wood* 1833 *Yarb*, 1837 *TA*. IRBY
HOLMES WOOD, *Holmes Wood* 1833 *Yarb*, cf. *Holme* 1602, 1612,
the Holmes 1638, 1662, 1697, 1748, 1762 all *Terrier*, 1812, 1833
Yarb, yᵉ Howme 1674, *yᵉ Houmes* 1668 both *Terrier, the Holm or
Ox pasture* 1690 *ib, Irby Holmes* 1824 O, *v.* **holmr**, varying
between the sg. and pl. MILL FIELD (lost, on the parish boundary
alongside the road from Irby to Swallow), 1812 *Yarb*, 1824 O,
1828 Bry, *– Plat* 1837 *TA, Mill field* 1800 *Yarb*, cf. *my mill at
Irby* 1772 *Field*, and *parkemylne de Hirby* 1383 Peace,

self-explanatory, *v.* **myln**, **feld** and **park**. MOAT, 1800 *Yarb*, *The Moats* 1824 O. NEW LANE (lost) 1828 Bry; it is the name of the lane eastwards from the village to Scrub Holt. NORTH'S LANE, named from a local family, cf. Francis *North* 1748 PR. ODESSA is *Pyewipe Hall* 1828 Bry; *pyewipe* is a common dial. term in L for the lapwing; the modern name Odessa is presumably a nickname of remoteness for a place close to the parish boundary with Beelsby. RECTORY (lost), 1828 Bry, – *House* 1822 *Terrier*, 1837 *TA*, *a* – 1864 *Terrier*, *One mansion or dwellinge house* 1612, *the parsonage house* 1638, 1662, *yᵉ Parsonage* 1671, *A Parsonage house* 1697, – *House* 1724, *One Parsonage house* 1762 all *ib*, *Parsonage Homestead* 1800 *Yarb*. RUSH HILLS COVERT, – *hill Cover* 1837 *TA*, *Rash Hills Cover* (sic) 1833 *Yarb* and is *Scrub Holt* 1828 Bry, cf. Scrub Holt *infra*. SCRUB HOLT is *Rough Close* 1828 Bry, and is *Irby Scrub Close* 1824 O, *Scrub Close Wood* 1837 *TA*, cf. *Scrub Close* 1800, 1812 *Yarb*. TRUNKASS LANE, *Trunkhouse Lane* 1828 Bry. WALK FM, cf. *Sheep Walk, Top* – 1800 *Yarb*, *The Walk* 1833 *ib*, *Walk, Top Walk* 1837 *TA*, *v.* **walk** 'a stretch of grass used for pasturing animals, especially sheep', common in L. WELBECK HILL, 1828 Bry, *the springes of Welbecks* 1658 HollesM, *South Welbeek* (sic) 1671 PR (Irby), *Welbeck* 1800 *Yarb*, *Well Beck* 1812 *ib*, for additional forms *v.* Welbeck Spring in Barnoldby le Beck, PN L **4**, 55, where it is pointed out that here there is a deep hollow with a spring rising from it and flowing to join Team Gate Drain. The hollow was full of water within the present generation and was used for bathing. The meaning of Welbeck is 'the stream rising from a spring', *v.* **wella, bekkr**.

FIELD–NAMES

Undated forms in (a) are 1837 *TA*; forms dated 1327, 1332 *SR*; 1375, 1381, 1382 Peace; 1602, 1612, 1625, 1638, 1662, 1668, 1671, 1674, 1679, 1686, 1690, 1697, 1706, 1718, 1724, 1748, 1762, 1781, 1822, 1838 *Terrier*; 1800, 1812, 1833 *Yarb*.

(a) Acre 1800, Acres 1812, The Acre 1833, 1837 (*v*. **æcer**); Ancient Lane in Seven Gardens; Ash Cl 1800, 1812 (*v*. **æsc**); Barnoldby le Beck Road 1822 (self-explanatory; Barnoldby is an adjacent parish); South Beacon Hill 1833, Beacon Fd 1800, 1837, Bacon Fd (sic) 1812; Beck Cl 1800, 1812, 1833, 1837 (*v*. **bekkr**); Beelsby Lane Plat (*v*. **plat**² 'a small piece of ground', as elsewhere in the parish; Beelsby is an adjacent village); Beelsby Sheepwalk 1833 (*v*. **shepe-walk**); Bormans Walk 1800 (named from the *Borman* family, cf. William *Borman* 1800, with **walk** 'a sheep pasture', as elsewhere in this parish); Bottom Cl; Far –, First Bottom Fd; Brick Kiln Cl; Burkitts Garden (named from the *Burkett* family, cf. David *Burkett* 1833 *Yarb*); Calf Cl 1812, 1822, 1833, 1837 (*the Calfe close* 1602, 1612); Carr 1800, 1812, The Car 1833, Car 1837 (cf. *Atte Ker* 1327, *atte Kerre* 1327, 1332 all (p), *v*. **kjarr**); Claytons Ings 1800 (named from the *Clayton* family, cf. Richard *Clayton* named in the document, with **eng** 'meadow, pasture' in the pl., as elsewhere in the parish); Cock Fd 1812; Coney Green 1800, 1812, Coney Green Cl 1833, Bottom –, Top Coney Green 1837 (cf. *a layne called Conegry layne* 1602, *the Conegry lane* 1612, *Conigry-lane* (sic) 1638, *Conygreene-lane* 1662, *v*. **coninger** 'a rabbit warren'); Cook Fd 1812; First –, Second Cook Fd 1833, First Cook Fd 1837 (named from the *Cook(e)* family, cf. William *Cooke* 1642 LPR); the Cottagers Plat 1822, 1838 (*Cottyers platt* 1625, *Erby cottyers platt* 1625, 1634, *Erby Cottagers platt* 1638, *yᵉ long Close alias yᵉ Cotagers platt* 1679, *the Long Close alias the Cottagers platt* 1686, *the Cotchers Plat* 1718, 1724, *the Cottager's Plat* 1781 (*v*. **plat**²; *Cottyer* and *Cotcher* are common alternatives for *Cottager* in north L); Cow Cl 1800, 1812, 1833, 1837, – Fd 1837, Cowfield 1800; Crab Yard Homestead 1800, Crab Yard & House 1812, Crab Yd 1833; Dean Davy's Garden (*Dean Davy* has not been identified, but *Davy* is a local surn., cf. Robert *Davy* 1749 PR); 8 Acres 1800, Eight – 1812, 1833, – acres 1837; 18 Acres 1800, Eighteen – 1812, 1833, (Far –, Long –, Middle) Eighteen – 1837; Eleven Acres 1800, 1812, – acres 1833, 1837; Farfield 1800, 1812, Far Fd 1833; Far Walk (cf. Walk Fm *supra*); First –, Second Fd; 15 Acres 1800, Fifteen – 1812, – acres 1833; 5 Acres 1800, Five – 1812, five – 1833; 40 shillings Fd 1800, Forty Shillings Fd 1812 (alluding to a rent or other payment); 4 Acres 1800, Four – 1812, 1833, 1837; 14 Acres 1800, Fourteen – 1812, 1833, Fox Cover 1800, the Fox Cover 1822; Garth 1800, 1812, 1833 (*v*. **garðr** 'an enclosure'); Gipsey Plat (*v*. **plat**²); G' Field 1800, Great – 1812; Green Lane ('an access way or occupation road'); Top Hastings 1800, Hastings 1812, 1833 (probably relating to *Hastings*, an early-cropping variety of pea); Hog Pitt long Fd 1800, Hog pit Fd 1812, – Pit Fd 1833, 1837 (*v*. **hogg**, **pytt**); Hollow Bridge 1800, Hollin

– 1812, Holland Bridge (sic) 1833, Hollow Briggs 1837 ('a bridge or causeway in a hollow' *v.* **brycg** (Scandinavianized in the 1837 form), **hol**[1] or **hol**[2]; Holme Walk Wood (*v.* **holmr, walk** and cf. Irby Holmes *supra*); Holton Cl (referring to Holton le Clay, a few miles to the SE); Home Cl (several), Bottom –, Top Home Cl; Home Fd 1800, 1833; Horse Cl; Ings 1800, 1812, 1833, – Cl 1837 (*the Inges* 1602, 1612, *the Inges close* 1602, – *Close* 1748, *Inges close* 1612, *the Inges closes* 1638 *y[e] Inges close* 1668, *Ings Close* 1671, 1706, *the Ings close* 1690, *Ings close* 1697, *the Ingsclose* 1724, cf. *y[e] Inges Walke* 1601, *the* – 1638, *v.* **eng** 'meadow, pasture'); High Intake 1800, 1833, – Intack, Low – 1812, Btm –, Top Intake (*v.* **inntak** 'a piece of land taken in or enclosed'); Johnsons Farm, – Wood 1800 (named from the *Johnson* family, cf. Joshua *Johnson* 1800); High –, Low Joint Cl (sic) 1800, – Joist Cl 1833, Joist Pasture, New Joist Cl 1837 ('the rented land, especially pasture' *v.* **agist**); Lane Cl 1800, – cl 1833; Lanker Lair 1800, Lunkerlease 1812, Lanker lees (sic) 1833, Laukan Ley (sic) 1837; Lea Cl; Ley Fd 1800, 1812 1812 (*v.* **lǣge** 'fallow, unploughed, lying untilled', **feld**); Lingard Cl (probably from the surn. *Lingard*); Little Fd 1812; Long fd 1800, – Fd 1800, 1812, 1833, 1837; Low Cl 1812; Lowfield 1800, 1812, Low Fd 1833 (cf. *the lower arable feild* 1602, 1612); Low Gdn; Middle Dales (*v.* **deill** in the pl.); Middle Walk (*v.* **walk**); Moat and Island (south of the road from Irby to Laceby and east of the church; it is different from Moat *supra*); New Fd; Nine Acres 1800, 1812, – acres 1833, 1837; Orchard (several); Oziers; Paddock 1833, 1837; Pattison Cl 1800, 1812, Paddison Cl 1837 (from the surn. *Paddison, Pattison*, cf. James *Paddison* 1727 PR, James *Pattison* 1782 ib); Pen Garth (*v.* **penn, garðr**); Pig Sties; Pig Yd; Pinfold Fd 1800, 1812, 1833, 1837 (*v.* **pynd–fald**); (Far) Pingle (*v.* **pingel** 'a small enclosure'); Pitt Fd 1800, Pit Fd 1812, 1833, (Great –, Little) Pit Fd 1837, Pit Walk 1837 (*v.* **pytt**); Plantation; First –, Second Plat (*v.* **plat**[2]); Plough Walk (*v.* **walk**); 17 Acres 1800, Seventeen – 1812, 1833, – acres 1837; Sheep Walk 1812, Far –, Little –, Near –, North –, South Sheep Walk 1833 (*v.* **shepe–walk**); Stack Yard 1833; Starlings 1800 (possibly from the surn. *Starling*); Steephill Side (self–explanatory); Stone Pit 1812, – Plat 1837 (*v.* **stān, pytt, plat**[2]); Stonepit Sheep Walk 1833; Stray Piece 1800; Strut Cl 1812 (perhaps a variant of Street Cl, cf. Barton Street *supra*); Swallow Plat 1837, North –, South Swallow Walk, South Swallow Sheep Walk 1833 (*v.* **plat**[2], **walk**); Swallow is an adjacent parish); Swardale Bottom; (Far –, Near) Ten Acres; Thistle Fd (*v.* **þistel**); Thomas Fd 1812 (probably from the surn. *Thomas*); Thorn Cl 1800, 1812, 1837 (*v.* **þorn**); 3 Acres 1800, Three – 1812, The Three acres 1833; Three Gardens; Top Cl; Top Fd 1800, 1812, North –, South Top Fd 1833, First –, Second –, Third

Top Fd 1837; Top Garden; Tup Pk 1800, 1812 (*v.* **tup** 'a ram'); 12 Acres
1800, Twelve – 1812, 1837, – acres 1833, The Twelve Acres 1833; Uffindale
(sic) 1837; Valley 1800; Washton dales 1762 (*Weston dale hedge* 1638,
Weston-dale 1662, *Westondale* 1706, 1724, *the Washtone Dale* (sic) 1748);
Well Garth 1800, 1812, 1833, 1837, – Yard 1800, 1812 (*v.* **wella, geard,
garðr**); Willows 1810, 1812, Willow Pingle 1781, 1822, 1838, Willows Cl
1833, 1837 (*the willow garth* 1602, *the willow close* 1612, – *willow pingle*
1625, *Willow pingle* 1634, – *Pingle* 1638, 1718, 1724, *the* – 1686, *v.* **garðr,
pingel**); Wood Cl 1833, 1837; Yard (*v.* **geard**).

(b) *Brygsele close* 1674 (referring to Brigsley, a nearby parish); *the
Common furres* 1638 (*v.* **furh** 'a furrow' in the pl.); *Croft de Irby* 1375 (p) (*v.*
croft); *Grene de Irby* 1381 (p) (*v.* **grene**²); *atte Hallegarth* 1332 (p) (*v.* **hall,
garðr**); *the kings high way* 1638; *kow pasture* 1602, *the kow* – 1612; *the long
close* 1634 (*v.* the early forms of the Cottagers Plat in (a) *supra*); *a furre-plat
of yᵉ Lords* 1638, *a parcell of furzground commonly called the Lords furzs*
(sic) 1724 (*v.* **fyrs, plat**²); *Moore dale* 1638 (*v.* **mōr, deill** 'a share of land');
the Orley close 1602, 1612; *the common pastures of Toft* . . . 1602, *the
common pasture of Tofte* . . ., *the Toft pasture* 1612, *toft lane & toft* 1638 (*v.*
toft 'a messuage, a curtilage'); *the upper close* 1602, *the upp close* 1612 (*v.*
upp, clos(e)).

Laceby

LACEBY

Lenesbi [*n* = *u*] 1086 DB (*Leuesbi* DBAbbreviatio), *Leves-,
Leuesbi* 1086 DB, 1130 P, 1132 (1403) Pat, *Leusebi* 1156 P
Leyseby c.1115 LS, 1204 FF (p), 1254 ValNor, 1266 Misc,
1272 *Ass*, (– "near" *Grimesby*) 1273 Ipm, 1274 Abbr, 1286
Ass, –*bi* 1276 RH
Leisebi 1145–54 (1394) Pat, 1155–58 (1334) Ch, Hy2 (1461)
Pat, –*by* 1272 *Ass*, *Leissebi* 1168, 1201, 1202, 1203 P *et
passim* to 1214 ib, –*b'* 1219 Fees (p), –*by* 1200, 1202 P both
(p), 1214 Cur, 1242–43 Fees, 1266 Ipm, *Leysseby* 1304
Abbr, 1315 Pat, 1315 Inqaqd, 1316 Orig, *Leysceby*
1240–50, 1306 RA iv, 1316 FA, 1335 Ipm, 1336 Cl
Laifsebi lHy2 Dane

Laisseby 1201 ChR, 1242–43 Fees, 1314 Pat, 1322 Ipm, *Laysseby* 1319 YearBk, 1327 *SR*, 1342 Cl, 1342 Ipm, 1369 *AD*, *Laisebi* 1202 Ass (p), *–by* 1314 Inqaqd, *Laysebi* 1259 Ipm, *–by* 1313, 1318 Cl, 1329 *Ass*

Laisceby 1240–53 RA iv, 1328 Pat, 1338 *HarlCh*, 1363 Pat, *Laysceby* 1258–63, a1260, 1306 RA iv, 1334 Ipm, 1372 Misc, 1375, 1381 Peace, 1383 BS, 1394 Pat

Layceby 1327 Ipm, 1329 *Ass*, 1332 *SR*, 1349 *Cor*, 1359 Ipm, 1365 Pat, 1373 Peace, 1380 Cl, 1402 *MM*, 1409 Cl, 1428 FA

Laisby 1293 *Ass*, 1602 *BT*, *–bie* 1592 ib, *Laysby* 1344 Ipm, *–bye* 1402 ib, *Laiceby* 1387, 1388, 1395 Peace

Leffebi (*–ff–* = *–ss–*) 1177 P, *Lessebi* 1177, 1180, 1181, 1182 P all (p) *et freq* to 1203 Cur (p), 1230 ChancR, *–b'* 1225 ClR, *–by* 1201 Memo, 1209 FF (p), 1210–12 RBE, 1227 Ch, 1234 Cl, 1234 FF, 1234 Ch, 1260 FF *et passim* to 1374 Ipm

Lesebi 1178, 1180, 1188 P all (p). 1196 ChancR, 1197 P, *–by* 1230 ib, 1282 Cl

Laceby 1327 Fine, 1395, 1401 Cl, 1431 FA, 1441 Cl, 1487 Ipm, 1490 Cl, 1490 Ipm, 1526 Sub *et passim*, *–bye* 1566 Pat, 1576 LER, 1609, 1611, 1624 *BT*, *–bie* 1564, 1570, 1586, 1598, 1607 *ib*

Laseby 1576 Saxton, 1610 Speed

Lasbye 1565, 1589, *–bie* 1600, 1607, *–by* 1601 all *BT*

'Leif's farmstead, village' from the ON pers.n. *Leifr* and **bȳ**. The pers.n. is not recorded independently in L, though it is in Y, *v.* SPNLY 185. It is very likely that spellings in *–ss–* are assimilated forms of *–fs–*.

Austin Garth, named from a local family, cf. John *Austin* 1566 *PR*, and **garðr** 'an enclosure'. Barton Street, cf. – *Close* 1840 *TA*. It is referred to in *regie strate versus Ludam* [i.e. Louth] a1260 RA iv and in *the street lane* 1601 *Terrier*, *the street* 1611 *ib*, *Street Close* m18 Monson, 1750, 1753, 1779 *PT*, 1840 *TA*, and *v.* the same name in Aylesby *supra*. Church Lane, cf. *Church &*

Church Yard 1840 *TA* and *Attekirke* 1284 Abbr, *atte Kyrk* 1304 ib, *v.* **kirkja**. COOPER LANE, 1724 *MiscDon 238*, cf. – *Close* 1753 *PT*, no doubt named from a local family, though the earliest reference noted is to William *Cooper* 1815 *BT*. COTTAGER'S PLAT, *cottagers' plot* 1779 *PT*, *Cottagers –*, *v.* **plot**, **plat**² 'a small piece of ground'. CROSS LANES HO (lost), – *Ho*. 1828 Bry, cf. – *Paddock* 1840 *TA*; it was at the junction of Barton Street and the Grimsby road, the modern A46. FIELD HO, cf. *camp' de Laysby* 1239 (Ed1) *Newh*, *campis de Laysby* c.1240 (Ed1) *ib*, – *Laysceby* a1260, 1306 RA iv, commemorating the open field of the village. FISH PONDS. GRIMSBY RD, *Grimesbygate* 1258–63 RA iv, *v.* **gata**. HOG PIT HILL, cf. *The Hogpitts* m18 *Monson*, *Hogpit* 1750 *PT*, *the Hog–Pit Close* 1753 *ib*, *Hog Pit Close* 1840 *TA*, self–explanatory. LACEBY BECK, 1831 *Monson*, 1838 *Brace*, *Le Beck* a1260, 1306 RA iv, cf. *terram Ricardi del Beck* 1230–53 ib, *atte Beck'* 1332 *SR* (p), *v.* **bekkr** 'a stream'. LACEBY HALL (lost), *the mansion, called Laceby Hall, which stands on a commanding eminence, is now (1841) unoccupied* 1842 White, cf. *Hall Field* 1840 *TA*. LACEBY HILL, 1824 O, 1831 *Monson*, 1838 *Brace*, cf. *Hill Ho*. 1828 Bry. LITTLE BECK, *Litelbec* 1240–53 RA iv, *little becks* 1609 *LincsD*, *Littlebecke* 1611 WillsL, *Little Beckes* 1631 *Cragg*, 1699 *HumbD*, *the little becks* 1635 *Foster*, *Litle Becks* 1645, 1681 *ib*, *Littlebecks* 1733 *Td'E*, *the little Becks* 1822 *Terrier*, *Little –* 1840 *TA*, cf. *Litelbechill* 1240–53 RA iv, *Littelbekhilles* 1258–63 *ib* (*v.* **hyll**), self–explanatory, *v.* **lȳtel**, **bekkr**. LITTLE LACEBY, 1828 Bry, 1840 *TA*. LOPHAM LANE, 1828 Bry, cf. *Lopham Close* m18 *Monson*, 1750, 1753 *PT*, *Far Lophams* 1840 *TA*, obscure. MANOR FM, *Manor F^m* 1828 Bry. MANOR HO, 1842 White, – *Lawn* 1840 *TA*. ROOKERY HO. SAND PIT. SCRUB HOLT. STUD FM. WALKS FM, cf. *The Walk* m18 *Monson*, *the Walks* 1753 *PT*, *Far –*, *First –*, *Middle Walk* 1840 *TA*, *v.* **walk**, which denotes land used for the pasture of animals, particularly sheep, hence the common *Sheepwalk*. WATERLOO INN, 1838 *Nelthorpe*, 1842 White. WILSON'S TERRACE, named from a local family, cf. John *Willson* 1581 PR.

FIELD-NAMES

Principal forms in (a) are 1840 *TA*. Spellings dated 1225 are ChR; 1230–53, 1240–53, 1258–63, 1306 RA iv; 1239[1] (Ed1), c.1240 (Ed1) *Newh*; 1239[2], m13 *HarlCh*; 1284, 1304 Abbr; 1286, 1329 *Ass*; 1313, 1318 Cl; 1327, 1332 *SR*; 1359 Ipm; 1375, 1395 Peace; 1586 *LincsD*; 1589 NCWills; 1601, 1606, 1609, 1611, 1625, 1634[1], 1662, 1668, 1671, 1679, 1686, 1718, 1724, 1762, 1781, 1822, 1836 *Terrier*; 1634[2], 1688, 1709 *Nelthorpe*; 1652 WillsPCC; 1733 *Td'E*; m18 *Monson*; 1744, 1745, 1765, 1771, 1772, 1790, 1795 *Field*; 1750, 1753, 1779 *PT*; 1773, 2776, 1780, 1782, 1824, 1834 *Yarb*.

(a) Allotment; Aylesby Cls (referring to Aylesby, an adjacent village); Allow Briggs Cl m18, 1750, Allow Briggs 1753, 1779, Hollow – 1840; Barn Cl; Barnolaby Seeds (sic) (referring to Barnoldby le Beck, a few miles to the south); Bennet's Wife House 1779 (named from the *Bennett* family, cf. Wiliam *Bennett* 1642 LPR); Far –, Top Bottom (*v.* **botm**); Bradley Road Cl (self-explanatory; Bradley is a few miles to the east); Brickkiln Cl; Bridge Pce (*v.* **brycg, pece**); Brumby Cl (from the surn. *Brumby*, cf. William *Brumbie* 1608 PR); Buckby (probably from the surn. *Buckby*); Bull Garth (*v.* **garðr**); Burks Cl 1779 (from the surn. *Buck(e)*); Burnt House Garth (*v.* **garðr**); Butcher Cl (from the surn. *Butcher*); Far –, First –, Rotten Carr (*v.* **kjarr**); Castle Hill (& Buildings); Chapel (*ad capellam* a1260, 1306, 1327, *de la chapele de Leyseby* 1286, *atte Chapel' de Layseby* 1329, *ad capellam* 1322, *atte Chapell of Layceby* 1359, *atte Chapell'* 1375 all (p), *v.* **chapel(e)**); Charity Thorp (perhaps 'land endowed for a charitable purpose' and in the same ownership as The Thorpes *v. infra*); The Cocking Cl m18, Cocking Cl 1753 (perhaps from the surn. *Cocking*); Cods Cl 1762 (named from the *Cod* family, cf. Thomas *Cod*, *Rector* 1642); ye fartherr Coney-Greens 1755 *PR*, Coney Greens (*v.* **conigre, coni, grēne**[2]); Cow Cl; a close called Cream Poke 1781, – call'd Creampoke 1822 (*a Close cal'd Cream Poke* 1724, a complimentary name for rich pasture, cf. the Cream Poke in the f.ns. (a) of Kirkby cum Osgodby PN L **3**, 55); Crow Holt (*v.* **crāwe, holt**); Deep Dales (*v.* **dēop, dalr**); East Cl (cf. North Cl, South Cl *infra*, which are adjacent); Far Cl; Farm Buildings and Walk Cl (*v.* **walk**); Fifteen Acres; The Furze Cl m18, 1750, the – 1753, Furze Cl 1779, (Little)

Furze Hill 1840 (*v.* **fyrs**); The Garth m18, Garth 1840 (*v.* **garðr**); Glebe Lds & Barn; The Grafts m18, 1750, the Graffs (sic) 1753 (*v.* **graft** 'a ditch, a moat'); Grantham Hill (probably named from the *Grantham* family, cf. Vincent *Grantham* 1758 *PR*); Grimsby Cl, – Fd, – Walk (*v.* **walk**; referring to Great Grimsby); Guy Wing; Hill side; Hogs Cl (perhaps from the surn. *Hog*(*g*), but cf. Hog Pit Hill *supra*); The Hoker Cl m18, Hooker Cl 1753, Low Hooker Barn Stack Yard etc, Hoker (sic); Holy Lands 1773, 1834, 1840, holy – 1776; Home Cl (several); Horse Cl; House, Buildings & Home Cl, House, Pleasure Grds and Buildings, House, Yard and Mill Cl; Humberstone Cl (probably from the surn. *Humberston*); (South End of) Jonathan Padddock (from the pers.n. or surn. *Jonathan*); King's two Cls m18, King Cl 1840 (named from the *King* family, cf. Thomas *King* m18); Laceby Cl m18, 1750, – Walk 1840 (*v.* **walk**; formerly Oldman Cl *infra*); Lane Cl, – Pce; Leys (*v.* **lea** 'a meadow, pasture' (OE **lēah**)); Locking Cl 1753; Lodge & Home Cl; Long Cl m18, 1750, 1753, long – 1779; High Low Fd; Lower Fd; Meadow Cl; Middle Cl; Middle Holt (*v.* **holt**); my mill at Laceby 1772, the Mill Pit 1812 *PR*, Mill House and Yard, Mill Lane, – Btms 1840; Milsons Cl m18, Milsons Cl 1753 (from the surn. *Milson*, cf. Edward and Thomas *Milson* 1642 LPR); Narrow Pce; New Cl; New Dykes m18, 1750, – Dikes 1840 (*v.* **dík**); North Cl (cf. East Cl *supra*); North Crofts (Btm) (*v.* **norð, croft**); North Plantation(s); Nuns furze 1780, 1782, Nun –1822, 1824 Nuns Furze 1822, 1824, nuns furres 1836 (*two leas of Furrs commonly called the Nunn furrs* 1611, *2 furr leyes . . . commonly called Nunnfurrs belonging to the Nuns of Great Grymsby* 1625, *Nun furres* 1634[1], *Nunns Furrs* 1634[2], 1709, *the nunfurrs* 1662, *Nun furrs* 1668, 1671, – *Furrs* 1679, *the Nun furs* 1686, *Nunnes furres* 1688, *Nun Furz* 1718, 1724, *v.* **nunne, fyrs**, the explanation is contained in the 1625 form and refers to the Augustinian nunnery of St. Leonard in Great Grimsby; note also the appellative use in *2 furr leyes supra* and *twenty Furr leas* 1679); Oat Cl; Occupation Lane; Oldmans Cl 1753 ("in the tenure of John Oldman"), Oldman's – 1779 (cf. Laceby Walk *supra*); Over Lds; Paddocks; The Park; Peasby (perhaps the same as *Pesebergh* 1240–53, *Peseberig* 1240–53, 1258–63 (*v.* **pise** 'pease', **be(o)rg** 'a hill, a mound')); Pelhams Lds (from the surn. *Pelham*); Pingle (*v.* **pingel**); Pit (*v.* **pytt**); Plantation (several), Plantations; Public House & Paddock; Ravensdale; Redding Poke; Robinsons Cl (named from the *Robinson* family, cf. Thomas *Robinson* 1601); Rockliffe Hill; Ruffhams (*v.* **rūh, holmr**); Salters Well Plantn (from the occup.n. or surn. *Salter* with **wella**); Sand Hill (*v.* **sand, hyll**); Scad Acre (perhaps from **scead** 'a boundary', in a Scandinavianized form); School Cl, School House etc.; Seven Acres; Sheet Cl; Shop on the waste (v. **scoppa** 'a hut'); Skaith Hill (perhaps from **skeið** 'a boundary', but earlier forms are needed to confirm this); Snapperdales (*Snapper* is obscure; the second el. is **deill** in the pl.); South Cl (cf. East Cl *supra*); South Plantation; Spaldermare 1765, – Cl 1771, Speldermare 1772, Speldermare Cl 1790, 1795, Speldon (sic) 1840 (*Spaldehow*, *Speldhou* a1260, *Spaldhowe* 1306, *the Spelders* 1652, *Spaldermare Close* 1744, *Spaldermare* 1745; Spalder, Spelder are no doubt modern relexes of *Spaldehow*, *Speldhou*, perhaps from **spald** 'a ditch', **haugr**, with (**ge**)**mǣre** in some later forms); Square Holt (v. **holt**); Stripes Bottom, – Hill (*certain closed* (sic) *called the Stripes* 1652, v. **strīp**, **botm**, **hyll**); Sunday School House and Yard; Ten Acres; the Thorpes 1779, Thorpes, Thorpes North, – South 1840 (*two . . . closes called Thorpes*, v. **þorp** 'a dependent outlying farmstead'); Top Cl; Town and Paddock; Town End Cl; Twelve Acres; Waste Wellow Pingle (v. **pingel**); West Plantation(s); Willows (v. **wilig** in the pl.); Wood Cl; Woodland Plantatiom (v. **wudu**, **land**).

(b) *Adlingmare* 1240–53 (the first el. is the ContGerm pers.n. *Adalin*, the second OE (**ge**)**mǣre** 'a boundary, land on or forming a boundary'); *Aylofbrigge* 1240–53 (from the ME pers.n. *Ai-*, *Aylaf*, an Anglo-Scandinavian form of ON *Eileifr*, with **brycg** in a Scandinavianized form); *a Back layne* 1611; *Barlands* 1240–53, *Barrelanges* 1258–63 (the second el. is **land** in the pl., the first ME *barre* 'a bar', the reference presumably being to plots of land marked off by a barrier, cf. *Barres* 1586); *Blindemires* 1240–53 ('the marshes concealed by vegetation', v. **blind**, **mýrr**); *Boytoft* 1240–53, 1258–63 (v. **boi**, **toft** 'a messuage, a curtilage'); *Brackley syke* 1586 (*Brackley* is probably a surn., with **sík**); *del Clay* 1327, *de Clay* 1332 both (p) (v. **clæg**); *Crimkelnoke* 1240–53 (probably from the ON pers.n. *Grímkel* and **nōk**, as suggested by Dr Insley); *Crosseberg* 1230–53, *Crossebergh* 1306 (presumably denoting a hill with a cross, v. **cros**, **berg**); *Crossewang* 1258–63 (v. **cros**, **vangr**); *Dicfurlanges* 1240–53, 1258–63, *Dicfurlang'* 1258–63 (v. **dík**, **furlang**); *Doflandes* 1240–53, *Dunelandes* 1258–63 (with *n* for *u*, i.e. *Duue-*) ('the dove lands', v. **dūfe**, **land**); *Goldeburg* 1230–53 (v. **gold**, **burh** 'a fortified place', the significance of which is not clear); *atte Grene de Layeseby* 1313, 1318, *Atte Grene* 1327, *Atte Grene de Layseby* 1329, *atte Grene* 1332 all (p) ('the village green', v. **grēne**[2]); *Grenebergmare* 1240–53 (v. **grēne**, **berg** with (**ge**)**mǣre**); *Grenemilne*, *Grenemilnegauel* 1258–63 (perhaps 'the mill at the grassy place', v. **grēne**[2], **myln**, with **gafol**[1] 'a forked piece of land, a narrow strip of land'); *haueracres* 1240–53, 1258–63 (v. **hafri** 'oats', with **akr**); *Ierlesholm* 1239[1] (Ed1), c.1240

(Ed1), *Jerlesholm* 1239², m13 (Dr Insley suggests that the first el. is the ON pers.n. **Jarl*, rather than the appellative ON **jarl** 'a nobleman, an earl' with **holmr**); *de Kychen de Laiceby* 1395 (p) (*v.* **cycene** 'a kitchen'); *Laceby Wood* 1589 (*v.* **wudu**); *Leuericroft* 1230–53 (from the OE pers.n. *Lēofrīc* with **croft**); *de la Lynde de Leysseby* 1304 (p) (*v.* **lind** 'a lime–tree'); *de La More* 1327, – *La more* 1332, *atte More de eadem* 1329 all (p) (*v.* **mōr**); *Musewell* a1260, 1306, *–welle* a1260 ('the spring infested by mice', *v.* **mūs, wella**); *the North End Platts* 1733 (*v.* **platt**²); *Nylofbrigge* 1240–53 (an erroneous form of *Aylofbrigge infra*); *curiam Rogeri le Paumer* a1260 ('Palmer's court', *v.* **court**); *the great Sleights* 1733 (*v.* **slétta** 'a smooth, level field'); *Stainholmes, Staynholmes* 1240–53, 1258–63 (*v.* **steinn, holmr**); *quodam fossato lavato in Lesseb'* 1225 ('a former wash–dike in Laceby', *v.* **wæsce–dīc**); *Whaylandes* (sic) 1230–53, a1260, *Whaytlandes* 1306 (*v.* **hveiti** 'wheat', **land**); *Wilgebrigge* 1258–63 (*v.* **brycg** in a Scandinavianized form; the first el. may be **wilig** 'a willow'); *Wranglandes* 1230–3, 1258–63 ('the crooked selions', *v.* **vrangr, land**); *Yukermare* 1240–53, *Thukermar* 1258–63 (both forms refer to the same piece of land, for *Y–* represents *Þ–*. The second el. is **(ge)mǣre** 'a boundary, land on a boundary'; the first is difficult but Dr Insley suggests it is the ON byname *Þunnkárr* 'the one with thin curly hair', with the loss of the nasalizing stroke over the *–u–*.

Scartho

SCARTHO

Scarhou 1086 DB, 1271 Cl, 1323 Inqaqd, *–ho* 1178, 1179 P
Scarfhou 1177 P, 1196 ChancR, *–ho* 1191, 1192, 1193, 1194
  et passim to 1214 all P, *–ou* 1195 ib
Scartho 1190, 1206 P, 1208, 1211 ChancR, 1212 P, 1218 Ass,
  1231 Welles, 1240 FF, 1254 ValNor, 1256 BC, 1278 Misc,
  1535 VE iv, 1554, 1558 InstBen, 1576 LER, 1576 Saxton,
  1610 Speed, 1634 VisitN, 1652 *Rad*, *–oo* 1499 Pat, 1526
  Sub, 1552 Pat, *–oe* 1699, 1720, 1738 *T'dE*, 1726 *Yarb*,
  1751 *NW et passim*, *Skartho* 1240 FF, 1601 *Terrier*
Scarthou 1219 FF, 1271 Cl, 1275 RH, 1289 RSu, 1294, 1308
  Pat, 1322 Misc, 1325, 1327 Pat, 1328 Banco, 1331 *DuLaCh*
  et passim to 1352 *MM*, *–oue* 1424 Pap, *–hou* 1286 *Ass*,

Scarthow 1256 FF, 1323 Misc, 1325 Cl, 1331 Ch, 1331 Pat,
1335 Ipm, 1388 Peace, 1428 FA *et passim* to 1695 *NW*, *–owe*
1292 Tax, 1323 Cl, 1331 Pat, 1375 Peace, 1377, 1383 Pat,
1383 Peace, 1389 Cl, 1406 Pat *et passim* to 1584 *MiscDon*
238, Skarthou 1316 FA, 1377 Pat, *–hou* 1322 Cl, 1322 Ch,
–owe 1380 Gaunt, 1384, 1388, 1391, 1402 Pat, 1405 Cl,
1539–40 Dugd iv, 1587 *MiscDep 62*, *–oe* 1545 *Td'E*
Scardho 1209 P (p), 1210 ib, 1210–12 RBE, 1212 Fees, 1219
Ass, *–howe* 1327 *SR*
Schartho 1231 Pat, 1256 (1318) Ch, *–ou* 1276 RH, *–owe* 1431
FA, 1626, 1628 *Td'E*, *–ow* 1548 *ib*
Scratho 1268 Cl, *–ou* 1328 Banco

The second el. of Scartho is clearly ON **haugr** 'a hill, a
mound'. The first, however, has been the subject of considerable
discussion. Ekwall, DEPN s.n., suggests that it may be the ON
pers.n. *Skarði* or ON **skarð** 'a gap, a notch'. Fellows–Jensen,
SSNEM 160, notes Ekwall's suggestions and rejects **skarð** on the
grounds that it is not topographically appropriate. On the other
hand, since the area is now built up it is well–nigh impossible to
determine the exact topography of the place. It may be pointed out
that here there are patches of Glacial Sand and Gravel and of
Alluvium lying on top of the Till. Fellows–Jensen on the evidence
of forms in *Scarf–* suggests that the first el. is perhaps ON **skarfr**
'a cormorant', drawing attention to the common interchange of *–f–*
and *–th–* in p.ns. The problem of these spellings is that they all
occur in one official source, Pipe Rolls, at times notoriously
erratic. It is strange, to say the least, that they are unsupported by
spellings from elsewhere and it should be noted that, even in P,
spellings in *–th–* and *–d–* are also found. The question must,
therefore, be posed as to whether these forms in *–f–* are
trustworthy, and the evidence clearly speaks against their having
any significance for the etymology of the name. On balance, as Dr
Insley points out, **skarð** provides an acceptable first el. for
Scartho, but 20th century development makes certainty impossible.

BELLSTRING HILL (lost), 1762 *Terrier*, 1787 *TCC*, 1828 Bry, *Bell String Hill* 1752 *Yarb*, cf. *Belstrings* 1638 *Terrier*, *a furlong called . . . Bellstrings* 1652 *Rad*, *Belstring wong* 1671 *Td'E*, *Belstrings* 1674 *Terrier*, *Bellstrings* 1706 *ib*, *Belstring Whong* 1723 *Td'E* (*v.* **vangr** 'a garden, an in–field'); presumably a piece of land the rent of which went towards the upkeep of the church bell–ropes. It denoted the area south of the boundary with Grimsby and north of Scartho Hall. CARR LANE, CAR PLANTATION, cf. *karfurlong* 1638 *ib*, *Carrfurlong* 1652 *Rad*, 1706 *Terrier*, *ye Carr* 1674 *ib*, *the –* 1697, 1706 *ib*, *Carr* 1724, 1762 *ib*, 1787 *TCC*, *Carforlong* 1778 *Nelthorpe*, *v.* **kjarr** 'a marsh, etc.'. CHURCH LANE, 1787 *TCC*. COLLEGE FM, from the holdings by Trinity College, Cambridge, cf. *Lease of Trinity Colledge in Cambridge* 1652 *Rad*. EAST END LANE, cf. *East ende Close* 1638, *– end Closes* 1667, *ye East end of Scartho* 1704, *the East end Closes* 1731 all *Td'E*. FERRIBY LANE, *Ferraby's Road* 1795 *EnclA*; Elizabeth *Ferraby* is named in the document. GLEBE FM, cf. *glebe lande* 1638, *Glebe Headland* 1697, *– headland* 1724, *– Leay* 1697, 1706, *– land*, *– headland* 1762 all *Terrier*, *Glebe Land* 1787 *TCC*, *v.* **land**, **hēafod–land**, **lea** (OE **lēah**). GOOSEMAN'S DRAIN is named from the family of Samuel *Gooseman* 1824 *Yarb*. PARSONAGE (lost), *ye parsonage howse* 1624, *No Parsonage House* 1697, *Parsonage house* 1706, *A –* 1724, 1762 all *Terrier*, *Pars. & Site of Hall* 1828 Bry, *One Slated dwelling house built in the year of our LORD one thousand eight hundred and forty six* 1862 *Terrier*. ROSE FM, cf. perhaps *Rowsey* 1624, 1697, 1706, 1762, *Rowsa*, *Rowso* 1724 all *Terrier*, *Rosy furlong* 1652 *Rad*, *Rowsoe furlong* 1787 *TCC*. SCARTHO HALL, cf. *atte Halle* 1332 *SR* (p) and *Parsonage supra*. SCARTHO TOP. SCARTHO WINDMILL (lost), *the mill*, *mill grene* 1638 *Terrier*, *the Mill* 1652 *Rad*, 1674, 1706 *Terrier*, *the wind Mill* 1667 *Td'E*, *– Winde Mill* 1691 *ib*, *Wind Mill* 1773 *Yarb*, *Windmill* 1786 *ib*, *Post Corn wind mill* 1811 *ib*, *– Wind Mill* 1826 *ib*, *Post Wind Corn Mill* (sic) 1850 *ib*, cf. *Millhill* 1697 *Terrier*, *mill hill* 1724 *ib*, *Mill hill* 1752 *Yarb*, *– Hill* 1762 *Terrier*, *Mill Hill whereon a wind mill lately stood* 1773 *Yarb*, *Mill Hill* 1786 *ib*, 1787 *TCC*, *mill Hill* 1811 *Yarb*, *Mill* 1824 O. SOUTHFIELD RD, cf. *Campus Austr'* 1457 *TCC*, *the South fielde* 1601, *The Southfeild* 1624, *the sowthe* *feild* 1638 all *Terrier*, – *South feild* 1652 *Rad*, 1691 *Td'E*, – *field* 1667 *ib*, – *Southfield* 1697, 1706, – *Field* 1724 all *Terrier*, 1752 *Yarb*, 1778 *Nelthorpe*, 1787 *TCC*, 1789 *Yarb*, commemorating one of the open fields of the village, *v.* **sūð**, **feld**, and cf. North Field in f.ns. (a) *infra*. TENNYSON'S HOLT, *Tennisons Holt* 1828 Bry, cf. *Tenison middow* 1778 *Nelthorpe*, named from the *Tennyson* family, cf. Mrs *Tennyson* 1789 *Yarb*, Susanna *Tennyson* 1792 *Td'E*. TOP CLOSE (lost), 1828 Bry; this is different from Scartho Top *supra* and was west of the village and south of Scartho Hall. WALTHAM RD (local), *Waltham gate* 1457 *TCC*, – *Gate* 1601, 1624, 1697, 1706, 1762, *Whattam gate* (sic) 1674, *Waltham high way* 1724 all *Terrier*; the road to Waltham, *v.* **gata**.

FIELD–NAMES

Forms dated 1327, 1332 are *SR*; 1336 Ch; 1351 *MM*; 1425 *Foster*; 1451–3, 1475–7 *MinAcct*; 1457, 1787 *TCC*; 1577, 1601, 1624, 1638[1], 1674, 1697, 1706, 1724[1], 1762[1] *Terrier*; 1587 *MiscDep 62*; 1609 *DuLaMB*; 1634, 1638[2], 1709, 1734, 1778, 1795 *Nelthorpe*; 1635, 1637, 1642, 1667, 1669, 1671, 1691, 1694, 1700, 1704, 1724[2], 1731[1], 1738, 1739, 1740, 1762[2], 1836 *Td'E*; 1652, 1657 *Rad*; 1725, 1726, 1730, 1731[2], 1737, 1752, 1773, 1789, 1804, 1819, 1850 *Yarb*; 1795 *EnclA*.

(a) Ballfurrs 1762[1] (*Ball furres* 1601, *–furres* 1638[1], *–furrs* 1674, – *furrs* 1697, 1706, *Balfurrs* 1724[1], *v.* **ball** 'a hillock', **fyrs**); Barrack 1778, 1836; Beale Cl 1762[1] (*Beale Close* 1638[1], *Beal close* 1674, 1706, – *Close* 1724[1], from the surn. *Beale*, cf. Peter *Beyll'* c.1539 *Inv*, William *Beale* 1574 *PR*); yᵉ Beck, Beckgar 1762[1], *–gars* 1778, – Gares 1787 (*Becke* 1638[1], *Beck* 1674, 1697, *the* – 1706, *Beckegares* 1638[1], *Beck gares* 1652, *–gares* 1674, 1697, 1706, 1724[1], cf. *Bekfurlanges*, *Bekleys* 1457 (*v.* **furlang**, **lea** (OE **lēah**) 'meadow, pasture' in the pl.) (*v.* **bekkr**, **geiri** 'a triangular piece of land' in the pl.); Bells Cl 1836; Blodram Carr 1787 (*Blotheram Carr* 1652, *v.* **kjarr**); Brack Side 1778; Bradlah Green (sic) 1778 (i.e. Bradley); Bradley Corner 1787; Bradley Gate 1752, 1762[1], – gate 1789 (the road to Bradley, a neighbouring parish, *v.* **gata**); Jⁿᵒ Brady's Cl 1762[1]; the broad half acre 1789; Brothcarr Side 1752, Broth Carr 1787, brothcar 1789 (*Brathcare*

1457, Broth carr furlong 1652, *-carr* 1697, 1706, *broth car* 1724[1]; this may well be identified with *Braythkarre* 1457, 'the broad marsh' *v.* **breiðr**, **kjarr**, a Scand. compound); Bullgrass 1762[1], – grass 1778, Bull Grass East 1787 (*the bull grese* (sic), *ye Bullgrese* 1638[1], *the* – 1674, *Bullgrass* 1697, 1706, *Bulgras*, *Bull Grass* 1724[1], *v.* **bula**, **græs**); Bull Thorn 1787; Candler Stile Whong 1787 (*v.* **vangr**); Carr Dyke 1836 (*Karrdyke* 1457, *v.* **kjarr**, **dík**); the Cillin house gath (sic) 1778, Kiln House Garth 1787 (*v.* **garðr**); Clark's Plott 1836; Colmeer 1762[1], Coulmare 1778, Coldmer Whong 1787 (*Colmerwange* 1457, *Cole mare* 1601, *Colmor* 1624, *Cole meere* 1652, *Colemeere furlong* 1657, *Colmear* 1697, 1706 (uncertain); The Common 1778; the Cow Pasture 1795; Daleground 1762[1] (*the dale grownde* 1601, *– grounde* 1624, *– deale grownd* 1638[1], *– Dale ground* 1674, *Dale ground* 1697, *Daleground* 1706, *Dale Ground* 1724[1], *v.* **deill**, the name here probably denoting a piece of a field); Dangate 1762[1] (*Dan gates* 1577, *–gates* 1624, *dangates* 1638[1], *Dan gates* 1674, *a furlong called Dangate* 1652, *Dangate* 1697, 1706, 'the Danes' way, road', *v.* **Danir**, **gata**, cf. Deanesgate in Great Grimsby *supra*); North –, South East Fd 1795; Elvin Fenn 1787 (*Elvin fenn side* 1652, *Elvin* is probably a family name here); Fields Meer 1762[1] (*the Fielde meare* (*banke*) 1577, *the fieldes meere* 1601, *ye feyldes meare* 1624, *the feildes –* 1638[1], *the feilds –* 1674, *fields Mear* 1697, *field – 1706, 'the boundary of the great field', *v.* **feld**, (**ge**)**mæǽre** and cf. *campus de Scarthowe* 1457, *in campis . . . de Skarthowe* 1587, *campos de Scarthoe* 1634, *Scarthoe feild* 1638[2]); Fleece Moor 1836; Gallows 1762[1] (1724[1], *ye gallowes* 1624, *the gallows* 1638[1], 1706, *a place called the Gallow* 1652, *the Gallows* 1674, 1697, *v.* **galga**); Goat Green (Whong) 1787 (cf. *Goate Ings* 1652, *v.* **grēne**[2] 'a green, a grassy place', **eng** 'a meadow, pasture'); Goosom Marrs 1787, Gooseham 1836 (*Goseholme* 1457, *a furlong Goosam* (sic) 1667, *– Goosham* (sic) 1691, *v.* **gōs** 'a goose', **holmr** 'raised land in marsh, etc.', cf. Stonams *infra* for the development); Goosemare 1804 (perhaps to be identified with *goosemarse* (sic) 1642, *–marshe* 1669, 'the marsh frequented by geese', *v.* **gōs**, **mersc**); Grassgarth 1787 (*v.* **garðr**); *y^e* Green 1762[1] (*Atte Grene* 1327, *atte –* 1332 both (p), *le Grene* 1451–3, 1475–7, *v.* **grēne**[2]); the Green Lane 1752; Haughton Gate 1787 (the road to Holton le Clay, *v.* **gata**); Hawcross Side 1787, Haw, Haw Cross 1836; Headings 1762[1] (for a discussion of *headings*, *v. ye headings* PN L **2**, 14); The Headland and Fellow 1778 (Mr Field points out this alludes to two headlands constituting a single unit and cf. similar names in PN L **2**, 12, where *fellow* is taken "perhaps in the sense 'a counterpart, a match'", and PN L **3**, 12, *v.* **hēafod–land**); Heneage farm 1762[1] (named from the *Heneage* family, cf. George *Heneage* 1695 NW); High Close Nook 1787 (*the hye close* 1624, *– High Close* 1667, 1731[1], *v.* **hēah**, **clos**(**e**)); Holme Acre

1787, – Dyke 1787, 1839 (*v.* **holmr, dík**); Holton Rd 1795 (*Howton gate* 1457, the road to Holton le Clay, *v.* **gata**); Honeyholes 1762¹, – Holes 1787 (*Hony holes* 1601, 1624, *–holes* 1697, *honiholes* 1724¹, *v.* **hunig, hol**¹ 'a hollow' in the pl., no doubt referring to sticky land); Hoober 1836; Horse Pasture 1795; Howhill 1762¹ (*Howe* 1457, *the howhill* 1601, *Howehill* 1638¹, *howe hill* 1674, *How hill ends* 1652, *Howhill* 1697, 1706, *how hill* 1724¹, *v.* **haugr** 'a hill, a mound', with **hyll**); Humberstone furrs 1762¹ (*humberstonefures* 1638¹, *Humber stone furrs* 1652, *Humberstone furrs* 1674, – *furs* 1697, *Humberston Furrs* 1706, *Humberstone Furs* 1724¹, *v.* **fyrs**), Humberstone Gate 1762¹ (*Humberstayne gate* 1457, *Humberston gate* 1601, *Humbersonegate* 1638¹, – *gate* 1674, 1697, *Humberston Gate* 1706, *Humberstone way* 1724¹, 'the road to Humberston (an adjacent parish)', *v.* **gata**); Humberstone hill 1762¹; Johnson Green 1762¹ (*Johnson grene* 1638¹, – *Green* 1674, 1697, 1706, 1724¹, named from the *Johnson* family, cf. Richard *Johneson* 1577 *Terrier*, with **grēne**² 'a grassy place'); Kilnhouse Garth 1787, Kiln 1836 (*v.* **garðr**, as elsewhere in the parish); Lamb coat more 1778, Lamb Cote 1836 (*Lamcote hyll, lytyllamcotemore* 1457, *Lam coates Meere* 1652 (*v.* **lamb, cot**, **(ge)mære**); Land Meer 1762¹ (*landmere* (*grene*) 1457, *land mares* 1601, *Landmare Dale* 1706, *Landmares* 1724¹, *v.* **land–(ge)mære** 'a boundary'); Laundike 1778 (*v.* **land, dík**); Lingmear 1762¹, Lingmer 1787 (*Lyngmare* 1457, *lyngmare* 1601, 1624, *Ling mor* 1624, *Ling meare furlong* 1652, *v.* **lyng** 'ling, heather', **(ge)mære**); Little Cl 1787; Long Syke Whong 1787, Long Sike 1836 (*Langesyke* (*grene*) 1457, *Long Sike furlong* 1652, *v.* **lang, sík**); Low Cl 1787; Maddison Farm 1762¹ (named from the *Maddison* family, cf. Sir Ralph *Maddison* 1642 *Td'E*); 2 Lands called Mare & Foal 1762¹ (*one land and One garing called the Mare & the fole* 1601, *Two Landes called mare & fole* 1697, *Two landes called by the name of Mare & fole* 1706, *mare and fole* 1724¹, probably referring to two contiguous selions of unequal size, cf. PN L **3**, 144); Meer Bank 1762¹ (*meerbank* 1724¹, *v.* **(ge)mære, banke**); mildike 1778 (*v.* **dík**; the first el. may well be **myln**); Mincemor 1762¹ (*Mansemare* (*grene*) 1457, *long Mans mare* 1601, 1624, *short Mansemare* 1624, *Manch more furlong* 1652, *Manch–moore* – 1657, perhaps 'the common or community moor', *v.* **mōr** presumably in the sense 'marsh'; the first el. may be **(ge)mænnes** 'community'); Mossom 1762¹, Mosshams 1787 (*mossome hill, mossoms* 1638¹, *Mosin hill* (sic) 1652, *Mosina hill* (sic) 1657, *Mossom hill* 1674, 1697, *Mossom* (*hill*) 1706, *Mosoms hill* 1724¹, *v.* **mos, holmr** 'higher ground in marsh'; forms in *–in–* are no doubt for *–m–*); the North Fd 1752, 1773, 1789, 1819, yᵉ Northfield 1762¹, the North fd 1778, 1850 (*in Campo boriali de Scarthowe* 1457, *the Northe fielde* 1601, *North field, the Northfeild* 1624, *the North Feild* 1642, *North feild* 1652, *the North field* 1667, 1731¹, – *feild*

1669, 1671, *the north field* 1697, *the Northfield* 1706, - *North Field* 1724[1], 1724[2], 1725, *v.* **norð, feld**; one of the open fields of the village); Northker 1778, North Carr 1787 (*Northcarre*, - *karre* 1457, -*carre* 1601, -*car* 1624, *v.* **norð, kjarr** and cf. Carr Lane *supra*); Nunns or College 1762[1] (*the landes belonging to the Nunnes of great Grymesbie, the Nunes grounde* 1577, *the Nunnes* 1601, *y*[e] - 1624, *the nvnes* 1638[1], *Nuns farme, the Nuns Land* 1642, 1669, - *Nuns* 1674, *Nunns* 1697, *nuns* 1724[1], *v.* **nunne**; the reference is to the nuns of St Leonard's Priory, Great Grimsby, and to Trinity College, Cambridge); Parsonage hedge 1762[1] (cf. *the parsonage headland* 1624, *v.* **hēafod–land** and cf. *Parsonage supra*); Peck Leys 1787; (the) Pinfold House 1752, 1789 (*v.* **pynd–fald**); Portnor Farm, - headland, - Leay 1792[1] (*Portnor* -, *Porner farm* 1724[1], named from the *Portner* family, cf. . . . *Portner* (no forename) 1724[1], with **ferme, hēafod–land, lea** (OE **lēah**) 'meadow, pasture'); Priestmeer 1762[1] (*Prestemare* 1457, *Prestmare* 1638[1], *prest mare* 1674, *Priest mear* 1706, -*mear* 1724[1], *v.* **prēost, (ge)mǣre**); Ring Dike 1795, High -, Low Ring Dike 1836; Scad(d) Carr 1787 (*Scadcarre* 1457, perhaps 'the boundary marsh' from a Scandinavianized form of **scēad** and **kjarr**); Scartho Cl 1762[1] (*Scarthoe Close* 1638[1], 1674, *Scatter close side* (sic) 1652, *Scather close* (sic) 1657, *Scarthoe Close* 1667, *Scartho* - 1697, 1706, 1724[1], *v.* **clos(e)**); Scartho Dykes 1762[1] (*Scarthow dyke* 1457, *Scarthoe dickes* 1577, 1638[1], *Skartho Dykes* 1601, *Schartho dykes* 1624, *Scatter Dike* 1652, *Scarthoe Dikes* 1674, *Scartho* - 1697, 1706, - *dikes* 1724[1], *v.* **dík**); Spittle Furrs 1762[1] (*the landes be longinge to the Spittle howse of great Grimesbie* 1577, *Spettell furres* (sic) 1638[1], *Spittle furrs* 1674, - *Furrs* 1697, - *Furs* 1706, *Spitle fures* 1724[1], *v.* **spitel** 'a hospital', **fyrs**, the reference being to the hospital of St Mary Magdalene and St Leger in Great Grimsby, *supra*); Springhead 1836; Stile Whong 1787 (*v.* **stigel** 'stile', **vangr**); (long -, short) Stonams 1762[1], Stone Holme 1836 (*Stonnames, long stonames* 1638[1], *Stone ham furlong* 1652, *Long* -, *Short Stonames* 1674, *Long* -, *Short stonams* 1697, *Stonam* 1706, 1724[1], *v.* **stān, holmr**; -*am* is a frequent reflex of **holmr** in north L); Stone Green 1836; Swanhill Bottom 1836; Teal Green 1787; the Tethering Paster 1778, the tethering Leys 1795 (*Tetheringe ground in Scartho* 1609, *the tethering* 1638[1], self-explanatory); Thompson yard 1778; Thorn hill 1778, -hill 1787 (*Thornehill furlong* 1652, *v.* **þorn, hyll**); Thorntree Leays 1762[1], - Leys 1787 (*Thorn tree leays* 1697, *Thorntree* -, from **þorn, trēow** with **lea** (OE **lēah**) 'meadow, pasture', in the pl.); West Thoudmear . . . sometimes called Thicking Green 1762[1] (cf. *Thykkyng* 1457, *Thickin* 1624, *v.* **picce** 'thick', **eng**, but the significance of 'thick' here is not clear), east Thoulmare (sic) 1778, East Thowlmare 1836 (cf. *West thoudmare* 1638[1], *Thawdmeer furlong* 1652, *Thawdmeere* - 1657, *west thoudmare* 1674, (*east*) *Tholmer Green*

1667, *the East Tholmer Green* 1691, *east thoulmare*, *west Thoulmare* 1724[1];
Thawdmeer, *Thoudmear*, etc. may represent *th' ould mear* 'the old
boundary, land on or forming a boundary', *v.* **ald**, **(ge)mǣre**); the Town
side 1778; Little Trankers 1778, Trancarr Green 1787 (*Trankar magna* 1457,
greate Trancker 1652, from **trani** 'a crane' and **kjarr** 'marsh', a Scand.
compound; Latin *magna* here is worthy of note); Tuplin headland 1762[1], *v.*
hēafod–land; James *Tuplin* is named in the document); Turgrave Hill 1762[1],
Torgraves 1778, Turf Graves 1787, Turf Groves 1836 (*Turgraves* 1457,
Turfgraues 1624, *Turfe graue* 1657, *a furlong called Turfe graves* 1667,
Turfgraves 1667, 1691, *Turgraue* 1724[1], *Turgraues hill* 1638[1], *Turgraus hill*
(sic) 1674, *Turgrave hill* 1697, 1706, referring to a place where turf was
dug, *v.* **turf**, **grǣf** 'a digging'); Water Well Head 1787; Welker hill 1752,
Wellcarr furs 1762[1], Welker 1778, Well Carr (Well) 1787, Well Carr 1836
(*Wellecarre*, *Welcarhyll* 1457, *Wellcarr hill* 1652, *Well Car –* 1667, *Wellcarr
furs* 1697, *– Furrs* 1706, *v.* **wella**, **kjarr** with **hyll** and **fyrs**); Wellow Syke
Green, – Well 1787 (*Wellow syke* 1547, *welhow sike* 1667, *Wellow sike*
1691, and cf. *Wellowhyll*, *Wellowange* 1457 (*v.* **hyll** and **vangr**) (the stream
or ditch (*v.* **sík**), is no doubt named from Wellow in Great Grimsby *supra*);
Wier Dike Drain 1795; Wissum (sic) 1762[1]; Wrendykes 1762[1] (*wrangdykes*
1601, *w'endickes* (sic) 1638[1], *wrendikes* 1674, *a furlong called Wrangdike
furlong* 1667, *Wrangdike furlong* 1691, *wrangdike hedge* 1667, *Wrangdike
– 1691 ('the crooked ditch', *v.* **vrangr**, **dík**, a Scand. compound).

　　(b) *the abbey hedge* 1601, *– Abbey hedg* 1624 (alluding to land held by
Wellow Abbey, Great Grimsby); *Akrhevedes* 1352 (*v.* ME **aker–heved** 'a
headland, the area at the end of an acre–strip land for turning the plough');
Balfra hill 1724[1]; *Barwyk* 1457 (*v.* **bere–wīc** 'a barley farm', 'an outlying
part of an estate, etc.', the first example of this name so far noted in north
L); *Bell close side* 1652; *the Signe of the Bird on hand* 1726 (presumably an
inn; it was formerly a cottage); *Blotryngcarre* 1457 (*Blotryng–* is obscure;
v. **kjarr**); *Bloxbrygwange* 1457 (perhaps the first el. is the pl. of ME **blok**
'a block' referring to the construction of the bridge); *a place called Bolin
end Acre*, *– the Bolin greene* 1652; *Bothumgrene* 1457 (*v.* **boðm** ' bottom',
grēne[2] 'green, a grassy place'); *Bradley dike* 1674, *– Dike* 1697, 1706, *–
land* 1457 (referring to the neighbouring parish of Bradley); *Brygsyke* 1457
(*v.* **brycg**, in a Scandinavianized form, **sík**); *Comenthinge* 1609 (*v.* **þing**
'property, premises'); *the common marfore* 1624, *– Mar furr* 1642, *–
Marfurr* 1669 (*v.* **marfur** 'a boundary furrow'); *ye dove cote closes* 1624;
the eastholme 1624 (*v.* **ēast**, **holmr**); *ye Fallow field or Common* 1738 (*v.*
falh in the sense 'land left untilled'); *una daila voc Feyrtpart* (sic) 1457 (Dr
Insley suggests that this is 'the part of land gone to ruin' from the past
participle form of ON *feyja* 'to let decay, go to ruin' and ME **part** and *v.*

deill); *Fowler grene* 1457 (from the occupational name or derived surn. *Fowler* and **grēne**[2]); *Franck thinge* 1609 (from the surn. *Frank* and **þing** 'possessions, property'); *le Gare* 1457 (*v.* **geiri**, as elsewhere in the parish); *Gatewange* 1457 (*v.* **gata, vangr**); *Goate Ings* 1652 (*v.* **gāt** 'a goat', **eng**); *Goldwange* 1457 (*v.* **golde, vangr**, perhaps an enclosure where gold flowers grow); *Gowland thinge* 1609 (from the surn. *Gowland* and **þing**); *Greenes Farm* 1669, *Green Farm* 1697, 1706 (from the surn. *Green(e)*, cf. John *Greene* 1590 *PR* and y[e] *Green supra* in f.ns. (a)); *the gresse headlonge* 1577 (*v.* **gærs, hēafod–land**); *una daila voc Gryme* 1457 (presumably 'Grim's share of land', *v.* **deill**); *Grymesby mere* 1457 ('the boundary with Great Grimsby', *v.* **(ge)mǣre**); *the ground called the Guild hallgarth* 1671 (*v.* **gild–hall, garðr**); *Hallyng* 1457 (*v.* **hall, eng**); *Ham Dike furlong* (sic) 1652, *Home Dike furlong* 1657 (*v.* **dík**); *Haughecrofte dyke* 1457, *Hawcroftes* 1637, *Hawcroft side* 1652, *Hawcrofts* 1700, *Hawcroft* 1730, 1731[2], 1737, 1740 (*v.* **haga**[1] 'an enclosure', **croft**); *Hawdelgryme, –hawe* 1457 (obscure); *the headelonge* 1577 (*v.* **hēafod–land**, cf. *the gresse headlonge supra*); *Hededail* 1457 (*v.* **hēafod, deill**); *Lamas Close* 1652 (*v.* **lammas**); *The Lovell deale* 1674, *Lovel dale* 1697, 1706 (from the surn. *Lovel* with **deill**); *the low close* 1624, *– Close* 1667, *South Close als Low Close* 1691, *the –* 1724[2], 1731[1], *– als the Low Close* 1725 (cf. High Close Nook *supra*); *the Meddow grownde* 1601, *medow grownd* 1638[1] (*v.* **mǣd**); *the Meir daill adioyning unto Grymesby feild* 1671 (*v.* **(ge)mǣre, deill**); y[e] *mote* 1624 (*v.* **mote** 'a moat'); *Munby Close* (sic) 1697 (named from the *Mumby* family, cf. Thomas *Mumbe* 1642 LPR); *Musholme* 1457 (*v.* **mūs** 'mouse', **holmr**); *old Mear* 1706 (*v.* **ald, (ge)mǣre**); *Outende* 1336 (*v.* **ūt, ende**); *Pacockwange* 1457 (from the ME surn. *Pacok* and **vangr**); *Parkers thinge* 1609 (from the surn. *Parker* and **þing** 'property, possessions', though the surn. has not been noted here before Edward *Parker* 1642 LPR); *Peake head land* 1666 PR, *Peak furlong* 1706 (*v.* Peaks Fm in Weelsby *infra*); *le Pyke* 1457 (*v.* **pīc** 'a point', though the sense here is not clear); *pratum Raulandi* 1457 ('Rowland's meadow'); *Raynals wange* 1457 (from the ME (OFr) pers.n. *Reinald* with **vangr**); *Rededayles* 1457 (probably from **hrēod** 'a reed' and **deill**); *Redyng* 1457 (probably from **hrēod** and **eng** 'meadow, pasture', as in *The Ridings* PN L **4**, 80–81); *Rowse wange* 1457 (probably from the surn. *Rows(e)* and **vangr**); *Rydynges* 1457 ('the clearing', *v.* **ryding** in the pl., a rare word in north L p.ns. and f.ns.); *South Close* (*v. the low close supra*); *the Spur Farm* 1704 (named from the *Spurr* family, cf. Henry and Thomas *Spurr* 1667 Td'E); Mr *Stampers farm* 1704; *Stayngrene* 1457 (*v.* ON **steinn** 'stone, stony', **grēne**[2]); *the thorpe garthes* 1601 (presumably *Thorpe* is a surn. here, *v.* **garðr**); *Tyllgrene* 1457 (probably from the ME pers.n. or surn. *Till*, a pet–form of *Matilda*, with **grēne**[2] 'a grassy place'); *Watergate* *furlong* 1652; *Waltham mere* 1457 ('the boundary with Waltham', *v.* (ge)mǣre); *Welle wange* 1457 (*v.* **wella, vangr**); *in occident fine de Scarthoe, the West end of Scarthoe* 1635, *the West endes* 1657, – *end* 1738 (self-explanatory, cf. East End Lane *supra*); *Westholme* 1425 (*v.* **west, holmr**); *Willow sike and Hill* 1652; *yᵉ windines* (sic) 1638[1], *the windins* 1674, *Windings* 1697, 1706 (a name noted in the f.ns. (b) of Immingham, PN L **3**, 173, as "perhaps a compound of **(ge)wind**[2] 'something winding' and **ing**[1], literally 'a winding place' in some topographical sense, apparently unrecorded in dictionaries. . . . Its exact sense is yet to be determined."); *Wolfou dails* 1457 ('the hill, mound frequented by wolves', *v.* **wulf, haugr**, with **deill** in the pl.); *Wormland* 1674 (*v.* **wyrm** 'a snake', 'earthworm', **land**); *wrone lands* (sic) 1638[1], *Wranglandes* 1652, *Ranglandes* 1657, *Wrung lands* 1697, *Wrunglands* 1724[1] ('the crooked selions', *v.* **vrangr, land**, cf. Wrengdykes in f.ns. (a) *supra*); *Wypeham* 1601, *One land at vipvm* (sic) 1638[1], *vipum* (sic) 1674, *Vipum* (sic) 1697, *wikum* 1724[1] (obscure).

Swallow

SWALLOW

> *Sualun* (sic) (7x) 1086 DB, *Svalun* (sic) 1086 ib
>
> *Sualwa* c.1115 LS, *Sualua, Svalue* 1159–81 (e13) *NCot, Sualue* 1200–10 RA ix (p), lHy3 *NCot, Sualwe* 1196–1203 RA iv, 1287 Ipm, *Swalue* a1155, eHy2, lHy2, e12 (e13) *NCot*, 1212 Fees, 1288, 1292, 1298 Ipm, 1428 FA, *Swalua* a1180 (e13) NCot, *Swalwe* 1163 RA i, 1196–1203, c.1200 (p) ib iv, 1272 *Ass*, 1281 QW, 1327 *SR*
>
> *Sualewa* 1143–47 Dane (p), *Sualewe* 1175 ChancR (p), 1188, 1190 *et freq* in P to 1206 ib, 1218 Ass, 1230 Welles, *Swalew'* 1218 Ass, *Swalewe* 1196 ChancR, 1203 P, 1205 ChancR, 1210–12 RBE, 1211 P, 1211–12 RBE, 1218 Ass, 1219 FF, 1227 Ch, 1231 Cl, 1240 FF, 1242–43 Fees *et passim* to 1361 Cl
>
> *Sualowe* 1212 Fees, *Swalowe* 1303, 1330 FA, 1340, 1359 Ipm, 1360 Pat, 1372 Misc, 1375 Ipm, 1375 Cl, 1379 Pat, 1385 Peace, 1388 *FF*, 1393 Pat *et passim* to 1531 *Foster, Swalow* 1346 FA, 1535 VE iv, *Swalou* 1332 *SR*, 1338 Misc' 1339 Fine

Sualu 1275, 1276 RH, 1281 Ipm, c.1300 RA iii, 1321 Misc, 1321 Cl

Swallowe 1369 *AD*, 1370 AD, 1373 Peace, 1499 HMCRep, 1526 Sub, 1543 LP xviii, 1547, 1552 Pat, 1576 LER, 1576 Saxton, *Swallow* 1610 Speed, 1658 *Foster*, 1680 *PT et passim*

Swallow is a very difficult name, for which no certain meaning can be suggested. Ekwall, DEPN s.n., suggests that it is "very likely an old river–name identical with Swale". He takes the latter, DEPN s.n., "to be related to *swallow* (the bird), belonging to the root *svel*– 'to move, plash', . . . The meaning of the name seems to be 'whirling, rushing river'". In his discussion of the R. Swale, RN 384–85, he points out that Swallow "is not on a stream, but in a well–defined valley, where a stream may be supposed to have run". In fact, a stream rises from an underground source and flows in an easterly direction, from a pond in the Rectory grounds, to the west of Swallow and disappears again immediately to the north–east. This must be the stream which gave its name to the place. Ekwall takes the base of the name to be **Swalwe* a weak fem. noun, the exact meaning of which "cannot be established", but which he suggests may have meant 'whirling, rushing, flowing'. The stream at Swallow, however, can hardly be described as whirling or rushing, but it does seem very likely that OE **swalwe* is the source of Swallow. Smith, EPNE s.v. ***swalwe**[2], accepts that this word "may be the source of the r.ns. Swale and Swallow" and suggests a meaning 'a whirlpool, rushing water', which again clearly cannot be the sense required here. Ekwall, RN 384–65, compares the English Swale, Swallow etc. with the German river–names Schwalb in Franconia (*Swalawa* c.802) and Schwale in Holstein (*Suale* 12th). Dr Insley draws attention to the fact that Hans Krahe, *Unsere altesten Flussnamen*, Wiesbaden 1964, 26, links the name Schwale to OHG, MHG *swal* 'a watercourse'. More recently, however, the name has been examined by Wolfgang Laur, *Historisches Ortsnamenlexikon von Schleswig–Holstein*, 2nd ed., Neumunster, 1992, s.v. Laur points out that there is also a Lithuanian river–name *Swale*, which has been linked to an Indo–European root *swel– with the sense 'burn'. He considers that the sense 'shine' might also be applicable and that the root can have the sense 'cool', cf. ODan, Modern Danish *sval* 'cool'. Laur suggests that the Holstein r.n. Schwale is pre–Germanic and belongs to the context of the 'Old European hydronomy', that is to an archaic phase of undifferentiated Indo–European. Dr Insley rightly considers that this explanation is also valid for the English Swale, Swallow, etc. and suggests that Swallow derives its name from an archaic Old European r.n. based on the Indo–European root *swel– in the sense 'shine', the Germanic base of which would be *swalwōn fem. This is the most plausible explanation of the etymology of Swallow which can be made with our present state of knowledge.

AYLESBY RD (local), cf. *Alesbie gate* 1580, *Ailsby –* 1601, 1697, 1709 1724 all *Terrier*, 'the road to Aylesby *supra*', *v.* **gata**. BARTON STREET, 1724, *– streate* 1580, *– strete* 1601, *– street* 1686, 1697, *barton –* 1709 all *Terrier*, the name of a presumed pre–Roman trackway leading to Barton upon Humber. BEELSBY RD (local), cf. *Beelsby Road Plot* 1832 *Yarb*, *Belesbygate* 1457 *TCC*, *Bielsbigate* 1580, *Beelsby gate* 1601, *Beilsby –* 1606, *Beelsby Gatte* 1697, *– gate* 1709, *Bielsby-Gate* 1724 all *Terrier*, 'the road to Beelsby', PN L **4**, 57, *v.* **gata**. BOWLANDS COVERT, *Bowlands Cover* 1824 O, 1828 Bry, cf. *Bowlandes* 1457 *TCC*, 1580, *Bowlands* 1601, 1686, 1697, 1724, *north –*, *South Bowlandes* 1606 all *Terrier*, *East bowlandes* 1652 *Rad*, *v.* **boga** 'a bow', used in some transferred sense not obvious from the topography, **land**. BRATTS LANE (lost), 1828 Bry, *v.* **brot** 'a small piece of land'; it was the lane leading eastwards from the village towards Beelsby. CAISTOR RD (local), cf. *Kayster gate* 1580, *Keaster –* 1601, *Caestergate* 1606, *Caster –* 1697, 1709, *Caistor-Gate* 1724 all *Terrier*, the road to Caistor, PN L **2**, 87, *v.* **gata**. CUXWOLD RD (local), cf. *le Cokeswaldgate* 1457 *TCC*, *the Steghe that leedithe to Cowxwolde* 1580, *a steye that goes to cuxwould* 1601 both *Terrier*, the road to Cuxwold, PN L **4**, 73, *v.* **gata**, **stīg** 'a path, a narrow road'. DAWBER'S WOOD, cf. *dowbar*, 1580, 1601, *Dowebarr* 1580, *Dawber* 1666, 1697, *dawber* 1709, *Daubar* 1724 all *Terrier*,

Dauber Hill 1824 O, *Daubers* – 1828 Bry; earlier forms are needed to suggest an etymology for *Dawber*. THE FOLLY, 1824 O, 1828 Bry, cf. *Folly Plot* 1832 *Yarb*; this is now the name of an area of land, but a building is marked here on 1824 O and 1828 Bry. THE HENHOLES, *Henne holles* 1601, *hen holes* 1606, *Hen holes* 1697 all *Terrier*, *Henholes* 1824 O, *Henhole* 1828 Bry, presumably 'the hollows where (wild) hens are found', *v.* **henn, hol**[1]. HOE HILL (lost), 1824 O, 1828 Bry; it was in the extreme south–east corner of the parish. IRBY RD (local), cf. *ewrbie gate* 1580, *Earby* – 1601, 1709 all *Terrier*, *Vrby* – 1652 *Rad*, the road to Irby upon Humber *supra*, *v.* **gata**. JACKSONS LEYS (lost, approx. TA 166 051), 1828 Bry, presumably named from the family of *Julion Jackson of Swallow* (sic) 1704 *PR* and the pl. of **lea** (OE **lēah**) 'meadow, pasture'. LIMBER RD (local), cf. *Limber gate* 1580, 1697, *Lymber* – 1601 all *Terrier*, leading to Great Limber, PN L **2**, 219, *v.* **gata**. LOW LINGS, 1828 Bry, 1832 *Yarb*, cf. *the Linges* 1580, – *Lynges* 1601, – *linges* 1606, *yᵉ Lings* 1686, 1697, *the highe Linges* 1580, – *hye Lynges* 1601, – *highe linges* 1606, *high Lings* 1686, *yᵉ high Lings* 1697 all *Terrier*, 'the places where heather grows', *v.* **lyng** in the pl. MIDDLE CARR (lost), 1828 Bry, *v.* **kjarr**; it was situated near Round Hill. RECTORY, *Rectorie* m16 *Cragg*, *The* – 1580, *one parsonage* 1601, *the parsonage house* 1606, *a Parsonage house* 1686, 1697, 1724, *one Personage house* 1709 all *Terrier*. RIBY RD (local), cf. *Rybygate* 1457 *TCC*, *Ribie*– 1580, *Ryby* – 1601, 1724, *Riby* – 1606 all *Terrier*, the road to Riby, PN L **2**, 249, *v.* **gata**. ROTHWELL RD (local), cf. *Rothewellgate* 1457 *TCC*, *Rowthwell* – 1580, 1601 *Terrier*, *Rowthwell* – 1652 *Rad*, 1697 *Terrier*, the road to Rothwell, PN L **4**, 154, *v.* **gata**. ROUND HILL, 1824 O, 1828 Bry, self–explanatory. SILVER HILL, 1824 O, *Selvarhill* 1580, *Selver* – 1601 both *Terrier*, *Silver hill furlong* 1652 *Rad*, *silver hill* 1686, 1697, – *Hills* 1724 all *Terrier*, 1833 *Yarb*, – *Fox Cover* 1828 Bry, probably named from the colour of the vegetation or of the soil, *v.* **seolfor, hyll**. SWALLOW DALES (lost), 1828 Bry is now Irby Dales in Irby parish *supra*. SWALLOW GRANGE, *Grangiam de swaulewe* (sic) 1187 (e13) *NCot*, *iuxta Grangiam* 112 (e13) *ib*; it was a **grange** of Nun Cotham Priory. SWALLOW VALE, 1824 O, – *Ho* 1828 Bry. SWALLOW WOLD, *Wold* 1806 *Plan* and cf. *Upper Wold F.* 1828 Bry. WHITE HART, 1828 *ib*, 1842 White.

FIELD-NAMES

Principal forms in (a) are *Yarb*; 1159–81 (e13), lHy2 (e13), l12
(e13) *NCot*; Hy3 (Hy4) *GCB*; 1300 Abbr; 1327, 1332 *SR*; 1388,
1389 *FF*; 1395 Peace; 1427 *GrimsCt*; 1457 *TCC*; 1491
GrimsExtent; 1580, 1601, 1606, 1612, 1697, 1709, 1724, 1822,
1830 *Terrier*; 1620 *LCS*; 1652 *Rad*; 1684 *TYR*; 1738, m18
Monson; 1806[1] *Map*; 1806[2] *Plan*.

(a) Becks Hill (cf. *Beckes* 1580, 1601, *the beck, – beckes* 1606, *Becks*
1697, *y* Becks* 1724, *v.* **bekkr, hyll**); Far –, Middle –, Near Bottom (*the
Botone* (sic) 1580, *v.* **botm**); Burnt hill Cl m18, Brant Hills 1832 (*a place
called Brantwell* 1652, probably 'the burnt hill', the 1652 form showing
confusion of *–hill* and *–well* as a result of weak stress); The Butt Cl m18,
Butt Cl 1832 (cf. *le Buttes* 1457, *v.* **butte** 'a strip of land abutting on a
boundary, etc.'); The Church Cl m18 (cf. *ad ecclesiam* 1327, *attekirk'* 1332,
atte kirk' de Swalowe 1388, 1389 all (p), *v.* **cirice, kirkja**), College Cl
(probably named from Trinity College, Cambridge, which held land here);
Corne Fd m18; the Cow Cl 1822, 1830; Croft (*v.* **croft**); Dixon's Cottage
& Croft (named from the family of William *Dixon* 1752 *PR*); East Fd 1806[1],
1806[2] (*le orientali campo* 1457, *The East fielde* 1580, *the est feld* 1601, *–
east feild* 1606, *– East Feeld* 1697, *– Easte Feeld* 1709, *– East Field* 1724,
one of the great fields of the parish, *v.* **ēast, feld**); Eight Acres; the fallow
Fd m18 (*v.* **fealu, feld**); Fardingworth Hill (*Farthingsorth hill* (sic) 1606);
Fox Cover (cf. Silver Hill *supra*); Furze (*v.* **fyrs**); the Great Cl m18; High
Ling(s) (cf. Low Lings *supra*); Home Cl m18, 1832; Horse Pasture 1806[1],
1806[2]; House Garden & Pleasure Grd; (Far) Ings, Ings Hill (cf. *Enges
furlonge* 1580, *the inges, – inges Bottome* 1601, *– Inges, – bottome* 606, *y*
Inggs, – Ings bottom* 1697, *great –, littel Ings Close, – the Ings bottom, –
hill* 1709, *great –, litle Ings close, Ings-hill, the Ings Bottom* 1724 (*v.* **eng**
'meadow, pasture', **hyll, botm**); The Lane Cl m18; Lusby's Cottage & Croft
(named from the family of John *Lusby* 1727 *PR*); Moor 1806[1], 1806[2] (*the
mooer* 1580, *– more* 1601, *more leas* 1606 (*v.* **lea**), *moor* 1697, *v.* **mōr**);
North Flg; Orchard (*the Orcharde, orchayrde* (sic) 1580, *the orchard* 1697,
1709, *The Orchard* 1724); Paddock; The Pingle m18 (*v.* **pingel**); Plantation;
Rails Plot (perhaps from the surn. *Rail*); Robinson's House & Garden
(named from the family of David *Robinsonne* 1642 LPR); The Round Cl
m18; The Royalty Sheep Walk m18 (*v.* **royalty, walk**); Simons Cl m18

(named from the family of Henry *Simon* 1680 *PR*); Sink Amoor (sic); Far -, First Six Acres; Skill plot (cf. *Longeskull, Short-* 1580, *Longskell* 1601, 1606, *Shortte skell* 1601, *Shortskell* 1606, *short Skell* 1697, *Long* - 1697, 1709, *Short Skel* 1709, 1724, *Long* - 1724, *v.* **skial** 'a boundary'); Spring Hill (cf. *iuxta fontem* 1159–81 (e13), *Sprenge garthe* 1580, *the Springe garthe* 1601, *the Springclose* 1606, *yᵉ Spring Garth* 1697, *the Spring Garth* 1724, *v.* **spring, garðr**); Stamps House & Croft (named from the family of John *Stamp* 1732 *PR*); Stone Pit Cl ((*the*) *Stone pitt* 1580, *the stone pytt, - stonne pytte* 1601, *yᵉ Stone pitt, - Stone gate* (*v.* **gata**) *that coms to the Stone pitt* 1697, *the Stone pitt* 1709, *Stone pitt Close* 1724, self-explanatory, *v.* **stān, pytt**); Triangle (referring to the shape of the field); 13 Acres; the Warren m18 (*v.* **wareine**); West Cl m18; Westfield 1806² (*in occident' campo* 1457, *West field* 1580, *The West felde* 1601, *the west feild* 1606, *West feeld* 1697, one of the great fields of the parish, *v.* **west, feld**); Willow Holt (*v.* **holt**); Wood.

(b) *Bartlandes* 1580, *Burtlandes* 1601, *-lands* 1697; *beckwindens* 1580, *Beckewindens* 1601, *Becks windings* 1697, *bex* - 1697, 1709, *Becks Windings* 1724 (*v.* **bekkr**; for *windings*, *v. The wyndinges infra*); *Jn Bells Barn* 1738; *Biling dail* 1697 (*v.* **deill** 'a share of land', the first el. perhaps being the surn. *Billing*); *blindwell furlong* 1652, *blind wells* 1709 (denoting a spring hidden by vegetation, *v.* **blind, wella**); *ad pontem* 1327, 1332 both (p) (*v.* **brycg**); *Brigg gate* 1606, 1724 ('the road to Brigg', *v.* **gata**); *the broade Furres* 1580, - *Brode furres* 1601, *broade furrs* 1606, *Brad furs* 1697, *Broad Furs* 1709 - *Furrs* 1724 (*v.* **brād, furh** in the pl.); *One land called ye Calfe* 1606 (*v.* **calf, land** 'a selion'); *William Claytons Butt close* 1652 (cf. The Butt Cl *supra*); *Cowkehelles* 1580, *Cawke holles* 1601, *Cawk hill* 1697, cf. *Cawkwell hill, - bottome* 1606 (*v.* **calc** 'chalk' with a variation between **hyll** and **hol**¹ 'a hollow' in the pl.); *yᵉ Cottagers platt* 1724 (*v.* **plat**); *Cowxolde meare* (sic) 1580, *Cowxwold meare* 1601, *Couxwould mear* 1697, *Coxwold feildes* 1606 ('the boundary land, the fields of Cuxwold (an adjoining parish)', *v.* **(ge)mǣre, feld**); *John Cresy great pitt* 1709; *Estergate* 1457 (perhaps 'the way to the sheep-fold' from OE **eowestre** 'a sheep-fold' and **gata**); *campum de Swalwe* Hy3 (Hy4), *campis de Swalewe* 1300, *campo de Swalowe* 1457, *Camp'* - 1491, *Swallowe Feilde* 1612 (*v.* **feld**); *the fieldes meare* 1580, - *feldes meare* 1601, *yᵉ Feeld mear* 1697 ('the boundary of the open fields', *v.* **feld, (ge)mǣre**); *Fowrwelles* 1580, *Furwells* 1606 (*v.* **fēower** 'four', **wella** 'a spring'); *le Fyrth* 1457, *the Furth stead* 1606 (perhaps from **fyrhðe** 'a wood, woodland, wooded country' in some later sense as recorded in MED s.v. *frith* (2) 'a park, a woodland meadow', 'an enclosure' and in EDD s.v. *firth* 'a wood, plantation, coppice', 'unused pastureland', cf. *the* *forthsteade* in Caborne f.ns. (b), PN L **4**, 68); *Geflynghow* 1457, *Gresle"howe* (sic) 1580, *Gesleuehowe* (sic) 1601, *gesting how* 1606, *Geslive how* 1697 (*v.* **haugr** 'a mound, a hill'; the first el. seems to be a pers.n., but the forms are too late and too varied for any certainty); *Edw. Gills headland* 1606, *Gill headland* 1697 (*v.* **hēafod–land** 'the head of a strip of land left for turning the plough'); *golding pit* 1606 (*v.* **pytt**; the first el. is probably the surn. *Golding*); *grenegate* 112 (e13) ('the green, grassy way, road', *v.* **grēne**[1], **gata**); *haliwellecroft* 1159–81 (e13), lHy2 (e13), *Holywelles* 1457, *Holliwell headlandes* 1606 (a compound of **hālig** 'holy' and **wella** 'a spring' with **croft** and **hēafod–land**); *Hall farme* 1684 (*v.* **hall**); *the Highe close* 1606; *the highe streate* 1580; *holdlande(s)* 112 (e13) (probably 'the long–cultivated land(s)' or 'the worn–out land(s)' *v.* **ald**, **land**); *Holgate* 1457, *Howle–gate, Hawdgate* 1580, *Houlle gate, holle gate* 1601, *howlgates* 1606, *Howlgats* 1697, *howlgats* 1709, *Houldgate* 1724 ('the way running in a hollow' *v.* **hol**[1], **gata**); *Holme Hill* 1606 (*v.* **holmr**, **hyll**); *del hyll'* 1327, *– Hill'* 1332, *– de Swalowe* 1395, *del Hill de Swalewe* 1427 all (p) (*v.* **hyll**); *Kingeshallecroft* 112 (e13) (named from the *King* family, cf. Alan *King de Cukewald* 112 (e13) (a neighbouring parish), with **hall**, **croft**); *the Layethe Garthe* 1580 (*v.* **hlaða** 'a barn', **garðr** 'an enclosure'); *lankedale* 1606, *Langgal* (sic) 1697; *Thomas leckes close* 1606; *Linedale, the Lyne dyke* 1580, *Lyme daille, Lynedaille* 1601, *the lyne Dyke, – dykes* 1606, *Linepale* (sic) 1697 (*v.* **līn**, **lín** 'flax', **deill**, **dík**); *le Longefeld* 1457 (*v.* **lang**, **feld**); *luuemanacra* lHy2 (e13) (*v.* **æcer**; the first el. is the ME pers.n. *Loveman* < late OE **Luf(e)mann, v.* Reaney, s.n. *Loveman*, where the ultimate etymology is wrongly given as OE *Lēofmann*. OE **Luf(e)mann* is a derivative in *–mann* of the attested OE masc. pers.n. *Lufa*, as Dr Insley points out); *mapple dale* 1697 (*v.* **mapel** 'a maple–tree' with **dalr** or **deill**); *Melne Hill* 1580, *Mylne hyll* 1601, *the millen hill* 1606, *Milne Hill* 1697 (*v.* **myln**, **hyll**); *Mylnestees furlong* 1580, *Myln stees* 1601, *the millenstees* 1606, *Milne stees* 1697 ('the paths to the mill', *v.* **myln**, **stīg**, **stígr** in the pl.); *Murfarr furlong* 1652 (*v.* **marfur** 'a boundary furrow', **furlang**); *Norbarr, Norbarhed* 1580, *Norbare, Norbar headland* 1601, *Nor bar* 1606, *norber headland* 1697, *norbor* 1709, *Norbor* 1724 (*v.* **norð**, **be(o)rg** 'a mound, a hill'); *caput del nord, – nort* 112 (e13) (*v.* **norð**, **hēafod**, perhaps in the sense of a headland in a field); *nunappelton dale* 1580, *Nunappleton dale, Nunnappleton land* 1606, *Nanapeldaile* (sic) 1697, *Appleton Dale* 1724 (*v.* **deill**, **land**, with reference to the Cistercian nuns of Nun Appleton YW who held land here); *le Northburgh* 1457 (*v.* **norð**, **burh**, though the sense of **burh** here is not clear); *Nutfurlondes* 1580, *– forlands* 1601, *nutt furlonges* 1606, *nut furlands* 1697 (*v.* **hnutu**, **furlang**, of which *furlondes, forlands* are common variants in north L); *Owneby Gate* 1457, *owmbie gate* 1580, *Ownby gaite* 1601, *Ownby gate* 1697 ('the road to Owmby (in Searby cum Owmby)', *v.* **gata**); *ye Parsons platt* 1724 (*v.* **platt** 'a plot of ground'); *the Queen ma^{ties} hegh waye or streate* 1580, *the Queenes hye wey* 1601 (self-explanatory and perhaps cf. *the highe streate supra*); *Riebie dale* 1580, *Ryby daille* 1601, *– dale* 1697 ('the share of land belonging to Riby (a nearby village)', *v.* **deill**); *Riuulum q' currit a Rodewella usque ad Cuchewald* lHy2 (e13) ('the stream which runs from Rothwell to Cuxwold'); *the South bothome* 1580 (*v.* **sūð, botm**); *Sowslacke* 1580 (*v.* **sugu** 'a sow' or **sūð** 'south', **slakki** 'a small shallow valley, a hollow in the ground', a word found several times in north L, but usually associated with north–west England, cf. *Potterdale slacke* PN L **2**, 27); *Stanlate dale* 1580, *Stanlatte daille* 1601, *Stantley dale* (sic) 1606, *Stanly Dale* 1652, *Stantlay dayle* 1709, *Staintley Dale* 1724 (obscure); *Staynhill'* 1332 (p) ('the stony hill', *v.* ON **steinn, hyll**); *le Swynhowe* 1457 (*v.* **swīn** 'a swine, a pig', **haugr** 'a mound, a hill'); *le Syk(e)* 1457, *the syke* 1580, *Sikes* 1601, *the Syke* 1606, *– Sike* 1652, *ye Sike* 1697, *the sike* 1709, *the Sykebothome* 1580, *– syke bottome* 1601, *ye sike bottom* 1697 (*v.* **sík** 'a ditch, a stream', **botm**); *the Towne end* 1580, *The Townes –* 1601, *the townes –* 1606, *Toune Endes* 1652, *ye town ends* 1697, *the town –* 1709, *Town End(s)* 1724 (self-explanatory); *the wath stead* 1709, *ye Wathstead* 1724 ('the place where there is a ford', *v.* **vað, stede**, a compound not recorded in Sandred); *Whaplot –, Whaplote close* 1580, *Whaplotte –, whaplotte –* 1601, *Whaplot(t), Whaplott –* 1606, *Waplow – 1697, Wapley –* 1697, 1724, *Waplay (close)* 1709, *Wapley (close)* 1724 (obscure); *Water mill* 1620; *Wilsby gate* 1652 (apparently 'the road to Weelsby (a village some miles to the east)', *v.* **gata**); *Wrangdale* 1457, 1580, *wreng–* 1606, *wrang –* 1697, cf. *wrang dale hedlonde* 1580, *wrangdall headland* 1601, *Wrangdall bottom* 1652, *wrang dale headland, – windings* 1697 ('the crooked share of land' *v.* **vrangr, deill** with **hēafod–land** and *v. the Wyndinges infra*; in 1457 it is described as *a dala*); *the Wraye* 1580, *– wrey* 1606 (*v.* **vrá** 'a nook or corner of land'); *the Wyndinges* 1580, *– windens* 1601, *ye windings* 1697 (as noted in PN L **3**, 16 "*winding* in a topographical sense does not seem to be recorded in dictionaries; perhaps it is an **ing**² derivative of **(ge)wind**² 'something winding, a winding path etc.', . . . perhaps denoting a place or places where there is a bend or bends".

Tetney

TETNEY

Tatenaya 1085 (16) Dugd iii, *-ai* 1086 DB, c.1115 LS, *-eia* R1
  (c.1331) *Spald i*, *-ay* 1194, 1195 P both (p), 1250 FF
Tataneyo(sic) 111 (c.1331) *Spald i*, *-eine* (sic) Hy2 Dane, *-ay*
  1203 FF
Thateneia Hy2 Dane (p)
Tetanai eHy2 RA iv, *Tetenay* eHy2 *AD*, 1240 RRG, 1242–43
  Fees, 1275 RH, 1291 RSu, 1309 Pat, 1327, 1332 *SR*, 1333
  Pat, 1338 Misc, 1341 *Extent et passim* to 1428 FA, *-eia*
  1155–58 (1334) Ch, Hy2 (1314) ib, 1202 Ass (p), *-ey* 1226
  FF, 1267 Ch, 1316, 1428 FA, 1514 LP xi, *-eye* 1245, 1263
  FF, 1291 Tax, 1296 RSu, 1329 *Ass*, 1331 Cl, *-eya* 1254
  ValNor, *Tetenai* 1201 P (p), *-aia* 1212 Fees
Tetney 1381 Peace, 1412 Pap, 1431 FA, 1449 Fine, 1523–24
  MinAcct, 1526 Sub, 1535 VE iv *et freq*, *-eye* 1282 Ch, *-ay*
  1384 Peace, 1396 de l'Isle, 1435 *AD*, 1446 Cl, 1450 *Anc*,
  1474 Cl, 1506 Ipm, 1539 *AOMB 211*, 1546–47 *MinAcct*,
  -aye 1492 Fine, 1536–37 Dugd vi
Tettenai 1201 Ass, 1202 P (p)
Tetteney 1308 Inqaqd, 1327 Banco, 1331 Ipm, 1406 Cl,
  1421–23 *MinAcct*, 1451 Cl, 1477 *DC*, 1478 Cl, 1547 Pat,
  -eye 1314, 1351 Ch, 1355, 1359 *Cor*, 1402 Pat, 1402 FA,
  1413 Cl, 1435 *FF*
Tettnay 1536–37 Dugd vi, *-ey* 1537–38 ib iv, 1545 LP xx
Theteneio(sic) 1199 (1330) Ch, *-eyo* (sic) 1200 ChR, *-ey* Hy3
  (1409), 113 AD, *-ay* 1297 ib
Thedeneye 1303 FA
Tedeneye 1390 Pat, *-ey* 1391, 1392 Cl
Toteny 1303 FA, *-ay* 1309 Orig, 1325 Pat, *-aye* 1318 ib, *-eye*
  1342 Cl, *-ey* 1454 Pat (all *-o-* = *-e-*)

Dr Insley suggests that this is 'Tǣte's island of land', from the
unrecorded OE fem. pers.n. *Tǣte* (gen.sg. *Tǣtan*) and ēg 'an

island of land'. OE *Tǣte* is a hypocoristic form of fem. names in *Tāt* and as Dr Insley points out contains the Germanic *-jōn* suffix, which caused *i*-mutation of the stem syllable. He also notes OE *Tāte*, which is attested in independent use, and the masc. variant *Tāta*, which is also found quite frequently. Tetney is situated on a distinct island of land in a low–lying marshy coastal area, typical of places with names from OE **ēg**. Margaret Gelling has plausibly argued that p.ns. in **ēg** belong to "the earlier rather than the later centuries of the Anglo–Saxon period" and further that **ēg** is a topgraphical term which had a quasi–habitative significance, *v.* PNITL 38–39.

BISHOPTHORPE is *Tetney Ho*. 1818 Bry. THE CASTLES (local), *le Casteles* 1451–53 *MinAcct*, *le castelles* 1477 *DC*, *pasture . . . voc' Castels* 1496–98, *pastur' . . . voc' Castelles* 1523–24, – *Castell' iuxta fosat' maris* 1546–47, – *iuxta Fossat'* 1475–77 all *MinAcct*, "a Barkery & Grounds called" *Castells* 1585–86 Lanc, *pastur' vocat' Castle* 1608–9 *MinAct*, *yᵉ Castles* 1705, *the –* 1719, 1764, 1775 all *Haigh*, 1779 *EnclA*; the ground here is flat and there are no traces of earthworks; the significance of the name is not known. CHURCH LANE (local). COW MARSH LANE (local), 1828 Bry, cf. *Cow Marsh* 1781 *Terrier*, 1779 *EnclA*, – *Road* 1785 *Haigh*. COWSKIT BANK (local), 1779 *EnclA*, 1822 *Terrier*, 1828 Bry, cf, *Cowiskitt* 1523–24, – *skytt* 1546–47 both *MinAcct*, perhaps literally 'cow–dung', *v.* **cū**, **scite**, with the second el. influenced by the cognate ON **skítr**. It is the name of the road leading to New Delights *infra*. CROWN AND ANCHOR, 1842 White, – *Inn* 1828 Bry, 1860 *Padley*. EASTFIELD FM (local), cf. *Tetney East feild* 1609 *DuLaMB 119*, *the east feilde* 1630 Foster, – *East field* 1676 *Haigh*, *Tetney East feild* 1686 *Terrier*, *the East feild* 1687 *Haigh*, – *field* 1697 *MiscDep 161*, *(the) East Field* 1702 *Haigh et passim*; one of the open fields of the village, *v.* **ēast**, **feld**. GRAINSBY LANE, *Grainsby Gate*, – *Road* 1779 *EnclA*, 1808 *GDC*, *v.* **gata**, leading to Grainsby. HALLOWELLS HILLS (lost, approx TA 299 014), 1828 Bry. HOLME FM (local), *Tetteneyholm* 1314 Ch, *le*

Holme 1475–77, 1496–98, 1523–24, 1546–47, 1608–9 all *MinAcct, the* – 1697, 1717 *MiscDep 161, Tetney Holme* 1774 *Hill, Holmes*1535–46 *MinAcct,* 1560 *Barne, le* – 1551 Pat, *The* – 1828 Bry, 'the higher ground amidst the marsh', *v.* **holmr**. HOLME LANE, 1828 Bry, *Holmes* – 1779 *EnclA,* 1792 *GDC,* 1855 *Haigh, Louth Road or* – 1779 *EnclA.* HOOP END (local), cf. *the hoop* 1709 *MiscDep 161, (the) Hoop* 1719 *ib,* 1781 *Terrier,* 1779 *EnclA,* 1825, 1864 *Terrier,* perhaps from OE **hōp** 'a hoop' in some transferred topographical sense; it is situated in a marked curve at a junction of two roads. INGHAM'S LANE, *Inhams Lane* 1828 Bry, cf. *est Fenne Inholmes* 1535–46 *MinAcct, Inholme* 1537–38 Dugd iv, *the Inhams* 1702 *Haigh,* 'the inner holme', *v.* **in**, **holmr**, cf. Holme Fm *supra* and Out Holme Fm *infra*. MILL (lost, approx TA 305 015), 1824 O, *Wind Mill* 1705 *Haigh,* 1779 *EnclA, molendino . . . de Tetanai* eHy2 RA iv, *a little green by the Mill, the Mill house* 1676 *Haigh,* cf. *myll close* 1609 *DuLaMB 119, Mulnecroft'* 1421–23, *Milnecrofte* 1451–53, 1475–77, *–croft* 1496–98, *Mylnecrofte* 1546–47, *Milncrofte* 1608–9 all *MinAcct* (*v.* **croft**), *Milnedale* 1475–77, 1496–98, 1546–47, 1608–9, *Mylne–* 1523–24 all *MinAcct* (*v.* **deill** 'a share of land'; there is no marked valley here), *Milnegat* 1446 Cl, *millgate* 1690 Wild, *Mill gate(s)* 1702 *Haigh* (*v.* **gata** 'a road'; it is said by Wild 68 to be the old road to Waithe), *Milnwanges* 1560 *Barne, The Mill Wong* 1702 *Haigh* (*v.* **vangr** 'a garden, an in–field'), *Charnell milnewra* 1446 Cl, *Milnewra* 1451 ib, *Mylnwrayes* 1535–46 *MinAcct* (*v.* **vrá** 'a nook, a corner of land' also 'a cattle shelter'; for Charnell *v.* *Charnels maner* in f.ns. (b) *infra*). MOTHER DRAIN SLUICE (local), *Mother Drain* 1779 *EnclA,* 1860 *Padley, the Great* – 1855, 1877 *Haigh.* NEW DELIGHTS, *the springs called Bloe Wells or New Delights Wells* 1779 *EnclA,* no doubt a complimentary nickname, cf. Tetney Blow Wells *infra*. NEW PLANTATION (lost), 1824 O; it was in the north–east corner of the parish near the Humberston boundary and the sea. NEWTON MARSH LANE (local), 1828 Bry, – *Road* 1779 *EnclA,* 1840 *BH,* cf. *marisco de Neuton* Hy2 Dane, *Newton Marsh* 1578–79, 1588–89 Lanc, 1668, 1683, 1709, 1727, 1746 *Haigh,* 1737, 1746 *GDC,* 1776 *Haigh,* 1781, 1825, 1864

Terrier, named from the *Newton* family, cf. Simon *Newton de Tetnay* 1446 Cl. NORTH END, 1828 Bry, cf. *North end grene* 1609 *DuLaMB 119*, self-explanatory. OLD BANK (lost), 1824 O, 1828 Bry. OLDFLEET DRAIN, *a River called the Fleet* 1726 *GDC*, (*the*) *Old Fleet* 1777 *Haigh*, 1779 *EnclA*, *v.* **flēot** 'a stream, a drain'. OUT HOLME FM, *Outholme* 1671 *MiscDep 161*, 1779 *EnclA*, 1780 *GDC*, – *Holme* 1779 *EnclA*, –*holmes* 1779 *GDC*, 1779 *Haigh*, 'the outer holme', *v.* **ūt**, **holmr** and cf. Ingham's Lane *supra*. PARK FM, cf. *Parklis* (sic) 1690 Wild, –*lese* 1698 *MiscDep 161*, – *Lese* 1717 *ib. v.* **park**, **lǣs** 'pasture, meadow–land'. PYEWIPE HALL (lost, approx TA 329 037), 1824 O, 1828 Bry, cf. Pyewipe (Inn), PN L **1**, 34, where it is pointed out that it alludes to the lapwing, *Vanellus vanellus*, by the dial. term not uncommonly used as a farm name. SEA BANK HO (lost, now in the sea by Tetney Haven), 1828 Bry. SOUTH MARSH LANE (local), 1828 Bry, – *Road* 1779 *EnclA*, cf. *Sowthmarshe* 1564–65 Lanc, *South Marsh* 1586–87 ib, *the south marsh* 1609 *DuLaMB 119*, *the South Marsh* 1668 *Haigh*, 1697, 1709, 1717, 1719 *MiscDep 161*, *South Marishe* 1671 *ib*, 1726 *GDC et freq* to 1780 *ib*, *cf. maresco Tataneine* (sic) Hy2 Dane, *marisco de Tetney* 1546–47 *MinAcct*, self–explanatory. TETNEY BECK, 1686 *Terrier*, apparently an alternative name for Humberston Beck *supra*. TETNEY BLOW WELLS, 1824 O, *the Below Wells* (sic) 1808, 1819, 1825 *GDC*, *Ponds or Pools of Water called the Below or Blow Wells* 1825 *ib*, *There are several Blow Wells . . . and they constantly send forth copious streams of pure water* 1842 White, *v.* Blow Wells in Great Coates *supra*. TETNEY DRAIN, 1824 O, 1828 Bry. TETNEY FITTIES, *wast lands in Tetney called greaves or Fyttes grounds lyeing without the Auntient Seabancks* 1609 *DuLaMB 119*, *the Fittys* 1779 *EnclA*, *Tetney North –, Tetney South Fittys* 1775 Yarb, 1779 *GDC*, *the North Fittys*, – *South Fittys by the Fleet Clow* 1777 *Haigh*, *North –, South Fittys* 1779 *EnclA*, cf. Humberston Fitties in Humberston *supra*. TETNEY FM (local), *Tetney F^m* 1828 Bry. TETNEY GRANGE, 1570 Pat, 1824 O, 1828 Bry, *grang' de Tetney* 1381 Peace, – *Tetnay* 1384 ib, *Tetnaye Grange* 1525–36 ChronLP, *Tetney graunge* 1535–46 *MinAcct*, *Tetny Graunge* 1647 *Foster*, *the* *grange of Tetney* 1649 WillsPCC, *Tettney Graunge* 1674 *LCS, the Manner . . . of Tetney called the North Graunge* 1664 *Dep, the north grange* 1706 *Foster, the Farr grange* 1609 *DuLaMB 119, the Farre Grange* 1702 *Haigh,* cf. *Grange Hill* 1687 *ib*; Louth Park Abbey held a **grange** in Tetney. TETNEY GROVE (lost), 1828 Bry, *The Greves* 1577–78 Lanc, cf. Tetney Fitties *supra, the growes* in South Ferriby, PN L **2**, 114 and *marsh called the Groves or Greaves* in East Halton, ib, 155. *Grove* and *greave* appear to be alternative dial. terms in north L and indeed in the Fenland for a place where digging (perhaps for turf) took place. Tetney Grove denoted an area around Sluice Gate. TETNEY HALL FM is *Old Hall* 1828 Bry. TETNEY HAVEN, 1775 *Yarb, Tetteney Havene* 1551 Cl, *portum de Tetteney* 1451–53, *port' de* – 1475–77, *portam* (sic) *de* – 1496–98, *portam de Tetney also Tetney Haven'* 1523–24 all *MinAcct, v.* **hafn**. TETNEY HIGH SANDS is *Sand Haile Flats* 1824 O. TETNEY LOCK, 1779 *EnclA*, 1824 O, 1828 Bry, on Louth Navigation. TUTTLE HO, cf. *Tuttyll haven* 1609 *DuLaMB 119, Tuttle Ramper* 1828 Bry; Tuttle Drain forms part of the boundary between Tetney and North Coates, *v.* PN L **4**, 145, where it is suggested that Tuttle means 'the look–out hill', *v.* **tōt–hyll**. VICARAGE (lost), *y*ᵉ *. . . vicarage* 1561, *The Ecclesiastical Commissioners . . . do hereby grant . . . to the Vicarage of Tetney . . . One Capital sum of One Thousand and four hundred pounds sterling . . . towards defreaying the cost of providing a new Parsonage* 1667, *the Vicarage* 1679, *A Vicaridge house* 1690, *the Vicarage House* 1781, *Vicarage House* 1825, *The Vicarage* 1864 all *Terrier*. WESTFIELD HO, cf. *le Westefeld'* 1535–46 *MinAcct, the West feild* 1676 *Haigh,* 1697 *MiscDep 161, – field* 1702 *Haigh,* 1726 *GDC, – Field* 1717 *MiscDep 161,* 1719, 1775 *Haigh,* 1779 *GDC, West Field* 1779 *EnclA, the West Fields* 1705 *Haigh,* one of the great fields of the village, *v.* **west, feld**. WORLDS END (lost), 1828 Bry; this was an area of land on the coast between Louth Navigation and the parish boundary with North Coates, a nickname of remoteness.

FIELD-NAMES

Forms dated m12 are *AD*; Hy2 Dane; ll3 AD; 1289 *Holywell*; 1314 Ch; 1327, 1332 *SR*; 1329 *Ass*; 1341 *Extent*; 1355, 1359 *Cor*; 1375 Works;1421-23, 1451-53, 1475-77,1496-98,1523-24, 1535-46, 1546-47, 1608-9 *MinAcct*; 1435 *FF*; 1446, 1451 Cl; 1450 *Anc*; 1477 *DC*; 1537-8 Dugd iv; 1545 LP xxii; 1551 Pat, 1554 (1686), 1561, 1781[1], 1825[1], 1864 *Terrier*; 1560 *Barne*; 1564-65, 1577-78, 1578-79, 1585-86, 1586-87, 1588-89 Lanc; 1569 *Tur*; 1579, 1630, 1706 *Foster*; 1609 *DuLaMB 119*; 1626, 1653, 1654, 1656, 1668, 1671, 1679, 1687, 1688, 1697, 1698, 1709[1], 1717, 1719[1] *MiscDep 161*; 1634 *HumbD*; 1664 *Dep*; 1668, 1676, 1683, 1684, 1687, 1696, 1702, 1704, 1705, 1709[2], 1712, 1719[2], 1737[1], 1746[1], 1757[1], 1764[1], 1775[1], 1776, 1777[1], 1778[1], 1779[1], 1780[1], 1785, 1786, 1826, 1861 *Haigh*; 1686 LNQ xviii, 1690, 1772[2], 1780[2] Wild; 1726, 1726 (1819), 1737[2], 1746[2], 1751, 1757[2], 1764[2], 1765, 1778[2], 1779[2], 1780[2], 1781[2], 1792, 1808[1], 1819, 1825[2], 1832 *GDC*; 1775[2] *Yarb*; 1779[3] *EnclA*; 1808[2] *Dixon*; 1815, 1836[1] *CC*; 1836[2] *Falk*; 1840 *BH*.

(a) the Back Cl 1779[3]; Big Fd 1840, The Brickyard, Brickyard Garth (*v.* **garðr** 'an enclosure', as elsewhere in the parish); Burkitt Cl 1778[2] (1737[2], Birkett Close 1737[1], named from the *Birkett* family, cf. William *Burkit* 1613 *BT*); Brigsley Rd 1779[3] (the road to Brigsley); Caborn Cl 1779[3] (*Caborne Close* 1690, *Cabourne Close* 1702, named from the *Cabourne* family, cf. Richard *Caburne* 1554 *Inv*); the Canal Bank 1777; the Manor or Chief Mansion called Cannon Garth 1836[2] (*v.* **garðr**; *Cannon* may be a surn. or may refer to a religious community of canons, *v.* **canoun**); Cat Garth 1777[3] (*v.* **cat(t)**, **garðr** and the early forms of Cowe Cl *infra*); Coal Shore Rd 1779[3], 1785, the – 1808[1]; the Coat Garth 1764[1], 1778[1], 1779[3], Cowd Garth (sic) 1779[1], Court Garth 1779[2], Coat Garth 1785 (1702, 1704, 1709[1], 1717, *the Coat garth* 1668, *Coat Gath* (sic) 1687, *The Coat Garths* 1705, *the Coatgarth* 1719[2], *Pinder Close otherwise Coat-garth* 1737[1], *v.* **cot** 'a cottage, a shed', **garðr**); Commissioners' Drain 1840; Cowe Cl 1779[1], Cow Cl otherwise Cat Garth (sic) 1780[2] (*Catgarth* 1609, *Catt Garth* 1709[1], 1719[1], *Catgarth Close* 1737[1], 1737[2], *v.* Cat Garth *supra*); Cuthbert Folly 1836[2] (from the surn. *Cuthbert* and **folie**); Draykmoor 1764[1], 1778[1] (*Dreyk more* 1705, *v.* **mōr** 'a marsh'; Dr Insley suggests that the first el. appears to be ME **drāke** 'a dragon', perhaps used here in connection with popular superstition); Great –, Little East Cl 1861; the East Fenn 1777, – Fen 1779[1] (*le Est Fenne* 1535–46, *Estfenne* 1560, *the Easte Fen* 1609, *theast fene* 1626, *the East fenne* 1671, *the East Fenn* 1717, 1737[1], *East Fenn* 1746[1], *v.* **ēast, fenn**); the East Garth 1779[3] (*v.* **garðr**); the East Homestead 1836[2]; The Eight acre mdw 1825[2]; Eleven Acres 1825[2], 1838; Fauldings platts, – plots 1819 (from the local surn. *Faulding*, cf. John *Faulding* 1779[3], with **plat**[2] and **plot**); the Fleet Clow 1780[1] (from **flēot** 'an inlet', 'a rivulet' and *clow* 'a dam for water', 'a sluice or floodgate'. For the history of this word *v.* NED s.v. *clow* sb[1], 1a); Friar Hill 1779[3]; The Gall Holme 1764[1], the Gallholme 1778[1], Galls Holme 1779[1] (*Gall Holme* 1609, 1746[1], *the Gallholme* 1705, 1719[2], *Galeholme* (sic) 1737[2], *v.* **galla** 'a barren spot in a field, spongy ground', **holmr** 'raised land in marsh', as elsewhere in the parish); Gilliatt's Cottage 1777, Giliatts – 1779[1], 1780[2] (*M*[r] *Gilliatt* is mentioned in the 1777 document); Greens Cl 1808[1], 1825[2], the Greens Cl 1819, 1825[2] (*Greens Close* 1746[1], probably named from the *Green* family, cf. John *Green* 1603 *Inv* and cf. *Ashelmore . . . Close* in f.ns. (b) *infra*); one other private Carriage and Driving Road to be called Greens Road 1779[3], the Greens Road 1808[1]; Hammond Lane 1779[3] (named from the family of William *Hammon* 1609 *BT*); Hewson's Lane 1779[3] (from the family of Michael *Hewson* 1642 LPR); North –, South Holme Close 1836[2] (cf. Holme Fm *supra*); North –, South Hoodick East, – West (sic) 1836[2] (*a place called Huddick* 1687); Houghton low lane 1779[3], Holton low Road 1785 (leading to Holton le Clay, an adjacent parish); Humberston Drain 1777; Humberstone Closes Rd 1779[3], Humberston's Cl 1786 (named from the family of Thomas Frederick *Humberstone* 1779[3]); The Hurds Cl 1779[3] (named from the family of Alexander *Hurd* 1605 *BT*); The Inggs 1757[1], – Ings 1764[1], The Ings of Tetney 1776, 1785 (*the Ings* 1609, 1697, 1702, 1709[1], 1719[1], 1746[1], *the Ingges* 1668, – *Inggs* 1717, – *Inngs banke* 1609, *v.* **eng** 'meadow, pasture', as elsewhere in the parish); Lidgett Lane 1779[3] (probably from a surn.); Lock Pits Cls 1780[1], Lock Pit Cls 1780[1]; the Lock Rd 1825[2] (named from Tetney Lock *supra*); Long Cl 1779[3]; Louth Rd 1779[3], 1808[1], 1825[2] (leading to Louth a few miles south of Tetney); Low Grounds 1779[1], 1780[2], 1781, the – 1779[2], Southlow grounds 1836[2]; Ludlams Lane 1779[3] (named from the family of John *Ludlam* 1730 Wild); Long Merry Lands 1815, 1836[1]; the Narrow Lane 1777; Navigation Bank Rd 1779[3] (leading to Louth Navigation); the new Cls 1776, 1785 (*the New Closes* 1668, 1712, –*Closes* 1684); the New Drain 1777; New Sea Bank

1779³, the delph of the new Sea Bank 1785 (cf. *fossatum maris de Tetteney* 1451–53, *Fossat' maris . . . in Tetney* 1546–47, *intra fossat' maris . . . in Tetney* 1608–9, *Tetney Bank* 1554 (1684), self–explanatory); the Nine Acres Cl 1825²; North Marsh 1765, the – 1778² (*Northemerssh'* 1341, *le Northmerssh'* 1421–23, – *northe m'sshe* 1535–46, *North'mersshe alias le Cowpastur'* 1523–24, – *al' le Cowpasture* 1546–47, *Northmershe* 1560, *North Marsh* 1586–87, 1737, *Northmarsh als' Cowpasture* 1608–9, the *North Marsh* 1668, 1676 *et freq*, 1746², *yᵉ* – 1683, *the North Marshe* 1717, *v.* **norð, mersc**); the Out Gates 1764¹, – Outgates 1778¹, Outgates 1779³, the Outgates Cl 1786 (*the Outgates pastures* 1668, *yᵉ Outgates* 1705, *v.* **ūt, gata**); the Oxholme 1751, 1765, 1776 *et freq*, 1826, Oxholme 1779¹, 1779³, Oxpastures or Oxholme 1779³, East –, North –, South –, West Oxholme 1836² (*Oxholme* 1609, 1746¹, *the Ox holme* 1668, 1726, 1746², – *Oxholme* 1709², 1726, – *Oxholm* 1737¹, *v.* **oxa, holmr**); Petch Holme 1764¹, 1778¹ (*Petch holme* 1705, 1719², named from the *Petch* family, cf. William *Peyche* 1557 *Inv*, John *Petch* 1702, 1737¹, with **holmr**, *v.* also Webster Holme *infra*); Pinder Cl 1779² (*Pynders Mawer als Pynders Close* 1626, *Pindar Close otherwise Coat–garth* 1737¹, *pindar close otherwise Coate–garth Close* 1737², from the occupational name *Pinder* or its derived surn., cf. Richard *Pynder* 1626; *Mawer* 1626 represents ME *maure* 'a saltern, a salt–hill', *v.* further PN L **4**, 119, s.n. *Cawthernsome Lane*); the Rabbit Hills 1779³; the Raison Rd 1825² (referring to Market Rasen, a few miles to the south–west); Robinson Garth 1779³ (from the *Robinson* family, cf. William *Robinson* 1779³, with **garðr**); the Round Cl 1779³; Salt Coat Holme 1764¹, Salt Coatholme 1778¹ (*Saltcoteholme* 1451–53, 1496–98, *Saltecote holme* 1523–24, *Saltcoteholmes* 1535–46, *Saltcoat holme* 1705, *Salt Coat holme* 1719², *v.* **salt–cote** 'a saltern', **holmr**, cf. *unam placeam ad faciendum salinam* m12, *Saltcote* 1421–23, *unius Saltcote holme* 1475–77); the Salt Fenn 1776, Salt Fen 1779³, East –, Middle Salt Fen 1836² (*Salt'fennes, le Saltfenne* 1421–23, 1451–53, 1475–57, *Saltfennes* 1451–53, 1523–24, *le Salte Fenne* 1535–46, *Saltfenne* 1546–47, *the salt fen* 1609, – *Salt Fen* 1668, 1709², *yᵉ Salt Fenn* 1683, *v.* **salt, fenn**); Lord Scarborough's Cl, – Cottage, – Croft 1777, 1779¹; Sea Holme 1836²; Sedgewick Holme 1764, 1778¹ (*Sedgewick holme* 1705, 1719², named from the *Sedgewick* family, cf. Elizabeth *Sedgewick* 1720 *Haigh*, with **holmr**); The first –, the second seven acres Cl 1825², Seven Acres 1840; Shepherd's House 1808² (perhaps named from the family of James *Shepherd* 1509–10 Wild); Dʳ Sibthorpe's Croft 1777 (*v.* **croft**), – Cl 1779², Dʳ Sibthorp's – 1779¹ (the Dr Sibthorpe is Humphrey *Sibthorpe* 1779³); the Sixteen acres or Lamb House Cl 1825², – or Lamb house cl 1838; the Skorneholme

1764[1], the Skerneholme 1778[1] (*the Skerneholme* 1705, *The* – 1719[2], *v.* **holmr**; Dr Insley suggests that the first el. is ON *skarn* 'dung', cf. ME *sharn*, *shern(e)* etc. 'dung, manure'); Gt –, Lt Slabs 1836[2] (*the Slabbs* 1690, – *Slabs* 1701); Small Sinks 1779[3] (*v.* **sink** 'a gutter, drain, sewer', and for a discussion of the word, *v.* PN L **2**, 199–20); South gate Holme 1779[1] (*v.* **sūð, gata, holmr**); The South River 1780[1]; Sowgirt Moor 1779[3] (it is tempting to suggest that *Sowgirt* is from the surn. *Sowgrift*, *Sawgrift* found in the parish in the 16th and 17th centuries, cf. Thomas *Sowgrift* c.1541, John *Sawgrift* 1621 both *Inv*; the second el. is probably **mōr**, presumably in the sense 'marsh'); Gt –, Lt Square Folly 1836[2] (*v.* **folie**); Tetney New Bank 1775[1] (probably the same as New Sea Bank *supra*); the Thorough Fair 1776, a place called – 1785 (*v.* **thoroughfare**); Town End Green, Town Green 1779[3], Townend Green 1808[1] (*Attegrene* 1327, *attegrene* 1329, *atte Grene* 1332 all (p), *Toungrene* 1546–47, *Townegreene* 1608–9, *the grene* 1609, *v.* **tūn, ende, grēne** 'a village green'); Townside Rd 1779[2], the Town side – 1785; the Town St. 1777, 1779[2] *et freq*, 1832, The town St. 1825[2], Town St. 1864; Twafleet (sic) 1757[1], –fleets 1764[1], Two Fleets 1779[3] (*Twaflete* 1446, *–flattes* 1535–46, 1560, *the Towfleets*, *Tway-*, *Tetney Twyfleets* 1609, *the twofleets* 1697, *the two Fleets* 1705, 1709[1], *Towfleets* 1717, *the two Fleets* 1719[1], *The Two* – 1746[1], *v.* **twā, flēot**, and *v.* the same name s.n. *Tuafletes* in Holton le Clay f.ns. (b) *supra*); the Twelve Acre Mdw 1825[2], – twelve Acre Mdws 1838, Twelve Acres 1825[2], 1840; the twenty Acres or Line Cl 1779[3]; Upcote Lane 1780[2] (cf. *Vpcoate hill* 1608–9, *v.* **upp** 'upper, higher up', **cot**); Ussledike 1779[3]; Warth Beck Cl 1779[3]; Wash Dike Cl 1779[3], 1746[1] (*Wash Dike Close* 1746[1], *v.* **wæsce, dík**); Webster Holme and Pinder Cl 1779[1], Webster Holme 1779[2] (*the Webster Holm otherwise Petch Holme* 1737[1], cf. *Webster smale Sykes* 1609, named from the *Webster* family, cf. Thomas *Wibstar* 1573 *Inv*, with **holmr, smæl**, and **sík**, *v.* also Coat Garth, Petch Holme *supra* and *le Smalesyche infra*); The Well Cl 1825[2], the – 1832 (*v.* **wella**); West Cl 1779[3]; The West Fen 1778[2], 1792 (*Westfene* 1446, *–fenne* 1451–53, *le* – 1535–46, – *West Fenne* 1545, *the West fen* 1609, *West Fenn* 1726, 1746[2], – *fen* 1726 (1819), *v.* **west, fenn**); Great –, Little Witchcap 1836[2] (perhaps a shape–name, alluding to the conical hat tradionally worn by witches); Wright's Garth 1779[3] (from the surn. *Wright*, cf. Richard *Wright* 1642 LPR).

(b) *Acreyeddis* 1535–46 (*v.* **æcer–hēafod** in the pl.); *Aluehou* m12 (apparently 'the mound haunted by elves', from ON *álfa*, gen.pl. of **álfr**, and **haugr**); *Asgardaille* 1446, *dalam voc' Alsgardale* (sic) 1535–46, *unum le dale vocat asgardale* 1560 (*v.* **deill**; the first el. is a partially anglicized form of the Scand. pers.n. *Ásgeirr*, in which OE *-gār* has replaced ON *-geirr*); *Ashelmore otherwise Greens Close* 1737[1], *Ashmore otherwise* - 1737[2] (*v.* **mōr** in the sense 'marsh'; *Ashel*- is perhaps 'the hill where ash–trees grow', *v.* **æsc, hyll**; *v.* also Greens Cl in f.ns. (a) *supra*); *Beane holme* 1609 (*v.* **bēan, holmr**); *Beasum* 1690, *Bearam* (sic) 1702; *Bilbourn close* 1554 (1684) (named from the *Bilbourn* family, cf. . . . *bylborn on East* (no forename), mentioned in the document); *Bissell hill* 1690 (*v.* **hyll**; the first el. is a surn., *v.* Reaney, s.n. *Bushell*); *braken* m12 (*v.* **brakni**); *Brentlake* 1451–53; *Brigesley hedg* 1609 (the hedge with Brigsley, a neighbouring parish); *Britendale* 1421–23, *Brotendale* 1451–53, *Brottendale* 1475–77, *Brokendale* 1608–9 (*v.* **deill**); *Bronnesmare* 1421–23, *Bronesmerr'* 1451–53, *Bronnesmere* 1475–77, *Bromesmede* 1546–47, *Bromesmeare* 1608–9 (*v.* **(ge)mǣre**; the first el. is uncertain; it should be noted that forms from *MinAcct* are very erratic and many are untrustworthy); *atte Brygg de tetenay* 1359, *at Brygge de Tetnay* 1450 both (p) (*v.* **brycg**); *terr' in Tetney called le Burgh in le mersshe* 1546–47, *- in le Marshe* 1608–9 (obscure; there is a Burgh le Marsh in LSR); *Busseland'* 1421–23 (the first el. is probably the ME surn./byname *Busse*, for which *v.* Reaney, s.n. *Buss*, with **land**); *Carr Mylwrayes* 1626, *- Milwrays* 1687, *- Mil–wray* 1688, cf. *Car Holme* 1698 (*v.* **holmr**) (the earlier forms are from **kjarr** with **myln, vrá**, 'a nook', cf. *Sheffield Milnwraies infra*); *Champiundayl* 113 (from the family of Henry *de Campania* 1314, with **deill**); *man'io de Tettenay vocato Charnels maner* 1435 (from the family of Robert *Charneles* 1332); *Chatholme* 1421–23, *Cat*- 1451–53, 1475–77, *chatbyme* (sic) 1546–47, *chatbyne, Shat*- 1608–9 (probably *v.* **catt, holmr**; the later forms doubtless represent scribal errors as elsewhere in *MinAcct*); *Clemetry wong* (sic) 1687 (*v.* **vangr**. *Clemetry* is presumably for *Cemetery*); *Clodacres* m12 (*v.* **clodd** 'a clod', **æcer**); *the upper & lower Closes* 1696; *Cocholme* 1451–53, *Cok*- 1475–7, *Saltholme vocat' Coxholmes* 1608–9 (*v.* **holmr**; the first el. may well be a pers.n. or surn.); *Cock green* 1702 (*v.* **grēne** 'a grassy place'); *College lands* 1690 (Clare College held land in the parish); *Comp'holme* (sic) 1451–53, *Saltcote holme . . . voc' Calholme* (sic) 1546–47, *Saltcot holme in Tetney voc' Cowpeholmes* 1608–9 (*v.* **holmr**; the first el. is uncertain, but may well be the surn. *Coupe*, for which *v.* Reaney, s.n. *Coope*; this was a saltern); *Cornesholm'dale* 1421–23, *-holmedale* 1451–53, 1475–7, *Corneholmes* 1546–7, *Cornisholmedale* 1608–9 (the first el. is perhaps a surn. with **holmr** and **deill**); *Cosens headland* 1690, *Couzen head lane* (sic) 1702 (no doubt from the family of John *Cosyn* 1332, William *Cossing* 1558 *Inv*); *Cottwell* 1702 (*v.* **wella**); *Coulthornes* 1586–7, *Colthornes* 1588–89 (*v.*

þorn; Dr Insley suggests that the first el. is possibly ME *cōl, coul, coyl* 'cabbage, kale, colewort, rape, mustard, or some other plant of the genus *Brassica*, also any cultivated leafy vegetable, garden greens, potherbs'. The name would then refer to a thorn–bush situated where a plant of this type was grown); *Cowholme* 1679, – *Holme* 1717 (*v.* **holmr**); *Crossedale* 1421–23, *Crossedale* 1451–53, 1475–77, 1608–9, *the Crosse Cloase* 1561 (*v.* **cros, deill, clos(e)**); *on deadman Shank* 1702 (*Shank* is no doubt being used topograhically here to indicate an outlying strip of land, as Mr Field points out; *deadman* refers to land on which a corpse has been found, *v.* **dede–man**); *le dic* m12 (*v.* **dík**); *douueholm' butt'* 1421–23, *Douueholme* 1451–53, – *butt'* 1475–77, *douueholme* 1546–47 (perhaps *v.* **dūfa** 'a dove', **holmr** with **butte**); *dovyngholme* 1451–53, *unius Saltcoteholme voc'* *dovyngholme* 1475–77, *Saltcote holme . . . voc' Douyngholme* 1546–47, *Salcotholme voc' Devingholme* (sic) 1608–9 (*v.* **holmr**; the first el. is obscure; it is the name of a saltern); *drentendale* 1421–23, *drentall* 1451–53, *Trentall'* 1546–47, *Trenkle* 1608–9 (obscure); *Ebercotgarthe* 1535–46 (*v.* **garðr**; the first el. is probably a surn.); *Erlsgate* 1451 (*v.* **gata**), *Erliscote* 1477, *Earles Coate* 1586–87, 1588–89, – *Cote* 1586–87, *Erles coote* 1588–89 (*v.* **cot**), *Barcarie voc' Erlescrofte* 1523–24, *Erlescrofte* 1546–47 (*v.* **croft**), *Earle marfurr balke* 1609 (*v.* **marfur** 'a boundary furrow', **balca**; perhaps all refer to a family called *Earl*); *campum de Teteney* 1289, *campo de Tetteney* 1421–23, 1451–53, *Campis de Tetney* 1475–77, *campis –* 1546–47, *campis –* 1608–9 (*v.* **feld**); *the Fenn Close* 1668, 1717, – *Fen Close* 1688 (*v.* **fenn**); *Fornesmare* 1421–23, 1475–77, *fornesmare* 1451–53, *Formesmare* (sic) 1523–24, *formare* (sic) 1546–47, *Formestoue* 1608–9 (*v.* **(ge)mære**; the first el. is probably the ON pers.n. *Forni, as suggested by Dr Insley. If so this name must be of considerable antiquity. The form dated 1608–9 does not represent an alternative variant in **stōw**, but is merely a garbled spelling); *Fowler garr Furlonge* 1609 (named from the *Fowler* family, cf. Agnes *Fowler* 1562 *BT*, William *Fowler* 1564 *ib*, with **geiri** and **furlang**); *furewelle* m12 (*v.* **wella**; the first el. may be *feor* 'far', cf. *Tetnaie furwelles infra*); *the furr Close als Rough Holme* 1696 (*v.* **fyrs, rūh, holmr**); *Gairedale* 1421–23, *Kairdale* (sic) 1451–53, *Karedale* 1475–77, *Kirdale* 1546–47, *Caredale* 1608–9 (*v.* **geiri** 'a triangular piece of land', **deill**); *Gairegrene* 1421–23, *Gar-* 1475–77, 1523–24, *-greene* 1451–53, *Garegrene* 1546–47 (*v.* **geiri, grēne**[2]); *Garr wong* 1554 (1684), 1579, *Garr Wong* 1686, *Garwong* 1706 (*v.* **geiri, vangr** 'a garden, an in–field'); *Grangerhirne* 1446 (*v.* **hyrne** 'an angle, a corner of land'; the first el. is probably the surn. *Granger*); *Greneholme* 1609,

Greene holme 1687 (*v.* **grēne**[1], **holmr**); *Gresham hedge* 1554 (1684) (probably from the surn. *Gresham* and **hecg**); *The Greves* "near the Sea" 1577–8 (*Gre(a)ve* (and *grove*) are dial. terms for sites where digging (for turf) took place throughout the Fenland, *v.* also PN L **2**, 155 and ib **4**, 128); *the Guild hall* 1609 (*v.* **gild–hall**); *le Hagh'* 1421–23 (*v.* **haga**[1]); *Hakebrigam* Hy2 (*v.* **brycg**); *the Hardings* 1696 (*v.* **heard** 'hard to till', **eng**); *Hawds Close* 1609; *the lane by the highway side* 1702; *the Hill* 1705, *that Hill or peice of ground* 1719[2] (*v.* **hyll**); *in le hirne* 1332 (p) (*v.* **hyrne**); *Holmersshe* 1546–47; *Honelandal'* 1421–23, *Honylandale* 1451–53, 1546–47, *Hony landale* 1608–9 (*v.* **hunig**, **land** with **deill**, probably referring to sticky soil); *Honey hale* (sic) 1687 (*v.* **hunig**, **halh**); *Honnesdale* 1421–23, 1451–53, *Huddesdale* (sic) 1546–47, *Hunsdale* 1608–9 (*v.* **deill**; the first el.is probably a surn.); *hough* 1475–77, *le Hogh'* 1496–98, – *Hough, Howe* 1523–24, 1546–47 (*v.* **hōh** 'a spur of land'); *ye House Close* 1696; *Isoldgrene* (sic) 1421–23, 1451–53, *Ingoldgrene* 1475–77, *Ingoldegrene* 1523–24, *Ingoldegrene* 1546–47, *Ingoldgreene* 1608–9 (*v.* **grēne**[2]; the first el. is a pers.n., ME *Isolde*, replaced in later forms by Scand. *Ingaldr*); *kestendale* 1421–23, 1451–53, 1475–77, 1546–47, *Kessendale* 1608–9 (probably from the surn. *Kesten* with **deill**); *Kingholme* 1451–53, *Kinges-* 1475–77, *Kynges-* 1546–47, *Kings-* 1608–9 (presumably from the surn. *King* with **holmr**); *placea* "of land . . . in" *Kirmanfen* "to make a salt–pan" 1314 (cf. *Kirmond Holme* in North Coates f.ns. (b), PN L **4**, 149; it is derived from the *Kirmond* family, cf. William *Kyerman* 1548 *Inv*, Nicholas *Kyrmond* 1558 *ib*); *Krakethornhilmare* m12 (from **kráka** 'a crow, a raven', **þorn**, with **hyll** and **(ge)mǣre**); *Kynholme al' Daunce holme* 1475–77 (*v.* **holmr**); *Lady moure* 1446, *Close . . . called Ladymore* 1746[1], *five Acres . . . called Ladymore* 1746[2] (*v.* **hlǣfdige**, **maure** 'a saltern' and cf. Pinder Cl in f.ns. (a) *supra*); *lairlandes* m12 (*v.* **leirr** 'clay', **land**); *the Land Close* 1696 (*v.* **land**, **clos(e)**); *Liddiardlane*, *–wonge* 1451 (from the surn. *Liddiard* with **vangr**); *littlegate* 1702; *Long Marfrey* 1690, – *Bank* 1702 (*v.* **marfur**, of which *marfrey* is a variant in north L); *Mamhole* 1626, 1668, 1687, 1688, 1717, *Mamholes* 1668, *Mam holes* 1671, *Mammhole* 1687 (perhaps from **malm** 'sand, sandy, chalky soil' with **hol**[1] 'a hole, a hollow'); *Marflett* 1702 (*v.* **(ge)mǣre** 'a boundary', **flēot** 'a stream'); *le Merssh'* 1421–23, – *Mersh'* 1451–53, – *mershe* 1475–77, *Marsh heads* 1676, – *Heads* 1698, 1717 (*v.* **mersc**, **hēafod**); *Marshall's wong* 1690 (from the family of John *Marshall* 1702 and **vangr** 'a garden, an in–field'); *three Parcells of Lands called the Mawers* 1671 (for *Mawers*, *v.* Pinder Cl in f.ns. (a) *supra*); *de Mydeby* 1327, – *Middeby*

1332, – *de Tetteney* 1355 all (p) (cf. Midby, PN L 2, 19, where it is suggested that this may be a partial anglicization of Scand. **miðr í bý** 'middle in the village' and comparable with *Northiby* and *Suthiby* respectively 'north in the village' and 'south in the village'); *Mire lease* 1687 (v. **mýrr, lǽs** 'pasture, meadow–land'); *Mundale* (sic) 1421–23, *Nundale* 1451–53, 1475–77, 1496–98, 1608–9 ('the nuns' share of land', v. **nunne, deill**, probably referring to the nuns of St Leonard's Priory in Great Grimsby); *new–croft* 1554 (1684), *New Crofft belonging to Humberston* 1684, *Humberston new croft* 1698, – *new Croft* 1717 (v. **nīwe, croft**, from the neighbouring village of Humberston); *the New Dyke* 1702; *Newlands* 1609 (v. **nīwe, land**); *the North Ings* 1609 (v. **eng**); *Nordlangblamild* m12 (from **blá(r)** 'dark; cold, exposed', **mylde** 'soil', with **norð** and **lang**); *North Close Nook* 1676, *North Close* 1690; *osgotacre* m12 (v. **æcer**; the first el. is an anglicized form of the ON pers.n. *Ásgautr*); *Ostler als Ursula Tack* (sic) 1709[1], *messuage . . . commonly called by the name of Ostler als Ursula Tack* 1719[1] (named from the *Ostler* family, cf. Thomas *Ostler* 1671; Ursula may refer to another person but may well be an erroneous form of *Ostler*; *tack* (ON **taka**) a Scottish or Northern English term for 'leasehold tenure, a leasehold tenement' is rare in L); *othemare* m12 (from **(ge)mǽre** 'a boundary', prefixed by 'on the'); *Parker Thinge* 1569, *landes called parker thing* 1664 (named from the *Parker* family, cf. *Alyes Parkare* 1586 BT, with **þing** 'property, premises'); *Pottewellis* 1535–46, *potwelles* 1560, *Pottwells* 1609, *Potwell dale* 1717 (v. **potte** 'a hole, a hollow', **wella** 'a spring'); *Pastur' voc' pittes* 1546–47, *the Pytts* 1608–9, – *Pyttes* 1671 (v. **pytt**); *a place called Pytwells* 1609 (v. **pytt, wella**); *Ryebrigge* 1375 (v. **rȳge** 'rye', **brycg** in a Scandinavianized form; the significance of 'rye' is uncertain); *Sand ham gate, Sandam Gate* 1702 (probably from **sand** and **holmr**; *ham* and *-am* are common reflexes of **holmr** in north L); *Sewitt Wong* 1702 (named from the *Sewett* family, cf. William *Sewete* 1562 BT, with **vangr**); *the garrs where the scyte hall some tyms stoode* (sic) 1609; *Sheffield Milnwraies* 1626, – *Milwrayes* 1687, – *Mill–wray* 1688, – *Mill Wray* 1717, – *Close* 1668 (v. **myln, vrá** 'a corner of land'; *Sheffield* is a surn. here, cf. Vincent *Sheffield* 1593 Wild); "a sheephouse called" *a shepecote* 1551; *Skipwith Holmes* 1653, – *holmes* 1654, *Eastholmes als Skipwith Holmes* 1656, 1671, 1719[1], – *als Skipwith holmes* 1709[1] (from the surn. *Skipwith* with **holmr**); *Small Dyke puttes* 1535–46, 1560 (v. **smæl** 'narrow', **dík, pytt**); *le Smalesyche* 1421–23, *Smallesikes, le Smalsike* 1451–53, – *Smale Sike* 1475–77, *Smalle sykes* 1535–46, – *Sykis* 1537–38, *le Smalesyke* 1546–47, *Smalley Sykes* (sic) 1551, *the smale sykes* 1608-9 (*v.* **smæl, sík**); *Southend greene* 1609, *the South End Green* 1737[1] (*v.* **sūð, ende, grēne**[2]); *Southfenne* 1421-23, 1451-53, 1608-9, *South'fenne* 1475-77, 1546-47, *south Fenne* 1535-46, *Southefenne* 1560, *the south fen* 1609 (*v.* **sūð, fenn**, cf. The East Fenn, The West Fen *supra*); *Staker maris* (sic) 1421-23, *Stakermarre* 1451-53, *- mare* 1523-24, *- mere* 1546-47, *Stockmore* (sic) 1608-9; *Stand dales* 1609 (*v.* **stān, deill**); *Stanner* 1702 (perhaps from **stæner** 'stony, rocky ground'); *the stringe close* 1609; *Tethings* (sic) 1609 (*v.* **tēoðung** 'a tithing'); *place called . . . Ten stongs* 1609 (*v.* **stǫng** 'a pole'); *Tetney dike* 1554 (1684), 1686 (*v.* **dík**); *Tetney East feild* 1686 (*v.* **ēast, feld**); *Tetnaie furwelles* 1579, *Tetney Furwells* 1630, 1634 (cf. *furewelle supra*); *Tounegreue* 1421-23, *Toungrave* 1451-53, *Townegraue* 1475-77, *Toungraue* 1523-24 (*v.* **tūn, græf**; probably where digging (for turf) took place for the village, cf. *The Greves supra*); *Tuttesfiondale* (sic) 1421-23, *Tutfrondale* 1451-53, *Trottesfondale* 1475-77 (obscure); *Tylholme* 1475-77 (*v.* **holmr**; the first may be ME *Tille*, a pet-form of *Matilda*, *v.* Reaney, s.n. *Till*, or it could be a name of some antiquity with the OE pers.n. *Tila* as first el.; this was a saltern); *Wallmore* 1535-46, *mora vocata Wallmere* (sic) 1537-38 (*v.* **wall, mōr** in the sense of 'marsh'); *Weather-Cock Close* 1737[1] (*v.* **weather-cock**); *West Close* 1690; *Westhenges* 113, *West Engez* 1446, *Westinggis, le Westynggys* 1535-46, *Westeynggis* 1537-38, *Westings* 1545, *le Westynges* 1551 (*v.* **west, eng**); *le Westmersshe* 1535-46, *- Westemershe* 1560 (*v.* **west, mersc**); *the wonge* 1609 (*v.* **vangr**); *Wyndynges* 1451 (for a discussion of *wyndyng*, *v.* PN L **3**, 16, where it is suggested that it perhaps denoted a place or places where there is a bend or bends).

Weelsby

WEELSBY

Wivelesbi 1086 DB, 1212 Fees, *Wiueles-* 1115 YCh iii, 1182, 1183, 1184, 1185 *et passim* to 1199 all P, 1219 Ass (p), *Wyveles-* 1266 Misc, 1276 RH, 1285 Ch, 1287, 1291 Ipm, 1293 *Ass*, (- "by Grymesby") 1294 Ipm, 1294 Ch, 1296, 1342, 1354 Pat, 1358 AD, 1393 Pat, *Wyvelis-* 1286 Ipm
Uiflesbi c.1115 LS, *Wyflesby* 1242-43 Fees, *-bi* 1275 RH, *Wifles-* 1272 *Ass*, 1282 *FF*, *- alias Weelsby* 1667 Td'E

Wevelsby 1314 Ipm, 1350, 1373 Cl

Weflesby 1372 AD

Wilesbi 1160–62 (1287) YCh iii, *Wyllesbye* 1537–38 Dugd iv,
   Willesbie a1567 LNQ v, *–bye* 1572 ChancP, *–by alias
   Weelesby* 1623, 1637 *BRA 437*, *– alias Wellesby* 1637 *ib,
   Wilsby* 1734 *Terrier*

Welesby 1341 *Extent*, 1349 Ipm, 1352 *MM*, (– "by"
   Grymesby) 1372 Misc, 1382 *AddR*, 1383 Peace, 1385,
   1387 Cl, 1406 Pat, 1431 FA, 1449 Pat, 1535 VE iv, 1610
   WillsL, 1611 *Nelthorpe*, 1617 (1658) HollesM, *Welis-*
   1316 Pat, 1316 Inqaqd, 1512 *BRA 437*, *Welys–* 1512 *ib*,
   1535 VE iv

Wellesby 1327 Cl, 1537 *AOMB 209*, *–bye* 1623 *Foster*

Weelsby 1527 HMCRep, 1632 *Foster*, 1635 *BRA 437*, 1654
   Foster et passim, *–bie* 1617 *BRA 437*

'Vífill's farmstead, village', *v.* **bȳ**. The first el. is the ON
pers.n. *Vífill*. In Scandinavia itself, this name is only certainly
attested in OWScand (Lind 1094–95). Fellows–Jensen, SPNLY
334 links this name to ON *vífill* 'beetle', but Dr Insley points out
that G. Muller, *Studien zu den theriophoren Personennamen der
Germanen*, Cologne–Viennas, 1970, 90, has plausibly suggested
that it is a sacral name belonging to a Primitive Norse form
*wīwilaR and having the sense 'the small one who has been
consecrated'. SSNEM 76 points out that ON *Vífill* is not attested
independently in L (or Y) and suggests that the first el. of
Weelsby may be the OE pers.n. **Wifel* or an appellative, ODan
*wiwæl 'pointed piece of ground', perhaps referring to the
pointed valley in which Weelsby lies. There seems little need to
consider any of these explanations. ON *Vífill* is a well attested
WScand pers.n. and it fits the recorded forms of Weelsby
perfectly.

BEACON HILL. CARLTHORPE (lost), *Karletorp* 1182, *Charletorp*
1183, *Carletorp* 1184, 1185 all P, 'Karli's outlying, dependent
settlement', *v.* **þorp**; alternatively it could be 'the outlying,
dependent settlement of the free men, peasants', *v.* **karl, þorp**,
since both would give rise to the same forms. There is no
indication of its situation, but it is linked with Weelsby in P.

CARR PLANTATION, cf. *Westcarre* 1457 *TCC*, 1592 *GrimsFC*, *North* -, *South Carr* 1788 *Heneage*, *v.* **kjarr** 'marsh'. CROW HOLT. FISH POND. HALL FM is *Weelsby F* (sic) 1831 *Monson*, - *Farm* 1838 *Brace*. HIGHFIELD HO, 1851 *Census*. PEAKS FM, *Peake* 1601, 1624, *Peeke* 1638, 1674, *Peak* 1697, 1706, 1762 all *Terrier* (Scartho), cf. *Peake Close* 1611 *Nelthorpe*, 1632 *Foster*, - *close* 1623 *ib*, *the Peeck Closes* 1625 *Heneage*, *Peak Closes* 1824 O, 1831 *Monson*, *Low peake furrs* 1652 *Rad*, *East Peaks Furze* 1788 *Heneage* (*v.* **fyrs**), *v.* **pēac** 'a knoll, a hill, a peak'; there is a very distinct rise in the ground here. PEAKS COVERTS, *Peaks Plantation & Cover* 1804 *Yarb*, *Peaks High Cover*, *Peaks Low* - 1824 *ib*. THE VILLA. WEELSBY HALL. WEELSBY HO, 1831 *Monson*, 1838 *Brace*. WEELSBY OLD HALL. WEELSBY PARK.

FIELD-NAMES

Forms dated 12 (l14) are *Gox*; 1358 AD vi, 1457 *TCC*; 1610, 1617[1] WillsL; 1611 *Nelthorpe*; 1617[2] AASR xl; 1617[3] (1658) HollesM; 1617[4], 1624, 1637, 1638, 1672[1] *BRA 437*; 1623, 1632 *Foster*; c.1625 *GrimsMap*; 1646 *GrimsCB viii*; 1672[2], 1697, 1722, 1726, 1731, 1764, 1771, 1774, 1826, 1837, 1845 *ThorGrims*, 1673, 1688 *GrimsCLeet*; 1788, 19 *Heneage*; 1824 *Yarb*; 1831 *Monson*; 1838 *Brace*.

(a) Abbey Hills 1788 (named from Wellow Abbey in Great Grimsby); East -, Old -, West Barn Cl 1788, Barn Cl 19; Brigsley Cl 19 (cf. *Brygeslay landes* 1457, from Brigsley, a neighbouring parish); East -, West Butcher Cl 19 (from the surn. *Butcher*); Calf Cls 1764 (*Calfe Close* 1617[1], 1617[2], 1722, *the* - 1617[3] (1658)); North Catbank 19, South - 1788 (*Cat Bank* c.1625, *Catt banke* 1673, *Cadbanke end* 1688 (self-explanatory); Cockers Cl 1788 (from the surn. *Cocker*); Dovecoat Cl 1788 (*v.* **douve–cote**); Field Moor Cl 19 (cf. *Welesbyfeld* 1457, *v.* **mōr**, **feld**); Franker Cl 19 (probably from a surn.); Furr Cl 1826 (1722, *furr close* 1726, *v.* **fyrs** 'furze'); Gate Ho 1851 *Census*; Great Walk 1788 (*v.* **walk** 'a sheep pasture', as elsewhere in the parish); Gunwells Cl 1837, Gunwell's Cls 1845 (*Gunwels* 1617[4], *Gunnwells* 1624, *the little Gun–wells* 1638, *Twoe Closes Called Gunwells* 1637, *Gunwell Closes* 1672[1], *Gunwells* - 1697,

1731; this is to be compared with *gunnel dyke* in Cleethorpes f.ns. (b) where it is suggested that it means 'Gunna's or Gunni's spring', *v.* **wella**. In fact the two names probably refer to the same feature); Haycroft Cl 1771, - Cls 1837, Haycroft's - (*Haycrofte* 1617[4], *-croftes* 1624, *Hey Crofts* 1637, *the little Haycrofts* 1638, *Haycrofts* 1672[1], 1672[2], *Haycrofte Closes* 1697, *Haycrofts Close* 1731, *v.* **hēg** 'hay', **croft**); East -, West high Fd 1788, Highfield 1868 Kelly (*y[e] Highefeild* 1646); higher Car 1774, Higher - 1826 (cf. Carr Plantation *supra*); North -, South Hogg Walk 1788 (cf. *Hoggclose* 1646; a *hog* is a young sheep before the first shearing, *v.* also **walk**); Holme Carr, - Hill 19 (cf. *Holmelands* 1457 and *terr' Thoē Holme* in the same document); Hooburg 1788 (obscure); House Cl 1788, 19; North -, South Intake 1788, Intax 1851 *Census*, - farm 1868 Kelly (*v.* **inntak** 'land taken in or enclosed'); Lea Cl 1826 (*Lea close* 1617[1], *my great* - 1617[3] (1658), *Lea Close* 1722 (*v.* **lea** (OE **lēah**) 'meadow, pasture'); Little Cl, near the Abbey 1824 (i.e. Wellow Abbey in Great Grimsby); Little Cl (triangular) (sic) 1824; North -, South little Walk 1788 (*v.* **walk**); Long Dyke Cl 1788 (*v.* **dík**); long Mare 1774, Long - 1826 (*Langmare* 1358, *Long Mare* 1722, 'the long boundary, land on or forming a boundary', *v.* **lang**, **(ge)mǣre**), Low Cl 1824; Middle Carr 1774 (*Midle Carre* 1617[1], - *car* 1617[2], *the midle Carr* 1722, *v.* **kjarr** and cf. Carr Plantation *supra*); Middle Cl 1826; East -, West Mill Cl, North -, South half Milne Cl, East -, West Mill Carr 19 (*v.* **myln**, **clos(e)**, **kjarr**); Nuns Cl 1824 (*Nonnes Close* c.1625, referring to the nuns of St Leonard's Priory in Great Grimsby, *v.* **nunne**); East -, Little -, North -, South Oxter Carr, Oxter Hill 19; Peak Cl 1824, Peaks Cottage, Peaks Crow Holt, Peaks Fourteen Acres, Peaks High -, Low Cover 1824 (named from Peaks Fm *supra*); North -, South Pontus (sic) 1788; Rush Cl 1788; Salt Cl 1788 (cf. *Saltecotecrike* 12 (l14), *v.* **salt**, **cot** with **crike** (ON **kriki**), no doubt the name of a saltern); Scarthoe Field Cl 1788 (from Scartho, an adjacent parish); Serjants Cl 1788 (from the surn. *Serj(e)ant* or *Sargent*); North -, South Sinks 1788 (*v.* **sink** 'a gutter, drain, sewer', discussed s.n. Sinks Covert, PN L **2**, 199–200); Stone Cl 1771, - Cls 1837; Stone's Cl 1845 (*Stones Closse* 1624, - *Close* 1637, 1638, 1672, perhaps from the surn. *Stone*); Stone Horse Carr 1788 (*v.* **kjarr**; a *stone-horse* is a stallion); Swine East Cl, Swines Middle Cl, Swines West Cl 19 (named from the family of William *Swine* mentioned in the document); Thimbleby Hill 1788 (presumably from the surn. *Thimbleby* from Thimbleby, LSR); East -, West Thorpe Garth 19; Washing Cl 1788 (perhaps a sheep-washing place); Whitehouse Cls 1771, 1845, - Cl 1837 (*Whitehouse Closes* 1617[4], 1697, *the Whitehouse Closses* 1624, - *White house closes* 1637, - *Closes* 1672[1], -

Close 1672², *-house closes* 1731 (presumably a reference to a white building).

(b) *the Ashe closse*, *- Little Ashe Closse* 1624, *- Ash Close*, *- Little Ash close* 1637, (*little*) *Ash Close* 1672¹ (*v.* **æsc, clos(e)**); *Bell close* 1611 (perhaps a close the rent of which went towards the upkeep of a church bell); *Knight Close* 1672² (named from the *Knight* family, cf. Alexander *Knight* 1731); *Marsshdyke* 1457 (*v.* **mersc, dík**); *Mudmare* 1457 (the first el. is obscure; the second is (**ge**)**mǣre**) 'a boundary, land on or forming a boundary'); *campus bor' de Welesby* 1457 ('the north field', one of the great fields of the village); *a little Pingle* 1617⁴, *a pingle* 1624, 1638, *the Pingle* 1637, *the Pingle Close* 1672¹ (*v.* **pingel** 'a small enclosure'); *pundow, lytylpundowe* 1457 (obscure); *Scuttlebelle* (sic) 1457 (obscure); *Staynmaregate* 1457 (*v.* **steinn** 'a stone', (**ge**)**mǣre**, with **gata**); *le Sykes* 1358 (*v.* **sík**); *Thorfgate* (sic) 1457 (obscure); *Trancard Close* (sic) 1610, *Tuckard Close* (sic) 1611, *Tanckard close* 1623, *Tancard Close* 1632; *Welles Closes* c.1625 (from the surn. *Welles*); *Welseby Closes* c.1625 (these lay on the boundary with Great Grimsby).

INDEX

This Index is based on the following principles:

    (a) It includes all the place-names in the body of the work.

    (b) It covers only the main reference to each place and no cross-references have been noted.

    (c) Street-names are included, but only those of Cleethorpes and Great Grimsby have been treated separately in the body of the text.

    (d) "Lost" names are printed in italics.

    (e) In grouping names no distinction has been made between those written in one word or two.

    (f) Only very few field-names (of special interest) have been included.